LET'S PLAY.

LAND ROVER

The complete guide to

FOUR-WHEEL DRIVE

Andrew St. Pierre White

About the author

Andrew St. Pierre White's career, as one of South Africa's leading authorities on off-road adventuring, was established with the publication in 1993 of the first edition of this book, "The Complete Guide to a 4X4 in Southern Africa". It was the first book of its kind written specifically for a Southern African audience, and an immediate best-seller. This, his latest book and eleventh on the subject, is the fourth comprehensive update of that work. Between these editions there have been several 4x4 Trails books and 4x4 videos and DVDs, now popular in many countries. In stark contrast, Andrew's other leisure activity is flying and making aviation documentaries.

Andrew lives in Cape Town with his wife Gwynn and three daughters, Stephanie, Erin and Kate.

From the author

This book is not just the work of the author, although credit for such tends to go that way. Many people contributed to the information in this book, which has been collected over more than a decade. As the 4x4 hobby grows, so knowledge about the subject grows. The subject is vast and it is fair to say that experienced off-roaders may disagree with some things that have been written here. Fortunately most of them have a deep love of the subject and are happy to share their experiences with me. What I have to do is to assimilate all this information, judge against my own background and understanding of the subject and hopefully reach conclusions that all who read will respect.

The beauty of this subject is that its growth seems infinite. Everytime I drive my vehicle, go on a trip, watch as someone coaxes a vehicle over an obstacle, chat to equipment suppliers or even walk around a well equipped vehicle, I learn something new.... boy I love this job!

The complete guide to

FOUR-WHEEL DRIVE

Andrew St. Pierre White

International Motoring Productions
a division of Andrew White and Associates CC
PO Box 3785, Somerset West 7129.

ISBN 0-9584701-4-6

© Andrew St. Pierre White 2004

Photographs: © Andrew St. Pierre White, unless otherwise indicated
Diagrams: © Andrew St. Pierre White, unless otherwise indicated
Design: Cornelle Ellis
Printed by Paar Print, Paarl, Cape Town

Fourth edition, 1st imprint.
This is the fourth edition of this book, the previous title being
'The Complete Guide to a Four Wheel Drive in Southern Africa',
first published in 1993.

CONTENTS

1. BASIC PRINCIPLES 02

Engines • Four-wheel drive transmission systems • Ground Clearance and Suspensions • Other features to consider • Buying second-hand

2. VEHICLES 34

Soft-Roaders • Lightweights • Work horses and double-cabs Station-wagons • Specialist and unusual vehicles

3. AUXILIARY EQUIPMENT 80

Body mounted accessories • Suspensions modifications Auxiliary tanks • Auxiliary lighting • Gauges • Electrics Roof Racks • Snorkels • Miscellaneous

4. WHEELS AND TYRES 110

Tyre selection • Radials, cross-plys, tubed and tubeless Spare wheel location • Wheel rims Repairing a puncture • Tyre index tables

5. DRIVING 128

Using four-wheel drive transmissions • Tyre pressures Off-road driving • 4x4 Driving schools

6. RECOVERY 160

Winches • Recovery Accessories • Kinetic/snatch straps • Jacks Sand ladders • Anchors • Recovery techniques

7. TRAILERS AND TOWING 192

Trailers versus roof racks • Towing equipment Trailer design • Towing on-road • Towing off-road

8. ON THE TRAIL 206

Vehicle packing • Portable refrigeration • Bush camping • Solar recharging • Water and survival • Packing lists • Conversion tables

9. MAINTENANCE AND BUSH REPAIRS 252

Maintenance • Breakdowns • Welding on a vehicle Filters • Handling fuel

10. NAVIGATION AND COMMUNICATION 270

Navigation • Communication

11. CONSERVATION 294

On the beach • Camping • Responsible behaviour

INDEX 303

1. BASIC PRINCIPLES

ENGINES

FOUR-WHEEL DRIVE TRANSMISSION SYSTEMS

GROUND CLEARANCE AND SUSPENSION

OTHER FEATURES TO CONSIDER

BUYING SECOND-HAND

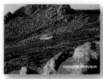

FOUR-WHEEL DRIVE VEHICLES have changed a great deal since first produced in any number; but at no time has this change been as swift as in the past 15 years. Between 1948 and 1968, vehicles like the Jeep CJ, Toyota Land Cruiser and Land Rover changed very little – they remained utilitarian, functional machines. In the late 1960s and early 1970s the market changed and Jeep built the Cherokee with power steering; Toyota produced a station wagon with wind-up windows, and Land Rover created a 4x4 with coil springs; the Range Rover. Even the Range Rover, the leader in the leisure 4x4 market for decades, was a year and a half in production before the introduction of carpets.

Comparing the sales brochures (left) of many of these originals with their modern equivalents reveals a completely different marketing strategy - vehicles that were once photographed climbing mountains are now seen in the polished environment of a shopping mall. This illustrates how the image for most 4x4s has changed from rugged work-horse to urban fashion statement. To compound the problem of choosing a suitable vehicle, manufacturers are creating 4x4s without true off-road ability and often advertise them as off-roaders.

It is true that in the modern world comfort is as important as off-road working ability, but many 4x4s are becoming so sophisticated that while being brilliant off-roaders they make themselves less suitable for wilderness travel. Sophistication makes servicing and repairs easy in the city but often impossible elsewhere.

As a result, all civilian four-wheel drive vehicles are a compromise between a town vehicle and an off-roader. Therefore, in selecting a vehicle designed for this double life, the buyer should ask this question: "How much time will I be spending on tarred roads and how much off-road?" and, "If I intend to go off-road, do I want to travel into the wilderness?" What follows is a guide to variations in design and original equipment and features that will be encountered when selecting a four-wheel drive vehicle.

ENGINES

The ideal power plant for an off-roader is able to produce its power at low RPM. Engines that do this can be driven in higher gear ratios in difficult terrain which is advantageous because the higher the gear ratio, the less chance of wheel-spin and the more delicately the driver can control the engine's power output. Engines designed with long piston strokes tend to do this.

Good off-road driving technique calls for selecting the right gear for the conditions. If the gear ratio selected is too high, a more powerful engine may still have the torque to get through, but if the

FROM TOP: Range Rover's first brochure of 1970; the 1976 and 2000 brochures; Mercedes G-wagen 1979 and 1990 brochures.

gear selected is too low, a big engine could, if not handled skillfully, cause excessive wheel-spin. For a novice driver therefore, high power is often a disadvantage but for the experienced it can be an advantage. For long distance travel, larger engines are more reliable because they rev slower with the penalty of higher fuel consumption.

PETROL VS DIESEL ENGINES

The comparison table that follows demonstrates the most important differences between petrol and diesel engines. Using these points and considering the difference in the price of petrol and diesel, the higher purchase price in many cases of diesel vehicles as well as the higher costs to maintain, the running costs between the two turn out in many cases to be similar. It is only at the fuel pump that the diesel has the edge. (In most countries) Everywhere else, even for operations in many Third World countries, petrol engines are the better choice. In addition to this, South Africa has some of the worst quality diesel fuel in the world and it plays havoc with turbo-chargers, reducing engine life to, in many cases, less than that of a petrol engine. However, the diesel quality problems are likely to be short lived.

A large capacity petrol engine is the choice off-road, even if its power output is similar to that of a smaller turbo-diesel. Turbo chargers boost power after the engine has, on average, reached 1000 RPM or

PETROL ENGINES	DIESEL ENGINES
Petrol engines are quiet	Some models are very noisy
More mechanics understand petrol engines	Fewer mechanics understand diesel engines
Many multi-valve petrol engines produce torque from low to high revs	Turbo-charged diesel engines produce little torque at low revs
Less frequent servicing required	More frequent servicing required
More complex electrical systems	More complex fuel systems
Less economical, less range	More economical, more range
Less expensive to service	More costly to service
Fuel less pungent but more volatile	Fuel more pungent, safer to transport

more. A petrol engine will work at much lower revs, down to 600 rpm in some cases. The difference here is a mere 400 rpm, which doesn't sound much, but low rev power is a distinct advantage off-road. Turbo-charged vehicles often have to take a tricky climb one gear lower than their petrol counterparts, because at some point in the climb, the revs drop to below where the boost is working and the engine stalls. Other terrain where small-capacity turbo-charged diesels often struggle is on dunes, where momentum cannot be maintained because of turbo-lag.

Like petrol engines, diesels are controlled by micro-processors. This is good and bad. It improves reliability and tuning accuracy. It also means that power output can be increased by the simple matter of adding a computer 'tuning chip'. Interestingly the Toyota Land Cruiser 79-series pick-up and its 4,2 diesel is the only non-computerised diesel on the market today. Another advantage of a turbo-charged engine is that altitude has less effect on performance than it has with a normally aspirated engine.

In Third World countries, fuel is frequently contaminated with dirt and water, with the result that fuel related problems cause more breakdowns than any other single factor. Ideally dual fuel filter systems should be fitted. At the very least, spare fuel filters must be carried.

Some turbo-diesels are fitted with an intercooler, a radiator which cools the hot air pumped by the turbocharger, which itself is powered by hot exhaust gases, before it enters the combustion chambers. They often increase power outputs by over 20%.

Third World fuels

Although there are still many parts of Africa where diesel and leaded petrol are the only fuels available, unleaded fuel is becoming widespread. Engines designed for both leaded and unleaded petrol are the most suitable for use as touring vehicles. Poor quality petrol found in rural areas can also create problems with sophisticated high compression engines, clogging fuel filters and affecting sensitive fuel injection systems. Ideally, petrol engines in long distance touring vehicles should be simple to maintain and spare fuel filters should always be carried. All modern 4x4s are being fitted with engines so complex that even basic servicing is designed to be done only at a dealer. In the Third World diesel is often more readily available than petrol.

Altitude also affects engine performance. A petrol engine with a compression ratio of about 8.5:1 will run well on 87-octane fuel above 5 000 feet or 93-octane at sea level. With a compression ratio higher than 8.5:1, a higher octane fuel would have to be used; 93-octane fuel at altitudes above 5 000 feet or 97-octane at sea level. It is important to consult the operator's handbook for recommended fuels. A fuel's octane rating is calculated from the rate at which the fuel burns. Running a low compression engine on high octane fuel will do no damage. In contrast, running a high compression engine on low octane or poor quality fuel could cause serious damage.

Although a heavy vehicle, the Land Cruiser 100, 4,5-petrol is an excellent performer on dunes because of its powerful engine that delivers high power at low revs. An aggressive driver with a heavy right foot might say the opposite, as wheelspin becomes a constant companion and the vehicle is seen to struggle.

Engine modifications

The four-wheel driver's vehicle has two kinds of life – on and off road. However, modifications to improve on-road performance may have detrimental effects on the vehicle's off-road abilities. Vehicle manufacturers always strive to increase engine power without increasing the engine's size or weight. One of the ways of doing this

is to improve the engine's capacity to breathe. Increasing the amount of air that can be consumed by an engine during the combustion cycle increases engine power. Fitting larger carburettors, free-flow exhaust systems or grinding and smoothing inlet and exhaust ports will increase air flow.

ABOVE: A breakdown in a remote area is no fun if your vehicle is over-complicated and requires special tools to complete basic functions. Unfortunately modern vehicles are built this way. I can see a future when vehicles will have notice warnings on the bonnet: "No User-Serviceable Parts Inside".

Modifications to engine components to increase performance are many and varied. Some carburettor modifications are unsuitable for a vehicle expected to work in difficult off-road conditions, since many off-road vehicle carburettors are fitted with special float chambers which allow them to operate when tilted during steep ascents and descents. Fuel injection systems do not suffer when the engine operates at odd angles.

Free-flow exhaust systems

Free-flow exhaust systems consist of big bore pipes and free-flow silencers and are worth considering.

The advantages of free-flow exhausts are numerous:

- *They improve fuel economy and thereby increase a vehicle's range.*
- *They improve acceleration without negatively affecting the power and torque output rev-range.*
- *In many cases they are less expensive than a genuine factory part.*

Although not spectacular, individually these improvements are noticeable. For example, when fitted to a Land Rover V8, fuel consumption improved by about 1.5 litres per 100kms. I calculated at the time that for a new free-flow exhaust system to pay for itself in fuel savings, I would need to travel over ninety thousand kilometres!

If your existing exhaust system is due for replacement I recommend investigating fitting one of these systems. It is important to make sure that there are several mounting points and that the job is done well. Exhaust failures are common in rough country.

RIGHT: Choose a vehicle with an engine that you will be comfortable with. For example, if you know more about repairing petrol engines, is it wise to drive a diesel vehicle and take it into remote areas?

FOUR-WHEEL DRIVE
TRANSMISSION SYSTEMS

Transmission systems for off-road vehicles are unique. Unlike a normal road vehicle where the gearbox is a single unit, off-road vehicle gearboxes comprise three, four and sometimes five units:

1. Main gearbox

Similar to a normal road vehicle's gearbox but built to withstand heavier torque loads. Many 4x4s are made with a choice of manual or automatic transmissions.

2. Transfer gearbox

Power from the engine is transmitted via the main gearbox to the transfer gearbox which is a two-ratio unit reducing the overall gearing. The result is two individual sets of forward and reverse gears. The high ratio is used for normal driving and the lower gear ratio is used for off-road work or starting off on a steep slope when towing a heavy load. From the transfer gearbox power is transmitted to the front and rear prop-shafts. In the case of full-time four-wheel drive vehicles it first goes through a centre differential or centre viscous coupling. In the case of part-time four-wheel drive vehicles this 'centre' component does not exist. For the most part, soft-roaders do not have a transfer gearbox.

3. Centre differential/viscous coupling

Located between the front and rear prop-shafts in full-time four-wheel drive vehicles only, this component distributes the power to the front and rear prop-shafts. Because the front and rear wheels rotate at different speeds when turning a corner this component must permit a differential in rotation speeds. A differential unit is fitted between the front and rear prop-shafts to do this. For off-road driving this differential can be locked, preventing differential rotation, locking the shafts together. This differential lock must not to be confused with differential locks found on axles as the job they do is entirely different.

A viscous coupling, in brief, does the same job as the centre differential but locking is done automatically.

A full-time four-wheel drive with its centre differential locked is the same as a part-time four-wheel drive vehicle engaged in four-wheel drive, the front and rear prop-shaft are attached, as if it were a solid shaft. These shafts drive the wheels via the axle differentials.

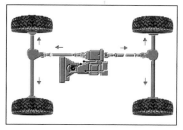

Four-wheel drive transmission layout

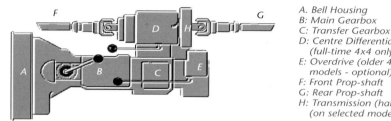

A. Bell Housing
B: Main Gearbox
C: Transfer Gearbox
D: Centre Differential
   (full-time 4x4 only)
E: Overdrive (older 4-speed
   models - optional)
F: Front Prop-shaft
G: Rear Prop-shaft
H: Transmission (hand) brake
   (on selected models)

Four-wheel drive central transmission components

4. Axle differentials

These components, one on the front and one on the back, distribute power from the prop-shafts to the wheels. Again, because of the different rotation speeds of the wheels when the vehicle turns, this differential permits this speed differential. (Hence the name differential) All wheeled vehicles have differentials for this purpose. Axle differential locks are fitted to some vehicles and are discussed later.

5. Overdrive unit

Fitted as optional equipment to some older vehicles, the overdrive is a gearbox that adds an additional high gear ratio. Overdrives are built for the relatively light duty of motorway cruising and are not intended for use with low gear ratios.

MANUAL VERSUS AUTOMATIC TRANSMISSION

There is much debate as to which transmission system is superior for a 4x4. Assuming that the vehicle will have the dual role of city vehicle and off-roader, here are my findings:

Because repairing 4x4 gearboxes is expensive, make it a priority to ensure that it is sound. In this case the Range Rover's inside had to be stripped in order to remove and refit the gearbox.

Advantages of manual transmission:

- *Engine braking down steep slopes is far superior where vehicle control is easier and safer.*
- *Easier to drive in very uneven terrain where as auto gearboxes tend to surge and can be difficult to control.*
- *The vehicle can be pull or push started.*
- *Manual gearboxes are easier to repair in the bush and more mechanics understand them.*
- *Manual transmissions are more economical to run and often less expensive.*
- *They run cooler when worked hard in heavy sand conditions.*

Automatic transmission enables smooth power application, an advantage in sand or slippery mud.

Advantages of automatic transmission:

- *Allows very gradual application of power to the wheels which would only be possible by slipping the clutch (with a manual gearbox).*
- *Technique of rocking, as a method of getting a vehicle out of a near-bogged situation in mud, is easier.*
- *Sand driving is altogether easier with auto gearboxes.*
- *More relaxed driving on road and on long bush tracks where there is a lot of slowing down and speeding up.*
- *Auto transmissions stress the vehicle less and are often a better choice when purchasing a used 4x4.*

Electronic Hill Descent Control (HDC)

Electronic Hill Descent Control first appeared in the Land Rover Freelander and Discovery Series-2 and is now commonplace in many modern 4x4s. HDC in conjunction with the anti-locking brakes (ABS) is used to slow a vehicle on steep descents.

I do not consider HDC a 'must have' and while it is useful in some situations it is more of a sales gimmick than a useful off-road tool. The trouble with it is that it engages at a speed that is too fast for most steep slopes. So the driver must use the brakes and transmission to slow the vehicle. In a well controlled descent it does not engage. HDC should therefore be considered as a kind of parachute should things go wrong; Release the brakes, hold on tight and steer the vehicle. HDC will assist in steering control albeit at a potentially unsafe speed. It should also be engaged when driving up steep slopes as it also engages in reverse and in the case of an uncontrolled rearward slide it could arrest a fast, dangerous descent.

Traction Control (TC)

Various systems have been developed to cancel out the wheel-spin that results from tractionless wheels on open differentials, normally accomplished by axle differential locks. These range from electronic traction control working with the anti-lock braking system, first seen in the Mercedes M-class, Discovery Series-2 and Range Rover. Jeep's Quadra-drive is hydraulic powered and does a similar job. These systems are beyond the scope of this book to illustrate in detail, however it is enough to say that they assist traction when wheels leave the ground or spin when the surface gets slippery. They do not, as advertised, make off-road driving easier but instead change the techniques required. In most cases traction control is harder on the vehicle and environment than axle differential locks, which in effect, do the same job. Chapter-5 illustrates this in detail.

One of the first vehicles to make full-time 4x4 fashionable was the Range Rover, launched in 1970. This is an early production model, the author's first vehicle, chassis number 0002492.

PERMANENT/FULL-TIME VERSUS SELECTABLE FOUR-WHEEL DRIVE

Full-time four-wheel drive

Full-time four-wheel drive has been an option for the off-road motorist for many years but only in the last 20 has it been recognised as the most user friendly type of four-wheel drive transmission. It has been fitted to vehicles such as the Jeep CJ-6 and CJ-7 and Range Rover since the early 1970s, the Land Rover 110 since the mid eighties, and the Mercedes-G and the Toyota Land Cruiser in the 1990s. The Mitsubishi Pajero/Shogun's transmission offers the options of part-time, full-time and true four-wheel drive with a system called 'Super-Select'.

1948, when 4x4s were far from fashionable, the Jeep CJ2 was probably the best off-road car available. This one was the second ever to succeed the climb up Sani Pass between South Africa and Lesotho. The climb was done without the trailer.

Most full-time four-wheel drive vehicles have a centre differential located between the front and rear prop-shafts to prevent wind-up caused by the different rotation speeds of wheels on sealed surfaces. (In the case of some vehicles with automatic gearboxes it is a self-locking hydraulic viscous coupling).

The advantages of full-time four-wheel drive transmissions are numerous and include safety, even tyre wear and better control and handling. Its only disadvantage is frequent misuse by those who operate it.

The trouble is that a full-time four-wheel drive vehicle with the centre differential unlocked is not operating in true four-wheel drive and drivers operate the vehicle as if it is. Hundreds if not thousands of high-speed roll overs on gravel roads around the world could be avoided if drivers lock the centre diff and drive in true four wheel-drive! More about this in chapter-5.

Contrary to popular belief, the full-time four-wheel drive system decreases tyre wear and does not affect fuel consumption greatly. Although there is no rule for the increase in fuel consumption caused by four-wheel drive while cruising, from the reports I have heard it may be as much as 5% – hardly significant considering the increase in safety it provides.

Selectable/Part-time four-wheel drive

This system is less expensive to produce owing to the absence of a centre differential, which is not required, since the front prop-shaft is disengaged when driven in two-wheel drive.

When a vehicle with part-time four-wheel drive is engaged in four-wheel drive, it is equivalent to a permanent four-wheel drive vehicle with its centre differential locked. With part-time systems, because the rotation of the front axle side shafts and prop-shaft do not serve

any purpose when travelling on firm surfaces, free wheeling hubs disconnect these components and will improve fuel consumption.

Part time 4WD vehicles pay a penalty in that the rear tyres (those used for driving the vehicle when in two-wheel drive) wear out before the front. This is especially true of vehicles driven in rough conditions where four-wheel drive should have been engaged but was not, often because the driver did not feel it was necessary.

Super-Select four-wheel drive

Super-Select four-wheel drive is found in the Mitsubishi Shogun/Pajero. This system gives the operator the full range of traction options: part-time four-wheel drive, full-time four-wheel drive with a centre differential unlocked and then true four wheel drive when this diff is locked. In some respects this is the ideal system. Again, its only disadvantage is drivers not using the system to its best advantage and not engaging full-time and true four-wheel drive when they should. Unless this expensive and complex system is used properly, the buyer has spent his money on nothing more than a gimmick.

Hydraulic viscous coupling

The hydraulic viscous coupling solves all of the problems of axle wind-up while at the same time operating as a non-slip differential. It works like a centre differential which is permanently locked but still absorbs all differential wheel speeds caused when driving on firm surfaces.

DIFFERENTIAL LOCKS: CENTRE, AXLE LOCKING AND LIMITED SLIP

The subject of diff locks is one of the most confusing and misunderstood aspects of four-wheel drive vehicles. This is illustrated by the way many magazine buyer's guides indicate this in their expansive charts; Indicating a 'yes' or 'no' is too simplistic and confuses the issue because not all diff locks have the same function. What a diff lock does depends on which differential is being locked AND what kind of 4x4 transmission is fitted.

For example let's compare a Defender's full-time 4WD with a diff lock and an Isuzu Frontier's part-time 4WD, also with a diff lock. Yet when both of these vehicles are in four-wheel drive with their diff locks engaged, the configuration of the drive to the wheels is different. This is because the Land Rover's diff lock is locking a centre diff, locking the front and rear prop-shafts together while the Isuzu's diff lock is located on the rear axle locking the left and right rear wheels together. With the Land Rover, although its 'diff is locked', the wheels on the rear axle remain unaffected, driven by an open, unlockable differential. It is in effect in the same configuration as the Isuzu with its diff unlocked.

ABOVE: The two production civilian 4x4s fitted with the ultimate traction configuration of locking front, centre and rear differentials is the Mercedes G series and the Toyota Land Cruiser 100 GX.

Differential locks on individual axles

An axle diff lock prevents differential wheel speeds on that axle, preventing wheel-spin on opposite wheels. They help tremendously in sticky situations particularly when two wheels on the same side drop into a trough and the axle is grounded, or when opposite front and back wheels leave the ground when traversing a ditch at an angle. Without axle diff locks, two airborne wheels, one on the back and one on the front, spin helplessly and the vehicle stops.

Axle diff locks can be a hindrance when engaged on flat ground where the surface is slippery but traction is similar on all four wheels. This is because a locked axle differential always causes understeer. Understeer causes disturbance and therefore increases the rolling resistance of the tyres which can cause a vehicle to bog down. Typical terrain on which this occurs is on a flat beach. It is not uncommon for the inexperienced driver, who tends to use every tool at their disposal to prevent difficulty, to create more problems for themselves by locking an axle differential. In this case only the centre diff (if you have one) should be locked.

When diff locks are fitted to both the front and rear axles it is imperative that the rear lock is operated first. A vehicle moving over slippery ground with a locked front axle and an unlocked rear diff will want to spin out and may become very difficult to control. Front diff locks severely inhibit steering control.

BELOW: Full-time 4WD on tar means that an open centre differential between front and rear prop-shafts drives all four wheels but permits wheels to rotate at different speeds. Don't be fooled: 4WD with an open centre diff will not give the safety and traction of true 4WD on slippery surfaces. Only locking the centre differential will do this.

Limited-slip differentials (LSD)

A limited slip rear differential does the same and gives the same advantages as a lockable differential but, as the name suggests, the advantage is limited. There is some slip, which can be an advantage and a disadvantage (see the table below).

In most cases limited slip differentials are fitted on the rear axle only. This is usually advisable, for when fitted on both front and rear axles, some limited slip differentials can alter the vehicle's handling characteristics and cause instability at speed.

ARB locker differential (top) and compressor (bottom).

Vacuum/Pneumatic differential locks

Until fairly recently the most common type of locking device was the air-locking diff, so called because it required a compressor to actuate the locking mechanism. These systems are still available and come from the USA, Australia and Great Britain. The ARB air-locker is one of the best available. Engine-vacuum powered differential locks are also made in South Africa by Gearmax. They are simpler, less costly but because they rarely disengage on demand are unsuitable for front diffs.

Post-delivery differential locks

Don't fall into the trap and believe that a four-wheel drive vehicle must have an axle diff lock before it will be effective off-road. It is true that there are some obstacles that only vehicles with a lockable diff will negotiate with ease, but these can in so many cases be overcome with driving skill. However, if you intend tackling the very toughest off-road conditions then axle differential locks are essential.

A rear axle diff lock is a 'nice to have' item and a front axle diff lock can be described as 'I want to be unstoppable!'.

COMPARISONS:
LOCKING DIFFERENTIAL VS LIMITED SLIP DIFFERENTIAL

LOCKING DIFFERENTIAL	LIMITED-SLIP DIFFERENTIAL
Engage/disengage controllability from inside the cab	No controllability
Misuse can lead to handling difficulties and excessive tyre wear	Misuse is not possible
Full locked position gives the best possible traction as the two wheels are locked together	Some compromise to traction as wheel slip can still occur, although far less than an ordinary differential
Additional wear and tear is negligible	Modern limited slips do not need regular rebuilding as do older types
Fairly costly	Less costly

Automatic locking differentials

Auto-lockers such as the Detroit Locker are automatic locking differential devices that lock when traction is needed, and disengage when a wheel needs to rotate at a different speed due to the vehicle turning on firm ground. No conscious decision has to be made to lock the differential – maximum traction is permanent. Automatic diff locks are a disadvantage in soft sand when the vehicle is turned, as the locking rear axle tends to cause drag on the outside wheel hampering progress. Contrary to what the manufacturers claim, I do not advise fitting an auto diff lock to a front axle as it can cause severe handling difficulties on slippery surfaces. Because they cannot be manually disengaged when steering becomes difficult, I must assume that they are unsuited to front axles.

Gearmax after-market differential locks can be fitted to any South African-made rear axle.

FREE-WHEEL HUBS

Fitted to part-time (selectable) 4x4 vehicles, free-wheel hubs fit on the front wheel hubs and enable the side shafts and prop-shaft to be disconnected from the wheels. The one and only purpose behind free-wheel hubs is to prevent these components from rotating unnecessarily and thereby reduce fuel consumption when driving on a firm surface.

Can free-wheel hubs, if engaged and operated on the road, damage the transmission? This is a very common question. The answer is no. However, the opposite is true: if hubs are left unlocked for long periods the following damage can result:

Bearing damage

On some vehicles the lubrication of the front hub bearings depends partly on axle rotation which sends oil to the bearings. With the front hubs disengaged, the axle remains stationary and the hub is not effectively lubricated.

Spline shaft damage

Spline shafts are located in the side shafts (in the case of vehicles with independent suspension) and in the prop-shafts (in the case of vehicles with solid axles) that allow for suspension travel as the vehicle moves over uneven ground. In conditions where the drive shafts are rotating, wear will be spread evenly over the splines. Should the drive shaft or prop-shaft remain stationary for long periods, as will occur if the hubs remain disengaged, the splines wear on a single plane. If serious uneven wear has occurred, drive shaft vibration will result. It is therefore important that, should you have free-wheel hubs fitted to your vehicle, drive with them engaged once in a while.

Auto and manual free-wheel hubs. Their only function is to save fuel on the open road. They must be engaged (manual) at the front wheels before the vehicle can be driven in four-wheel drive.

If free-wheel hubs are not offered as standard equipment and you wish to fit them, do not skimp – cheap units fail when the going gets tough.

Automatic free-wheel hubs

Automatic free-wheel hubs engage the front wheels automatically when the front prop-shaft rotates under power, i.e. when four-wheel drive is selected in the cab. Old types of automatic free-wheel hubs did not lock when compression braking (descending steep slopes) or moving in reverse. Modern auto free-wheel hubs do operate when moving in reverse and down steep slopes.

Modern auto hubs are engaged simply by engaging four-wheel drive. Auto-hubs have improved and have become as reliable as the manual types. For this reason many manufacturers are fitting these in preference to the manual types. Many serious off-roaders still prefer manual types.

PORTAL AXLES

Reduction gearboxes fitted at each wheel hub serve to increase axle ground clearance. While it increases ground clearance it also means that once the vehicle has bogged, it is very much deeper and therefore much more difficult to extricate.

Four-wheel drive transmissions - summary

1. *Part-time four-wheel drive transmissions have two differentials; one on the front axle and one on the rear axle.*
2. *Full-time four-wheel drive systems have three differentials. One on the front axle, one on the rear axle and one in the centre, driving the front and rear prop-shafts.*
3. *A differential lock on an axle prevents differential rotation between the two wheels on that axle. (Left and right).*
4. *A differential lock in the centre prevents differential rotation between the prop-shafts. (Front and rear)*
6. *It is possible to have all three differentials lockable (full-time 4wd), or two differentials lockable (part-time 4wd). This is the ultimate traction configuration.*
7. *Free-wheel front hubs are used to save fuel. They are fitted to part-time four-wheel drive vehicles only. They cannot be damaged by leaving them locked.*

GROUND CLEARANCE AND SUSPENSION

It is a bad idea to take a vehicle manufacturer's minimum ground clearance claim and base off-road performance on it. For example, a Land Rover Freelander has a higher ground clearance than a Mercedes Geländewagen. The Freelander's independent suspension enables it to have a reasonable clearance which is measured from the chassis. In the case of the Mercedes, the clearance is measured from the differential housing, which is attached to a live axle suspension which moves up as the wheels ride over obstacles. So when they go off-road the Mercedes's clearance increases and with the Freelander it decreases. The result: The Freelander has inadequate clearance for driving off road and the Mercedes, which while it is not over endowed with clearance, must rate as one of the best off-roaders of all time.

Because of this, clearance together with the type of suspension must be considered. Therefore clearance should be measured not only under the lowest point of the chassis but in front of, behind and between the axles as well. The front and rear overhangs (approach and departure angles), wheelbase in relation to wheel size (break-over angle) and centre of gravity (roll-over angle) are important factors which affect a vehicle's off-road ability. A vehicle with a 'wheel in each corner' configuration, a short wheelbase and large wheels will be most effective off-road. However, this 'ideal' often gives the vehicle poor on-road handling characteristics.

Approach Angle
The maximum angle a vehicle can approach an obstacle without any part of the vehicle striking that obstacle.

Departure Angle
The maximum angle a vehicle can leave an obstacle without any part of the vehicle striking that obstacle.

Break-over Angle
The maximum angle a vehicle can ride over without striking the obstacle between its axles. The longer the wheelbase the larger this angle is. On some vehicles, parts of the transmission protrude below the chassis and this has a detrimental effect on the break-over angle.

If you are fitting protective equipment or towing apparatus to your vehicle, it is important to consider the negative effect it may have on these angles and therefore the vehicle's off-road ability.

When clearance specifications are given in data sheets issued by vehicle manufacturers they are normally the measurement taken from the lowest part of the vehicle to the ground on a flat surface. When a vehicle moves over ground this clearance moves constantly, more so if the suspension is of the independent type.

Approach Angle   Break-Over Angle   Departure Angle

Important angles that just by looking at them will give some idea of what sort of off-road performer the vehicle might be.

Wheelbase

The choice of wheelbase should be determined by the kind of work the vehicle is likely to undertake and the loads to be carried. Long wheelbase vehicles can carry heavier payloads and have a higher seating capacity. They handle better on the road, on corrugations and on fast unsurfaced roads.

Short wheelbase vehicles have a few advantages when off-road. An improved break-over angle is the most significant. They are generally lighter, more manouverable and more economical. Short wheelbase is a disadvantage on gravel roads and corrugations as they tend to have less straight-line stability and are more prone to slide.

The maximum climb angle, which can be represented as degrees from horizontal or a percentage of a one-in-one slope (100% = 45°) Figures supplied by manufacturers are based on a vehicle moving on a traction-perfect flat surface. In the real world, things are very different.

Roll-Over Angle

This is the angle at which a vehicle will roll when traversing a slope at right angles. This value is a result of the distance of the vehicle's centre of gravity above the ground. Anything above 40° is good and below 35° is poor.

CHOICE OF SUSPENSION

No compromise made to improve off-road ability or on-road comfort is more noticeable than those made to the suspension. The type and rating of the springs, the configuration of the axle location and the axle design all have a significant effect on a vehicle's ability off-road and comfort both off and on the road.

Two types of axles are fitted to off-road vehicles – independent and live/solid beam axles.

With a low centre of gravity and well-tuned suspension such as the Mercedes Geländewagen has, at no time during this obstacle did the vehicle feel as if was going to roll over. If this vehicle had been equipped with a roof-rack, I would not have attempted this obstacle. Note the rear wheels firmly on the ground.

Solid/live axles versus independent axles

If the vehicle is going to spend most of its time in the bush or will be worked hard in very rough country, rigid, solid beam axles, also known as 'live axles', are stronger and perform better than independent suspension.

When a wheel on a solid axle rides over an obstacle and lifts, it lifts the part of the vehicle closest to the ground (the differential) with it, thereby increasing ground clearance and clearing the differential over the obstacle. Because solid axles are very heavy, independent suspension reduces the unsprung weight contributing to ride comfort on-road.

With independent suspension, as a wheel rides over an obstacle the differential is left in a vulnerable position closer to the ground. Although independent suspension is able to offer superior axle articulation because the axle is independent of the differential, this is rarely the case with the current range of vehicles. In general, vehicles with the best axle articulation are those with solid axles and coil springs front and back.

Axle articulation

No single compromise to the suspension system is more noticeable than axle articulation. Axle articulation is the suspension's ability to allow the wheels to move vertically, to drop into deep ruts and follow the contours of the ground without leaving it and lose traction. Articulation is therefore very important to an off-road vehicle but to a road cruiser it is a curse because it allows the body to roll uncomfortably as the vehicle is cornered. In general, independent suspension gives less articulation and body roll than does solid axles.

Top: Solid or 'live' axle. Bottom: Independent front suspension showing the suspension as it is fully extended.

SPRINGS AND SHOCKS

Three types of springs are fitted to off-road vehicles – coil springs, leaf springs and torsion bars. Solid beam axles are either fitted with leaf or coil springs while independent axles are fitted with coil springs or torsion bars, or both. Another system, based on pneumatic cylinders in place of springs, permits variable ride-height adjustment from the cab. This highly sophisticated system is controlled by a computer and is fitted to top-spec 4x4s like the Range Rover and Land Cruiser V8.

Coil versus leaf springs

Coil springs make for a better ride both on and off the road. This is because they absorb vibration better than leaf springs and suspension designers can take advantage of unrestricted axle articulation offered by coil springs.

Vehicle designers must decide how much vertical axle movement, or articulation to allow. Too little means poor off-road performance, too much means uncomfortable body roll on the tarmac. What designers of modern vehicles do is to limit the articulation and then compensate with devices such as electronic traction control or axle diff locks.

Coil spring designs require axle location arms to locate the axle to the chassis – a job which leaf springs do themselves. These arms come in the form of radius arms at the front, trailing arms at the rear and panhard rods or similar to locate the axle laterally. These suspension systems can absorb irregularities in the road surface so efficiently that vehicles get damaged often long before the driver realises the damage he is doing. One of the philosophies behind maintaining the production of 4X4s with leaf spring suspension for so long was the fact that an uncomfortable ride limits the driver's endurance before limiting the vehicle's.

Axle straps

Some vehicles, often those equipped with leaf springs, have heavy duty nylon straps attached to the chassis and looped around the axle at each hub. These prevent spring and shock breakages where suspension travel over uneven ground allows the axle to drop too far.

Shock absorbers

Shock absorbers control the oscillation of the road springs. When operating on rough surfaces they work hard because axle travel is greatly increased which in turn increases shock absorber temperatures. Shock absorbers are a vital part of the suspension system and in most cases, those supplied by the vehicle manufacturers are the minimum required for safety and vehicle controllability.

If you use your 4x4 off-road and on gravel roads and are considering improving the ride, handling and off-road performance, upgrading the shock absorbers is the first thing to consider. Gas shock absorbers and other suspension modifications are discussed in detail in chapter-3.

The original Range Rover's axle articulation is the best of any vehicle in its class (79cms) and makes the vehicle very easy to drive over rough ground. The downside is high body-roll when cornering. Full-time four-wheel drive compensates for this by ensuring negative steering and outstanding road holding

SUSPENSION CONFIGURATIONS

These diagrams illustrate the variations in suspension systems fitted to off-road vehicles.

Front coil springs and a solid axle are always combined with a similar setup on the rear. This setup offers the best combination for off-road ability. Examples: Land Rover Defender, Mercedes Geländewagen and Unimog, Toyota Land Cruiser 80 and 100GX, newer Nissan Patrol and first and second generation Range Rovers.

(DIAGRAM COURTESY OF NISSAN)

Rear coil springs and a solid axle are also combined with independent front suspension such as the Mitsubishi Pajero/Shogun and Isuzu Trooper.

Front independent coil springs or torsion bars are found on vehicles such as the Mitsubishi Pajero/Shogun Isuzu Trooper, Ssangyong Musso and bakkie-based vehicles like the Nissan Tracker, Sani and Hardbody, Ford Courier, Mazda B, Isuzu KB and Frontier.

(DIAGRAM COURTESY OF SSANGYONG)

Rear leaf springs and a solid axle are found on all bakkie-based 4x4s such as the Nissan Sani and Hardbody, Ford Courier, Mazda B, Isuzu KB and Frontier, first Pajero.

Leaf springs on a front axle are found on older designs such as the Land Rover series I,II and III. Toyota Hilux, Land Cruiser FJ40, FJ60, FJ75, FJ60 and earlier models, Suzuki SJ40, Jeep CJ, old Chevrolet Blazer, old Nissan Patrol, SVM, Asia Rocsta, Mahindra and Jeep CJ. They are always matched with similar systems on the rear.

An all-four independent suspension configuration was until recent times fairly unusual, found on vehicles such as the VW Syncro Bus, Toyota Mega Cruiser and Styre-Puch Pinzgauer. Now it is found on many 'soft-roaders' such as the Land Rover Freelander, Nissan X-Trail and Toyota Rav4. Trends in vehicles are leaning toward this configuration as it gives the best on-road comfort. The Pajero was the first off-road 4x4 to adopt this followed by the third-generation Range Rover. Others, doubtless, will follow.

OTHER FEATURES TO CONSIDER

DIESEL TURBO FAILURES

Why is it that petrol engines seem to last so much longer than the average turbo-diesel? The answer is anything but simple. Try as I may, being simplistic about this issue isn't going to help. So here I am going to get a bit technical. So, if you own or are planning to purchase a turbo-diesel vehicle understand the pitfalls because some are very costly. I am not advocating staying away from diesel engines but rather an understanding of them will not only prevent huge repair bills in the future but also enable you to get the long life that a diesel engine can deliver if treated correctly.

Typical turbo waste-gate damage caused by excessive exhaust gas temperatures.

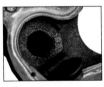

In 2000 owning a Mercedes 290GDT, I experienced an engine failure which resulted in a huge learning curve for me. It happened on a trip through Johannesburg so I called Steve from Steve's Auto Clinic. Having more experience with diesels than anyone else I knew, I felt confident I was in safe hands. To cut a long story short, a blocked air filter had caused an excessive exhaust gas temperature which caused turbo and injector damage. Two years later, just before this book was published, I purchased another used 290GDT. I remember the famous quote, "Those who do not learn from history are condemned to repeat it". I visited Steve and again I was on a learning curve. In just two years problems with damaged turbochargers in thousands of vehicles had spread from turbo failures to cylinder heads as well. I wanted to know why?

Steve uses an effective analogy. A new vehicle is like a healthy child, fit and energetic. The child's body is like the vehicle's engine. Once a child becomes a teenager some begin to smoke, drink or both. The body begins a path of deterioration, and becomes diseased. By forty, the equivalent of forty-thousand kilometers, doctor says, "Stop smoking!". So the smoking is stopped. Is the adult suddenly healthy because a bad habit is kicked? No. Damage has already been done.

A new vehicle drives energetically out of the showroom. In the case of a diesel engine it is often mishandled recklessly, like the teenager on a binge. Driving a turbo-diesel at full power for long periods, hauling heavy trailers up steep hills at full power, hour after hour of speeding down to the coast at 150 kph. That's how to abuse a turbo-diesel. These engines are not designed to work this way and it damages them! So if you want your vehicle to perform these tasks, buy a petrol! Petrol car engines are more suitable than diesels for running at full power over long periods.

A new vehicle is like a healthy child, fit and energetic. A child's body is like the vehicle's engine.

The advice on fitting exhaust gas temperature gauge early in the vehicle's life cannot be over emphasized. Drivers inadvertently abusing the engine, driving it in a manner which over stresses it will be warned by the gauge and buzzer. This is one of the problems with buying a used turbo-diesel. Fitting an EGT gauge after the vehicle has covered 50 000km is like a forty year old quitting smoking. The damage has been done. Not smoking at all is the most desirable: never abusing the engine because a gauge is telling you that you are. It's a bit like a government health warning, but instead it reads, "RUNNING THIS ENGINE LIKE THIS WILL SERIOUSLY DAMAGE YOUR WEALTH".

The Mercedes 290GD on the Dyna diagnostic bed at Steve's Auto Clinic's Vanderbijl Park centre.

Does the fitting of an EGT gauge effect the warranty? No and Yes. It can in no way have a negative effect on the engine as it is fitted to the exhaust. A bloody-minded dealership may claim it has an effect in an attempt at avoiding a claim, but I was told by Steve that never, in any one of their nine branches has Steve's Auto Clinic seen a warranty claim discarded due to an aftermarket fitment of either an EGT gauge or intercooler.

Modern diesels are mostly alloy head and block. With cast iron engines high EGT caused turbo and injector damage. With modern alloy engines high EGT often leads to head, valve and pre-combustion chamber damage as well. But how can he be so sure it is high EGT that's causing the damage? Writers in magazines have come up with other theories, but 99 out of 100 turbo-diesels in for turbo or cylinder head

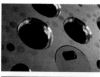

Top: A new cylinder head showing the three valve seats and the pre-combustion chamber.
Middle: A damaged pre-combustion chamber. The change in shape of the apeture and the cracks cause severe reduction of power output.
Bottom: A valve damaged by excessive heat. This damage in most cases is accompanied by valve seat and head damage. In many cases the entire head cannot be repaired and must be replaced. The costs are very high and leave many customers in tears. Sincere thanks to Steve Fisher of SAC for giving of his time and expertise for this section.

damage are clearly caused by excessive combustion temperatures. Heat fatigue shows itself by cracks as the metal changes its form.

I was one of the rare 'lucky' ones as my new G seemed to be in good shape.

"It happens very rarely that we see a turbo-diesel vehicle over 50K with no damage", Steve told me. He explained that many vehicles without particularly high mileage arrive for a conversion of some sort. Sometimes they even try to talk the customer out of it because a diagnostic test tells a tale that the engine is likely to have a major failure before 100 000 kms. While the damage has been done it is lying invisible inside the engine but it can't be proven without taking the engine apart. Should they do a modification, even an intercooler, it is often perceived to have contributed to the failure. It's a real problem.

Diesel engines are happiest when driven on or close to the revs that produce the highest torque. At higher revs, torque drops off and while power increases so does the temperature generated. The result is high fuel consumption and high engine temperatures. This is why above 140 kph most diesel engines will consume about as much fuel as a similar petrol vehicle. At this speed the petrol engine is happiest, revving high and burning its fuel efficiently, while a diesel is at high-stress, running hot and burning fuel inefficiently.

So when considering a new or used vehicle, think about what kind of driver you are. If you are towing, buy a petrol. If you want the economy of diesel, decide now that long stretches at high speeds are a thing of the past. If the vehicle is used, do a diagnostic test to see if damage has been done and if it's new, fit an EGT gauge without delay and reset the diesel pump on an active dyna to limit the combustion temperatures before damage is done.

LOADING CAPACITY

When travelling through remote or unpopulated areas; food, water, fuel, tools and camping equipment have to be carried. Therefore your vehicle should have a large enough loading capacity in terms of volume and weight. Water weighs one kilogram per litre and fuel almost as much. Heavy duty suspension should be fitted to those vehicles asked to carry loads close to their limits over rough ground. Heavy duty shock-absorbers will also assist.

When selecting a 4x4, it is worth asking how much weight can be carried on the roof. Unfortunately I have rarely seen this specification published in a sales brochure, because so often it is alarmingly low, so this information may be hard to find. The range of weight to be carried ranges from the lowest in vehicles such as old Range Rovers

at about 50kgs, a Land Rover Defender at 75kgs up to 200kgs on a Mercedes G-Wagen. (specs not verified)

Loading any roof rack too well forward will cause overloading of both roof pillars and front springs. Structural failures from overloading show themselves in the form of cracks in the windscreen and fading shock absorbers. If you have a winch, bull bar, power steering and air conditioning fitted, your front springs may well be pushed beyond their design limits. Overloading a vehicle's springs will quickly result in serious structural failures in rough terrain including chassis breakage.

DISC VS DRUM BRAKES

All-wheel disc brakes are an advantage on and off-road. Apart from not being affected by water, like drums, they operate effectively in reverse. This is where the disadvantage comes, which can be significant off-road, when drum brakes are fitted on the rear wheels. Picture the following situation: a vehicle stalls while moving up a very steep climb. The vehicle must be secured before the clutch is depressed and the engine restarted or the reverse-stall manoeuvre performed. The foot brake and hand brake are used to hold the vehicle. With the drum brakes on the rear axle doing almost all the work, and with a stalled engine and no brake-boosting assisting the effort, it may be impossible to secure the vehicle with brakes alone. In this case the vehicle must be left in gear and rocks packed behind the wheels to assist the braking effort before the clutch can be depressed.

Although all drum brakes are less effective in reverse than discs, not all drum brakes are totally ineffectual in reverse. Generally speaking, the older the vehicle, the worse they perform.

With many pickups and some station-wagon 4x4s, the spare wheel is carried under the load-bay. By fitting a rear-wheel carrier, like this one by IEF Engineering, a large fuel tank can now be put in its place, low down keeping the centre of gravity low.

POWER STEERING

Assisted steering is a great advantage when driving a heavy 4WD vehicle, both in the city and off-road. Although it adds mechanical complications should something need repair and adds weight it is highly advisable. Drive an old Land Rover Series-3 all day in heavy sand and you will realise the value of power steering in the bush.

VEHICLE RANGE AND PAYLOAD

A vehicle required to undertake journeys into unpopulated areas needs a good range to be effective. Because payload can be converted into range by carrying more fuel, either an economical engine or high

After driving through deep water, water can become trapped in brake drums making them ineffective. Sand can also collect in drum brakes damaging the shoes.

fuel tank capacity and payload is required for a vehicle to have a good range.

I suggest a range of no less than 1000 kms between fuel stops if you are planning to create a good expedition vehicle. Few standard vehicles will cover this distance without additional tanks or jerrycans. Auxiliary fuel tanks are discussed in chapter-3.

BUMPERS

One of the most useful auxiliary items for the vehicle that is going to drive off-road is the high-lift jack. It requires a suitable flat jacking surface on the vehicle for efficient use. Modern designs tend towards curved rounded body shapes and rounded bumpers. If you are purchasing a new vehicle and intend to take it off-road ensure that the bumpers are adequate in both shape and strength for use as jacking points and if not, suitable adaptations can be made so that a high-lift can be used with the vehicle. These modifications are rarely available from the manufacturers themselves but are often designed and fitted by off-road vehicle fitment specialists.

Vehicles that spend a lot of time on or near the beach will likely have rust problems. If they spend time launching boats or emersed to any degree whatsoever, the condition of the drive train and chassis is likely to be poor. Be particularly careful if it looks good - rust may be concealed by a new layer of paint.

BUYING SECOND-HAND

When the value of vehicles is calculated, the cost of the fountain of youth is included in the purchase price. The value of the probable guarantee claims is also added. The genuine mileage may not be genuine. I do not have a recipe for testing the authenticity of kilometre readings, nor can I tell you how and when to trust a used-car dealer. If a new car manufacturer puts its name behind a used-car, then you can be fairly sure that it will be covered by a worthwhile warranty.

With a second-hand 4x4, the mileage shown on the odo will not be an indication of how much life the vehicle still has in it. Due to the rough conditions that many 4x4s are subjected to, wear and tear levels are difficult to estimate by simply looking at and driving a vehicle. The experience of the vehicle's driver is worth evaluating. The experienced driver would have put far less strain on components than the inexperienced driver.

To buy second-hand from private sellers or used-car dealers, you will need to be able to inspect and test drive the vehicle with a mechanical mind. Off-road vehicles that have had a working life will wear in specific places. Keep the following in mind:

If the vehicle has been used to tow and launch a boat, axle oils may have been contaminated with water and axle oil seals may be corroded, particularly in salt water.

If the vehicle has been used on the beach, rust will be a major concern. Even aluminium bodied vehicles such as Land Rovers suffer from damage to body and chassis due to rust. No matter how good a vehicle looks, if you suspect that it may have been submerged by an incoming tide, don't touch it!

If the vehicle has been used for towing; clutches and gearboxes, although normally heavy duty on 4x4s, would have been worked hard. If overly heavy loads have been carried on the roof, the roof supports and windscreens often crack. Bush work takes its toll on suspension components, such as bushes, bump stops, shock absorbers and springs. Automatic vehicles are generally better mechanically than manual vehicles. This is because auto transmission is kinder to the drive train, absorbing shock loadings caused by aggressive driving off-road.

A well maintained vehicle means a great deal. In order to inspect a vehicle properly its body and chassis should be clean but not black painted. This can hide a hundred problems.

Your inspection should also include the following:

- *A service record is particularly important with diesel vehicles.*
- *Look for oil leaks under the engine and around the gearbox – they could mean trouble. Axle hub oil leaks are given away by oil splashed on the inside of the wheel rim/s. These oil seals are fairly simple to replace although if oil has contaminated the brakes the pads will have to be replaced. Oil seepage around the front axle constant velocity joints (the shiny round thing on each front wheel hub) is normal, but the oil should not drip.*
- *Bounce and rock the vehicle on all four corners. The bounce should stop quickly. If it does not, the shock absorbers may be worn. Worn suspension bushes will cause clunks and knocks.*
- *Look for rust. Beware of a newly painted chassis – it may mean hidden rust. Some common places where body rust may be found are under the vent in front of the windscreen, the chassis near the suspension shackles and underneath the doors and door sills. Cracked paint on any part of the body could be caused by rust forming underneath. Establish if the rust is structural or cosmetic. If the surrounding metal is in good order then it may be repairable.*
- *Open and close all of the doors, the bonnet and the tailgate and wind all of the windows up and down and test the lights and indicators.*
- *Look for damage to the chassis frame, cross members and floor panelling that could have been caused by careless driving over difficult terrain. Look for cracks in the chassis rails, particularly close to suspension location points. If there is absolutely no visual damage*

underneath the vehicle, it is an indication that the vehicle may never have been off-road, or if it has, it has been treated with care. If the chassis is too clean, beware. Fresh black paint could be hiding damage.

- Inspect the exhaust pipe. If it is not well secured, it may have been this way for some time and developed cracks.
- Inspect the tail pipe. If it is a petrol engine it should be medium to dark grey. It should not be sooty black as this could be the telltale sign of worn rings or valve guides. If it is a very light grey and has not just returned from a long run then the vehicle may have burnt valves caused by a too lean air-fuel mixture. Exhaust pipe colouration is no sure way to diagnose engine problems. Further tests, such as compression, should be made if in doubt.
- Open the bonnet. The engine should be clean and show signs that it has been well maintained. The battery terminals should not have white powdery deposits, but should be covered by a thin layer of grease, again signs of a well cared for vehicle.
- It may be difficult to establish whether a vehicle has been involved in an accident. Tap the bodywork all around, and the sound will change if body putty has been layered on thick. A small magnet used as a metal detector will also be useful. (This will not work with aluminium body panels.)
- Find the engine and chassis numbers and compare these with the registration held by the owner. Make sure that these numbers have not been tampered with in any way. If you suspect that this may have occurred, don't go any further. Legislation makes it illegal to own a vehicle whose chassis or engine numbers have been changed without appropriate documentation.

Here is a guide to what to look for when test driving a used 4x4:

- Start the engine. It should idle smoothly between 700 and 900 rpm. Some diesels running on high-sulphur fuel idle noisily.
- Warm up the engine. Have someone stand at the rear of the vehicle. Quickly push down the accelerator as far as it will go and then release it. There should not be excessive smoke from the exhaust. The engine should accelerate quickly and smoothly.
- Black smoke? Diesels that smoke heavily under acceleration mean an over-rich fuel mixture. This causes turbocharger damage if left for more than a few hundred kilometres. Testing the exhaust gas temperatures is the best way to know if turbo damage has occurred. Extended temperatures over 750°C likely mean trouble and an expensive repair.
- Blue smoke means oil in the combustion chambers and is likely caused by worn rings and valve guides. Repairs are expensive.

- Listen to the exhaust for escaping exhaust gas from anywhere but the tail pipe. Do this by putting your shoe over the end on the tailpipe. This forces gas to escape from any leaks. Rust at the tail end of the exhaust is common and not serious, but rust in silencers is a more expensive problem. When the engine decelerates it should not smoke. If it does, it may mean worn valve guides.
- Listen to the engine – does it clatter or are there any knocking sounds? Sounds like these can indicate worn bearings, cam chains, rockers, etc. If the engine ticks, it could mean a simple problem of valve clearances that require adjustment or worn hydraulic lifters. It is advisable to have an expert take a look and have a listen.
- Check the air filter – an excessively dirty one will mean a poorly maintained vehicle.
- Driving a 4x4 is different to driving a normal vehicle. Because of the complex transmission, and the heavy clutch and transmission backlash, smooth gear changes can be a little difficult to handle at first on some models.
- Test the brakes. Drive at about 50 kph and when it is safe, push on the brake pedal until the vehicle comes to a halt. There should be no tendency to veer from straight-ahead. The brake pedal should not sink all the way to the floor. If it does, there could be fluid seepage inside the brake master cylinder or wheel cylinder which would require a brake system overhaul.
- After driving for a few minutes, check the water temperature gauge. If it is equipped with an oil pressure gauge, check that also. Low oil pressure could mean worn engine bearings.
- Take the vehicle onto the motorway and run it up to a reasonable speed. There should be no undue vibration. Vibration could mean a simple problem such as wheel balance, or, at worst, an unbalanced prop-shaft which could have caused gearbox bearing and oil seal failure. A quick inspection of the gearbox at the prop-shafts for oil leaks may reveal the source of the problem.
- Test all gear ratios. Accelerate and decelerate sharply in all gears. Doing this may cause it to jump out of gear, a common problem with well used 4x4 transfer gearboxes.
- Testing a 4x4 off-road is not easy. It is not fair to the owner to go crashing through axle deep mud to see if the vehicle can cope – especially if you are an inexperienced driver. The best way to do this is to look closely at the vehicle specifications and compare them with other vehicles. Ask other owners of the same type of vehicle for their comments. Do this and you will have a good idea of what you are buying in terms of performance.
- Army surplus vehicles have normally been abused and will need a great deal of rebuilding work to get them into a reliable condition.

Steves Auto Clinic

The Country's Leading Petrol & Diesel Performance Enhancement Specialists

Home Page   **Road Tests**   **Enquiries**   **Contact Us**   **Brochures**

- Service, Repairs & Maintenance
- Cylinder head Conversions
- Intercooler Systems
- Plug & Play Systems
- Unichip Tuning
- Dyna Tuning
- Exhaust Systems & Performance Branches
- Performance Airfilters
- SAC Trucks

Just follow the leaders !

Boost Your Knowledge

Steves Auto Clinic up to speed on the information highway

Steves Auto Clinic, the country's leading petrol & diesel auto specialists, boasts a range of products and services well-suited to the freeways and byways of South Africa, but motoring consumers can also benefit from the company's skills on the information superhighway.

The SAC website is not only informative, but in the line with the company's reputation for creating vehicles that are both fast and efficient, it operates quickly too.

The overall design of the site is clean and refreshing with the emphasis on speed and user-friendlyness. No fancy bells and whistles, flash effects or other gizmos to slow the page down; just pure efficiency and loads of useful information

www.steves.co.za

2. VEHICLES

SOFT-ROADERS

LIGHTWEIGHTS

WORK HORSES AND PICK-UPS

STATION-WAGONS

UNUSUAL VEHICLES

THE TRICKY PART of choosing a four-wheel drive vehicle is that modern off-roaders have dual personalities. Most are required to cruise economically and comfortably and when the road ends these same vehicles are asked to climb hills more suited to a mountain goat. Armed with insight into how vehicles are designed to cope with these demands is of significant advantage to the buyer.

The comments that follow are derived from my own experience and the many off-road enthusiasts out there whose opinions I value. Remember, these should be regarded as opinions and not facts and while it is sometimes unusual to find objective criticism in the motoring press, the purpose of this book would be frustrated if the opinions contained herein were subject to pressure from advertisers.

1. *Soft-roaders: These are 4x4s without the key ingredients necessary for true off-road use i.e. Low-transfer gearing and adequate clearance. Not all soft-roaders are included here and vehicles I regard as useless in any off-road situation have been omitted. Vehicles that lie between the soft-roader and station-wagon categories, having low-range gearing but inadequate clearance, are in this category. With all soft-roaders, off-road, the automatics always perform better than the manuals.*

2. *Super-roaders: My term for a new category of 4x4s. Just like a soft-roader but with a super price tag. (Because you can't compare a Cayenne to an Xtrail). Some have low gearing and reasonable clearance but vehicles in this category are so costly and are built with a light-duty chassis design, that they cannot be regarded as true off-roaders. The autos always perform better than the manuals.*

3. *Lightweights. These vehicles fall between soft-roaders and working off-roaders. All have true off-road ability however many have very poor on-road performance.*

4. *Workhorses and pick-ups: These vehicles range from uncompromising workhorses like the Land Rover Defender to single and double-cab pick-ups. All have true off-road ability and on-road performance that ranges from adequate to excellent.*

5. *Leisure station-wagons. Vehicles in this categroy range between basic station-wagon off-roaders through to luxury wagons, all the way to off-road 'limousines'.*

Previous and current models are included in all these categories.

SOFT-ROADERS

KIA SPORTAGE

A Korean lightweight, the Sportage was introduced in the mid nineties. It has part-time 4x4 and low-range gearing but ground clearance is poor. While it is classed as a soft-roader its low-range gearbox extends its versatility greatly. It has proved itself to be unsuited to long stretches of rough gravel as its light-duty build soon shows signs of wear.

KIA NMOTORS

LAND ROVER FREELANDER

Land Rover's littlie is not so little. It is almost as big as an early Discovery on the outside and like an early Discovery a little cramped on the inside. Its main failing is the badge; Land Rovers have always been exemplary off-roaders, but not this one. Unfortunately many buyers fall into the marketing trap and expect the vehicle to do what it was never designed to do. The Freelander is not an off-roader.

LAND ROVER SA

To compensate for the absence of low gearing, electronic hill descent control is fitted but the system works at a too high speed to be really effective. Reliability problems are common but most accounts seem to centre on clutch failure. In most cases this is because frustrated drivers, believing that they have purchased an off-roader, slip the clutch to take obstacles and soon burn it out.

The Freelander performs well on gravel but suffers from clearance shortage on even modest sand tracks. On-road it is a joy to drive and the engine choices suit the vehicle well; the second generation engines are a big improvement. Interior appointments are typical Land Rover and exude style. The high driving position is the best part of the Freelander.

MITSUBISHI OUTLANDER

The Outlander is in my view a late starter and enters the soft-roader market where other models were two or so years ago. The styling, particularly the exterior, already feels dated. Performance on road is pleasant, but nothing special and while it is roomy the off-road performance is fair for this category. The engine is a 2,4 four-cylinder petrol linked to a 'Sportronic' four-speed auto transmission.

DAIMLER CHRYSLER SA

Full-time four-wheel drive is by a centre viscous coupling. Clearance of the Outlander can only be described as poor. One of its saving graces is its particularly roomy load area and a competitive price when compared with competitors like the X-Trail and Rav-4. Like many in this category the interior is fashionable and funky.

NISSAN X-TRAIL

Nissan's baby 4x4 is as close to a true soft-roader you can get without actually being one. Its off-road performance is one of the best in its class, performing well in sand and handling well on gravel. It impressed me in quite difficult sand conditions and on-road it's comfortable and easy to drive. In off-road driving, steep slopes and rocky terrain finds the X-Trail battling with no low gearing to continue. The diesel model is one of the best performing diesels in this category.

SUBARU FORESTER

The Forester is Subaru's step towards building a true off roader but their marketing stategy has always baffled me: Their 4x4 saloons have a reputation for reliability, performance and safety and the Forester is just the same. Why did they stop at a soft-roader? While driving the Forester I felt a sense of frustration because the vehicle has obvious potential as a true off-roader, its performance falling short due to a lack of low-range gearing. The Forester has a 2,5-litre 4-cylinder petrol engine, is well built and always nice to drive. Unfortunately the new models have even less clearance than the old.

TOYOTA RAV4

The first soft-roader on the market it was initially introduced as a concept car. While the early RAV4 had no low gearing, it had good clearance, and was quite a good off-roader. The old and new models come in two body styles – three and five door versions. Changes to the original design were a cosmetic upgrade in mid-1998 and in 2000 an all-new model with most of the ground clearance removed was launched. In terms of off-road use the second generation RAV4 is a poor replacement and although a little more comfortable, doesn't have the crisp road handling or off-road ability of the first.

SUPER ROADERS

BMW X3 and X5

Since the introduction of the Porsche Cayene and the Toureg the X5 is no longer the best performing super-roader. Off and on-road the Toureg beats it and on-road so does the Cayenne. On road it's the same story. The X5 is a beautiful road performer, the closest thing to a regular saloon car without actually being one. Off-road the automatics are capable but without the clearance its abilities are limited. Engines include a 3-litre straight six and two V8s of over 4-litres with either a 5-speed auto or manual transmission. The auto is better by far.

www.porsche.com

Because you can.
The Porsche Cayenne S.

Porsche Centre Johannesburg
Tel: 011 686 9000

Porsche Centre Cape
Tel: 021 914 8200

The king of the soft-roaders: Porsche Cayenne. The off-road package includes real off road ability at a switch. Selectable anti-roll bars, air suspension and body protection.

DCSA@MOTORPICS

MERCEDES BENZ M-CLASS

Like other in this class, sophisticated and a reasonable off-roader, the M-class has a highly effective traction control but inadequate clearance to take full advantage of it. On-road it is the least refined in its class by a wide margin and is a dissapointing drive. I have heard it said that the M-class is not a 'real Mercedes', owing to its lack of solidity and security felt in all other Mercedes cars. I agree. The M-class is a disappointment when compared to all supers and most softies.

PORSCHE

PORSCHE CAYENNE

While the Cayenne is seen as a top challenger in this category, but off-road it leads the pack, because it has real off-road potential. Ground clearance is better than average for the class. Full-time four-wheel drive with a traction control, a centre diff lock, low range and a rear diff lock turns the Cayenne into a vehicle that lies between super and genuine off-roader. Its variable air suspension (optional) provides a not under-generous brake-over angle and a wading depth of 500mm. The two most popular engine options are the 'S', a potent 250kw V8 or the 'Turbo', an unspeakably quick 331kW V8-turbo. Both are coupled to a silky six-speed tiptronic gearbox. The off-road package includes a button to disable the ant-roll bars! A spectacular drive!

VW PRESS@MOTORPICS

VW TAUREG

The Toureg's V-10 turbo-diesel belies its name and the big engined models perform like the Paris-Dakar rally cars that whip past the ponderous Taureg caravans plying the Sahara. Clearance is fairly good with adjustable air suspension. The interior is intimidating with its electronic wizardry. A stunning drive on road, in the rough the suspension feels harsh but sure. In my view, the Taureg is second only to the Cayenne in refinement and performance.

LIGHTWEIGHTS

ASIA ROCSTA

The Asia Rocsta is a Jeep CJ look-alike with basic features and dated technology. The makers use slogans like 'dirt cheap' and 'The most fun you can have with your top off' when describing their vehicle, which gives you some idea of the position in the market. On road it's noisy and slow and when off-road, light and manoeuvrable but nothing special. Ground clearance is not as good as one would expect for this type of vehicle. Engines are a 1,8-litre petrol or a 2.2 diesel 4-cylinder. Spare parts are hard to find almost anywhere.

ASIA MOTORS

DAIHATSU ROCKY and TERIOS

The Rocky is a Japanese lightweight Jeep style vehicle powered by a turbo diesel 4-cylinder 2,7-litre engine and is fitted with independent front double wishbone suspension and solid axle and coil springs at the back. The Terios is an altogether different vehicle; curvaceous and stylish, it tackles the Freelander, RAV4 and Grand Vitara market although it is considerably smaller than all of these. It has full time four-wheel drive with a lockable centre differential but no transfer gearing. Performance can be best described as ordinary.

DAIHATSU

JEEP CJ

The first mass produced light all-purpose 4WD was the American World War II Jeep. At the outbreak of the war, the US Army required a 'Light Command and Reconnaissance Car' for use in the conflict. Four-wheel drive was a design priority and the American Bantam Company soon had a prototype being tested by the US Army. Unfortunately for American Bantam, they could not cope with the volume of production that was required, so a number of other manufacturers were called in to evaluate the Bantam.

Both Ford and Willys-Overland took up the challenge and built their own versions to be assessed. Ford called their new vehicle the Pygmy or alternatively the Ford model GP, short for 'General Purpose'. Willys-Overland called theirs the Jeep, the name coming from a character in the Popeye cartoon series called Eugene – a little 4WD that could do virtually anything. So the 'Jeep' was born.

The final vehicle was a combination of the best of all three designs and built by all three manufacturers. Over 638 000 were built before the end of the war and after it Willys-Overland continued building light 4x4s, and the 'Civilian Jeep', the Jeep CJ series, came into being. Both the Toyota Land Cruiser and Land Rover's original design principles can be traced to the Second World War Willys Jeep.

DAIMLER CHRYSLER SA

*Top: Jeep CJ2.
Middle: Original CJ 3
in original condition.
Bottom:, 4.0 Wrangler
is the current
'CJ' equivalent.
Middle right:
Ex military CJ6 with
over-sizes tyres.*

The 'civilian Jeep' or CJ series was first offered as a military machine with minor modifications to suit the civilian market. The CJ2 was the first, and early models are now collectors' items. The second model, the CJ3, with raised bonnet to accommodate the new engine was first made in 1952. This machine is still made in India and is called the Mahindra, although with a different engine. All CJ Jeeps are excellent off-roaders, the CJ2 and CJ3 being the most favoured by the Jeep fanatics. Suspension is by solid axles and leaf springs. Depending on the model, they are available in part time or permanent four-wheel drive. Once built in South Africa by Volkswagen, there are few good second-hand units available.

New models are called Wrangler and come with a 4-litre 6-cylinder engine. A limited-slip rear diff, good low-down torque and fair clearance make the Wrangler great fun off-road.

LADA NIVA

The Lada Niva is built by AutoVAZ, 900 kilometres south of Moscow at Togliatti, a giant vehicle plant employing more than 130 000 people and turning out over 2000 units each day. Currently the factory exports over 140 000 vehicles every year and of these, 60% are Lada Nivas. No other Soviet vehicle has found the following that this unimpressive vehicle has and it is testament to the strength of the four-wheel drive market throughout the world that the only widely exported Soviet passenger car should be a four-wheel drive.

When looking closely at the Lada, it should only be compared to similarly priced vehicles, although it is the only station wagon in its price range. When this is done the Lada is great. It is very mobile, highly effective off-road and better on-road than most of its competitors.

Reliability problems and its total lack of anything resembling style continue to be the most serious drawback of the Niva.

The Lada has a live rear axle and independent front coil spring suspension, which has excellent articulation. Although the interior is reminiscent of a 1975 Fiat 124, suspension and transmission is of a fairly advanced design. It has permanent four-wheel drive with a lockable centre differential. Other minor changes have been made to cater for the Western market, namely improved sound-proofing, better seats, removable rear seats and an improved tailgate design allowing better loadability. Current models have a new 4-cylinder 1700cc engine. Spare parts, like many vehicles in this class, are only readily available in major urban centres.

Models available include the Standard, Safari, Cub, 5-door s/wagon, single cab and double cab pick-up. Advanced option packs include alloy wheels and sunroofs.

MAHINDRA

Based on the CJ3 Jeep, it is built in India from Willys' body panels and transmission parts mated to a Peugeot diesel or petrol engine. Some of the good points of the last true CJ3 Jeep remain, such as grease nipples on points of high stress axle and suspension areas. Bucket seats and a few niceties have been added. The Mahindra gives birth to intense boredom on the open road, managing a noisy 120kph downhill, with a tailwind, if you're lucky.

MITSUBISHI PAJERO - SWB

Many Pajero buyers, no doubt due to excellent marketing, believe that they are buying a vehicle that has won several Paris-Dakar rallies. The fact is that what is available to the public shares no more than technology with this "rally proven' space-age machine so successful in this event, and only in the very early events were production Pajeros entered. I mention this because I have had Pajero buyers read my criticisms of the vehicle and react alarmingly at my conclusions.

The Pajero SWB has few serious competitors in the pocket-sized four-wheel drive market because while it is an excellent town car it is also good off-road and has, through its evolution, retained the vital ingredients of a true off-roader, namely low-range gearing and good ground clearance.

The short wheelbase Pajero is not as good as its long wheelbase brother either on-road or off. On-road it is not quite as smooth and effortless but, in this sphere, is superior to anything in its class. One thing that struck me when driving the SWB well over the speed limit on a film shoot was its outstanding stability at high speed, not something normally associated with short-wheelbase vehicles. Off-road its ride is

DAIMLER CHRYSLER SA

bouncy and quite choppy and its severe lack of wheel travel on the front wheels soon becomes apparent when traversing uneven terrain. Despite this, this shortcoming can often be overcome by driving technique and the Pajero has gained a vast and devoted following. Some models have a rear diff-lock fitted, a significant advantage with this vehicle, more so than most.

The 2002 shape, distinguished by its rounded wheel arches and rally-car styling, is better off-road than it looks. Its bodywork, on first appearance looks low to the ground but off-road it's quite good, its auto gearboxes working brilliantly in the rough. Add some clearance with an after-market suspension kit and the Pajero SWB is very good. Interior, the SWB version is similar to the LWB but, with four adults, expect complaints about a severe lack of leg-room and packing space. For engine choice, read about the LWB later in this chapter.

NISSAN TERRANO

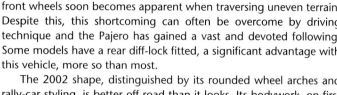

On first seeing the Terrano, particularly the short wheelbase version, one can be excused for making comparisons with the Freelander or RAV4. But this is wrong, because the Terrano is a true off-roader. So, comparisons should be made with the Suzuki Vitara, Kia Sportage and the Pajero SWB and the long wheelbase Terrano should be compared with the Isuzu Frontier. The Terrano out-performs the best of these in many respects.

Off-road the Terrano is terrific. It has part-time four-wheel drive without an axle diff lock and approach, break-over and departure angles are good, particularly with the short wheelbase version. Clearance under the diff is average. Wheel travel is fair and the suspension is on the stiff side. I pushed the suspension by driving over an axle twister a little too fast and it didn't complain a bit. The interior is pleasant; the high driving position just right and packing space is generous, even in the SWB version.

SSANGYONG KORANDO

Arguably one of the ugliest and tastelessly styled 4x4s ever made the Korando is based on a shortened Musso chassis and performance wise, the Korando is below average in most respects. Its front-end overhang is long and heavy which causes the front suspension to dive in, bottoming at the slightest provocation. Wheel travel is fair but clearance, especially between the front wheels is poor. While the Korando petrol versions feel powerful its road feel is heavy and ponderous for such a compact vehicle. The turbo-diesel model is the better choice. Overall the Korando doesn't shine in any aspect apart from its used vehicle prices which are usually low for this kind of vehicle. I guess they are not very popular. Not surprising really.

SUZUKI SJ 410 and SJ 413 SAMURAI

The diminutive Suzuki Jeep is not considered a serious off-roader because of its small size and inability to carry the kinds of loads needed for extended trips. It is also slow and uncomfortable. However, off-road ability is excellent due mainly to its small size and lightweight. On the beach and over dunes it will out perform most 4x4s but its limitations show when asked to climb hills on uneven terrain where its lack of weight and stiff suspension hamper ability.

Early models roll over very easily, so a novice driver should be very careful with obstacles taken too fast. When bogging down, even in the worst case, the Suzuki can be easily dug out. Suspension is by solid beam axles on leaf springs on older models and coil springs on the new. The current model is enlarged marginally and is called Samurai. It offers improved comfort and better features with its coil spring suspension and a wider track, making it more stable. The long wheelbase models are better working machines and are popular with aid organisations operating in Central Africa.

SUZUKI VITARA AND GRAND VITARA

Suzuki's other; more upmarket lightweight is the Vitara, a vehicle with two wheels in the softies category and two wheels in this category. Unlike many vehicles often compared to it, the Vitara has a low-range gearbox, equipping the vehicle with reasonable off-road ability. It does, however, suffer from a lack of clearance and this is the design's downfall. Despite this, and its road tyres and feminine looks, it is surprisingly agile off-road and has even been used for difficult long distance trips into Botswana by some who are more daring than me. High speed handling is vague and in a cross wind at over 100kph it's scary. The later Grand Vitara's ride is improved over the early models. It comes with features such as air conditioning and electrical adjustment for the exterior mirrors and with a choice of engines, a 2-litre V6 and a multi-valve 1,6-litre four-cylinder.

SVM MOHICAN

The SVM (Special Vehicle Manufacturers) Mohican is a 2-seater Jeep CJ style vehicle developed and built in small numbers in South Africa. It is a crude, robust design and an outstanding off-roader performing very well in competitive events. Suspension is by leaf springs that allow better-than-average vertical movement on a galvanised box section chassis. The body is glass fibre with steel reinforcing.

The SVM is a little overpowered, the engine a Ford Essex 3-litre V6 attached to a Borg Warner 5-speed dual-transfer gearbox and lockable rear diff. The SVM is no longer built but many found their way to the homes of serious off road enthusiasts around the world.

WORKHORSES AND PICK-UPS

FORD COURIER/RANGER

Ford's pickup has progressed beyond the 4x2 conversion it once was. Engines have improved, comfort increased and they can be regarded as true off-roaders. The suspension has been refined to cope with the dual lifestyle of this leisure vehicle. In the past the Ford Courier range was not a particularly popular 4x4 when compared to its closest rivals the Isuzu and Nissan but today things are changing.

There are two engine options, a 2,5-litre four-cylinder turbo-diesel and a 4-litre V6 petrol. The turbo-diesel is the better choice, in my opinion, for just about everything, even towing! It's lively, economical and pleasant to drive on road and off. The V6 is underpowered for a 4-litre and its performance towing was poor, being underpowered, thirsty and the auto gearbox was troublesome and awkard to drive. Off road the auto box needs skill to control with surge that can only be arrested with left-foot braking. Comfort for road cruising is excellent and I enjoyed the vehicle on the long haul. Suspension is typical in this class, independent torsion bars at front, leaf springs and solid axle at the back.

ISUZU KB

Isuzu's initial foray into the South African 4x4 world was in March 1972 with a 2-litre petrol pick-up badged 'Chev LUV'. The 4x4 derivative came seven years later together with the name change to Isuzu KB series. By now a 1,9-litre diesel engine had been included in the range that was available in the 4x4 chassis by July 1979. In March 1984 engine evolution placed a 2,3-litre engine in the 4x4. The range was still going strong until March 1987 when the entire range was given a face-lift and the 4x4 KB was available in 2,3-litre petrol and 2,5-litre diesel engine, both models being single cab layouts. In March 1993 the trend-setting 2,8-litre direct injection turbo-diesel and 2,6-litre petrol engines were introduced together with a double-cab body. For a while the top-spec model was called Reef and Frontier, (before the Frontier station wagon was introduced in 1998) a double-cab offered with both engine options. A third 4x4 variant is the 250D, a 2,5-litre normally aspirated diesel engine in a single cab.

In the nineties the Isuzu KB evolved into a respectable off-roader against stiff competition from Nissan, Colt and Mazda. Later it still managed to hold its own against the 1999 revamped Toyota Hilux, despite the Isuzu's design being by far the oldest in the range.

A rear differential locking mechanism, now becoming standard on many pick-ups, upgrades the Isuzu to an effective off-roader. The petrol 2,6-litre engine is a good engine but nothing special, and some report

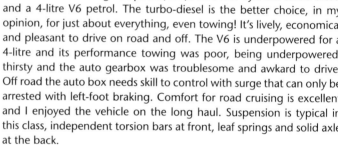

thirstier than some of the competition. However, the turbo-diesel engine gives ample power on the open road when carrying a load, good low-down torque, making it a good performer off-road. Lack of ground clearance is the Isuzu's biggest drawback and the standard towing attachment snags on obstacles. Late Frontier models, released before the rounded body shape was introduced, feature an aluminium bull bar, sump guard and a rear diff lock. The changes in the new models are largely cosmetic, excluding the V6, which is quieter and more powerful. The diesel-turbo-engine is still my favourite, and for a working 4x4 it is the better choice. Its the Isuzu's reliability and frugal diesels that keep this very old design so popular. An all new range is due for release mid 2004. (The Australian model is pictured right.)

LAND ROVER

The concept of a light, dual-purpose workhorse crossed the Atlantic in 1946 when the British Rover Company developed the Land Rover. Its designer, Maurice Wilks, then chairman of the Rover Company, was using an ex-military Jeep for work on his farm. He conceived the idea of a British equivalent – so the imperishable story of the "Landy" was born. The original Land Rover was announced in April 1948 and was remarkably like the Jeep. Fifty years later Land Rover Ltd is the

world's only vehicle manufacturer building nothing but four-wheel drive vehicles.

What made the Land Rover unique was its ability to accept power take-offs for driving agricultural equipment such as pumps, saws and winches, and it was marketed as a lightweight tractor that could also carry passengers. Its body was made of Birmabright (developed in Birmingham England) aluminium as a means of overcoming the government's steel rationing and as an aid in production as it could be hand-shaped, obviating the need for new machine presses. To save time the prototype was built on a Jeep chassis and had its steering wheel located in the middle. The idea of this was that farmers familiar with tractors would immediately be at home behind the wheel and there would be no need for right-hand-drive and left-hand-drive versions. This idea was soon dropped and the production vehicle had a standard layout and an all-new welded box section steel chassis was made for it. Listed among the first model's optional extras were doors, side screens, weather protection, a passenger seat, cushions, a heater, a starting handle and the tyre for the standard spare wheel.

Land Rover's design, being simple and easy to maintain, gave it the potential for worldwide use, and complied with the British government's post-war stipulation that new projects should be geared for export. It is ironic that the Land Rover idea was originally a stop gap to keep the Rover company busy until steel was available to produce more of the luxury sedans for which it was famous. Thirty years later it was the only part of British Leyland that was turning a profit.

By the end of 1949, 8000 Land Rovers had been delivered. These vehicles, known as the 'Series One', continued to be manufactured until 1958, with the only changes being to the engine and transmission. In 1950 the transmission was changed from its original permanent 4WD system that had a free-wheel inserted between the front propeller shaft and the transfer box to overcome the windup when driven on a sealed surface. The new system was truly selectable, allowing the driver to engage the front prop-shaft at will. This system continued until 1983 with the release of the full-time 4WD system in the newly developed Land Rover 110.

In 1954 the first change was made to the chassis. Still designated the Series-1, the new wheelbase was 86 inches (increased from the original 80 inches). The overall length increased from 11ft to 11ft 8.7 inches and the vehicle was 2.6 inches wider. The unladen weight had increased by over 200 lbs. 1954 also saw the introduction of the first long wheelbase version, its wheelbase measuring 107 inches. With 41 inches of additional load space and vastly increased payload it would keep the peace with the sales department. In less than four years this wheelbase was extended by 2 inches, from 107 to 109 inches, in

Early Land Rovers still make a worthwile purchase. They are easy to work on and if you are prepared to tinker they make great playthings. Also, the Land Rover cult is something incomparable in the world of 4x4s.

order to allow the fitting of the first engine alternative – a diesel unit producing 51 bhp at 3500 rpm and a torque of 87lb/ft at 2000 rpm. This option added 195lbs to the curb weight. The short wheelbase vehicles also undertook a chassis change for the same reason – the 86 inch wheelbase became 88 inches.

In 1957, nine years after it was launched, management decided that the Land Rover should be thoroughly reappraised and, owing to increasing pressure from the sales force, major improvements be made. The results appeared in April of 1958 and came in the form of the Series-2. Still very much a Land Rover, the changes in appearance were obvious. The front wings and body sides were slightly curved and the bonnet had a somewhat subtle shape change. The chassis frame and exhaust, once visible from the side, were hidden by adding additional bodywork below the side panels and doors.

Owing to the variations in Land Rover design during the last 46 years of production, it would take an entire volume to list the specifications of all of the different vehicles.

COMPARISON CHART.
1948-1953; THE FIRST JEEP, LAND ROVER
AND TOYOTA LAND CRUISER

	JEEP	LAND ROVER	TOYOTA
ENGINE			
Capacity	2199 cc	1595 cc	3386 cc
Cylinders	4 in-line	4 in-line	6 in-line
Bhp	60 @ 3600 rpm	50 @ 4000 rpm	85 @ 2300 rpm
TRANSMISSION			
Main gearbox	3-spd selectable 4wd	3-spd full-time 4wd	4-spd selectable 4wd
Transfer gearbox	1.97:1	2.52:1	no transfer gearing
Final drive	4.88:1	4.88:1	n/available
CHASSIS			
	Pressed steel channel	Steel box section	Pressed steel channel
SUSPENSION			
	Live axles on leaf springs	Live axles on leaf springs	Live axles on leaf springs
DIMENSIONS			
Wheel base	80 inches	80 inches	90 inches
Track front	48 inches	50 inches	54 inches
Track rear	48 inches	50 inches	53 inches
Length	133 inches	132 inches	151 inches
Width	62 inches	60 inches	65 inches
Weight	2315 lbs	2520 lbs	n/available

For the first time, concessions were made to driver comfort: easier operating pendant pedals, sprung seats, glass side door windows instead of Perspex and, on the 109 inch version, an adjustable driver's seat. Even a carpet covering the transmission hump between the two front seats was offered as an optional extra.

At this time the chassis layouts stabilised with the long wheelbases measuring 109 inches and the short 88 inches, which stayed this way until 1984. With the Series Two the track was increased by 1.5 inches and the rear springs were hung from the side of the chassis rail instead of directly beneath it. This gave an extra two inches of vertical wheel travel. Perhaps the most important mechanical improvement was to the engine line up. A new overhead valve 2.286 cc petrol engine was offered, although a few early Series Two 109" machines still had the older 1.997 cc engine fitted.

During 10 years of Land Rover production the engine power had risen by 40% and engine torque, so important to a working four-wheel drive, had increased by 50%. The price had increased too – by 40%. In the first year of production, 28 000 Series-2 machines were produced. Just 17 years after it was first produced the half millionth Land Rover was built. Only two years after the Series-2 was announced, vehicles with minor suspension refinements, known as the Series-2A were in the showrooms.

After the Land Rover 109-inch Forward Control came a military derivative in the form of the 101-inch wheelbase Forward Control light troop carrier. These vehicles have become collectors' items and are outstanding in off-road terrain. They are powered by the Rover 3500 V8 with Range Rover transmission components and solid axles on leaf springs. They are noisy and uncomfortable on the road but very versatile for the serious outback adventurer as the chassis layout offers enormous versatility for the fitting of additional fuel and water tanks, spare wheels, stoves, beds and all manner of other safari equipment.

In 1967 a six cylinder engine, originally fitted to the Rover 95 passenger car, was squeezed into the Land Rover's engine bay. The 2625 cc unit's output was reduced from that of the saloon car version. Camshaft timings were adjusted and the compression ratio was reduced to, in some cases, as low as 7:1 for Third World use. The engine was rated at 83 bhp at 4 500 rpm and a torque of 128 lbs/ft at 1 500 rpm. A high capacity oil bath air filter was also fitted and the engine produced the smooth pulling power famous in Rover's saloon cars. it was only offered with the long wheelbase version.

In the Land Rover Series-3, the most noticeable change was a new look front end with the headlamps being moved outwards (although this modification appeared during the last months of Series-2a production) and a brand new radiator grille. In Australia many outback travellers complained about the new plastic grille that could no longer be used for cooking over a fire.

With the new design, however, water cans could now be fitted in the recesses next to the grille without blocking the headlamps. In the cockpit the instruments were shifted from the centre of the dashboard to directly in front of the driver. It also featured a brand new gearbox with revised ratios, synchromesh on 1st and 2nd, bigger and better brakes and improvements to the seat cushions and ventilation system.

In June 1976 the one millionth Land Rover, a specially painted Series-3 short wheelbase version, was driven off the production line by the Mayor of Birmingham during a grand ceremony at the Solihull plant in the English Midlands. Production of the Series-3 ended in 1984 following the introduction in 1970 of the Range Rover and in 1983 of the One-Ten.

LAND ROVER SERIES 1, 2, 2a AND 3

Many of these workhorses are bought and sold second-hand. If they are well maintained, and you are prepared to spend some time keeping them running, they are a good purchase and are sure to last almost indefinitely. Although the body is aluminium it does corrode. Pay special attention to the chassis, which must be inspected closely. Areas prone to rust are in the area of the spring shackles and the rear cross member. By modern standards, they are unsophisticated vehicles and Series-1 versions are now collectors' items. Series-2 versions are prone to axle half-shaft breakages and spares should be carried to remote areas. Clean Series 3 versions can make an excellent second-hand purchase.

THE LAND ROVER CULT.
Unique in the world of 4x4s is the Land Rover cult. The passion associated with this vehicle, in particular the older Series 1,2,3, and Defender is unmatched in the automotive world. The glue is a bond of mutual respect, passion and love for their vehicles. Waves from complete strangers, flashing headlights and warm greetings in a camp site just because you drive a vehicle with the same badge is rarely understood by those who have never experienced it. So often outsiders see it as just a bond of mutual suffering. But it is so much more than that.

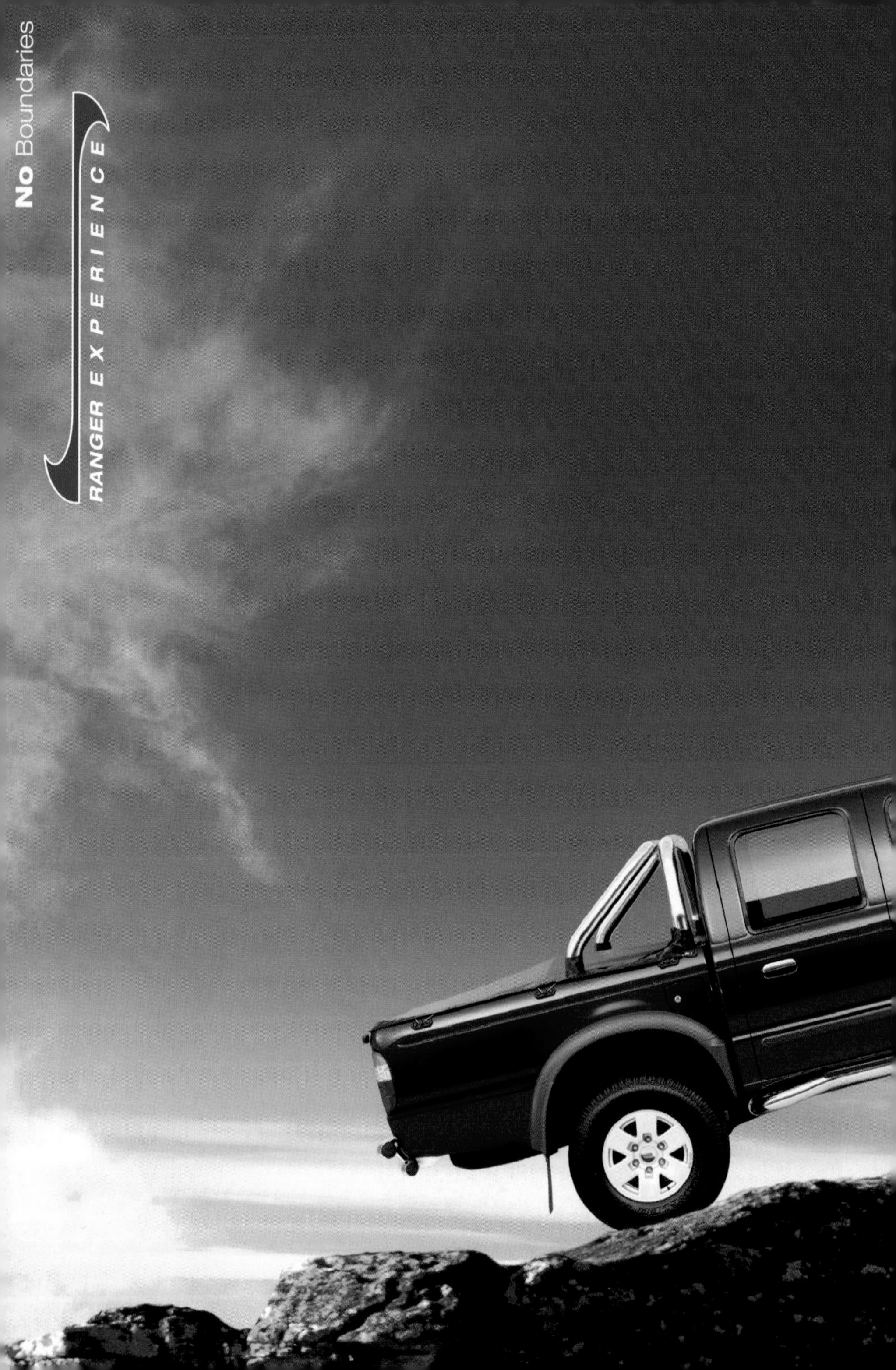
No Boundaries
RANGER EXPERIENCE

...And get a free off-road driving experience.

When you buy a Ford**Ranger** 4X4 or 4X2 with diff-lock, you are entitled to become a member of the Ranger owners club, AKA "Ford **No** Boundaries Ranger Experience". Included in the package is a free off-road driving course. Regular club activities include weekends away and trips to places like Lesotho, Swaziland, Mozambique, Botswana and Namibia. This is a club for the whole family. You'll also enjoy great discounts on things like tyres, GPS's, recovery equipment and reduced insurance. Not to mention the chance to win great prizes in our quarterly newsletter. So if you're looking for off-road excitement and adventure, buy a Ford**Ranger** and join the club.

Treat yourself to a new Ford**Ranger**...

A South African version of the Series-3 appeared in the form of the R6 – a 109-inch wheelbase chassis and a 12-seat station wagon body. Behind the very attractive flush grille was a 2.6-litre six-cylinder car engine and Spanish-assembled gearbox. It was a troublesome vehicle from the start and no matter how much redesigning work was done the overheating problems could not be overcome. They are common second-hand purchases and most continue to plague their owners with overheating. Another Land Rover that shared the flush grille of the R6 was the V8. This was the predecessor to the One-Ten. It had a V8 engine and Range Rover transmission but with lead spring suspension. As not many were built they too have become a favourite with collectors.

LAND ROVER DEFENDER 90/110/130

In 1982, with the success of the Series-3 and the Range Rover behind them, Land Rover decided to combine the two designs. Having made no significant change to the traditional Land Rover design for so long, this was a giant leap forward. The result was the Land Rover 110 (One Ten) and 90 (Ninety). The new vehicle was faster, better on the road and better off. It was smoother, stronger, more comfort with less noise. Although the vehicle appeared to be a Range Rover-Land Rover hybrid, it did not share as many components as one might think. The chassis design was Range Rover but, unlike the Range Rover, it was built to be strong enough for military use. Like the Range Rover coil springs, panhard rods and radius arms located the axles but the gearbox was new, although it also had full-time four-wheel drive. Much of the body was common to the Series-3 but, because the new axles had a wider track, wheel arch eyebrows were added. Engine options were a 4-cylinder 2.1/4-litre and 3.5-litre V8 petrol.

In 1990 both the One Ten and Ninety were named 'Defender' and produced in three wheelbases: 92,9, 110 and 130 inches, called the Defender Ninety, One Ten and One Thirty respectively.

The Defender is a truck. Its close cousins, the Discovery and Range Rover, are off-road cars. The Defender can best be described as an off-roader with acceptable road manners. It is not altogether suited to everyday suburban motoring and, although not uncomfortable, it is big and turns like a school bus. Luxury packages are called County or Hi-Line and include cloth seats, carpeting and air-conditioning.

In later years engine options were a 2800cc 6-cylinder BMW petrol, three versions of a 2500cc 4-cylinder turbo-charged diesel and a 5-cylinder turbo-diesel engine. The first diesel was the '100' engine and was plagued with over-heating problems. The second version, the '200' was a vast improvement, offering reliability combined with excellent economy. The last 4-cylinder, predictably called the '300', was again an improvement. A cam-chain tensioner modification to the 300 engine was necessary and if considering a second-hand purchase, make sure this mod has been done. If not, the clock is ticking to a huge engine rebuild bill should the timing belt fail! The BMW engine is thirsty and way overpowered for the chassis. With the Tdi 5-cylinder diesel gone is the tractor-like thump of the older diesels and almost gone is the severe turbo lag. Lots of low down torque and improved cruising has made a great vehicle greater.

Above: Land Rover Defender 90 and 110. Below: Land Rover Defender 110 Td5.

Between 1988 and 1991, V8 Defenders were fitted with a Spanish-assembled LT85 5-speed gearbox. A high percentage of these gearboxes were faulty due to under-sized bearings being fitted in the factory. These gearboxes are good for only about 80,000kms, though many have failed much sooner. Once the bearings wear, the gearbox becomes noisy in all ratios other than fourth. Purchasing a second-hand vehicle fitted with an untouched LT85 gearbox is risky. Virtually all Defenders have or have had waterproofing problems. I guess this is the last remnant of a 1950's design.

The double-cab 110 variant is another incarnation of the design, practical and ideal for expedition use. Back seat passengers quickly complain of lack of leg and head room and an overly high seating position. Double cabs are also built on the 130 high-capacity chassis.

Sadly, over the past 15 years, the build quality of Land Rovers has deteriorated to the point that they now have a widely held reputation of unreliability. Unlike the old days when electrics were a common problem, today repeated failures of engines and gearboxes are tainting the reputation of what I consider to be one of the most outstanding and highly versatile 4x4s available today. The result is scores of Land Rover owners are now looking at Japanese replacements.

MAZDA B-SERIES/DRIFTER

The Mazda-B 4x4 was introduced in November 1990 as a single cab version, followed by a double-cab variant that is still with us today, although it is now called the Drifter and is a well-developed and popular off-roader. Today, two engines are offered: a 4-cylinder 2.5-litre intercooled turbo-diesel and a 2,6-litre 4-cylinder petrol. The ubiquitous 3-litre V6 Essex engine has been discontinued. Suspension is independent double wishbone with coils springs at the front and leaf springs at the rear and automatic free-wheel hubs are now standard. The diesel version is the better vehicle in just about all driving conditions and performance of the diesel is the same as the Ford Ranger, where the chassis, engine and drive-train is so similar.

MITSUBISHI COLT

Introduced in November 1994, the Mitsubishi Colt is a twin-cab 4X4 based on a two-wheel drive pick-up modified to compete with the wide range of double-cab vehicles. It has part-time four-wheel drive with automatic free-wheel hubs. Some early Colts had transfer gearbox failures, a problem which was sorted out fairly early in the vehicle's production run, so buying second-hand should be fairly safe.

The second generation Colt is happily not an old Colt with some fancy body panels and interior – it is all new. Off-road the improvement is outstanding. Gone is the harsh ride and lack of wheel travel. The Colt had become an accomplished off-roader to take its place with the best of Toyota, Isuzu and Nissan. The V6 engine is also excellent off-road. Driving up steep banks I deliberately maintained revs at below 1000 and it still pulled strongly. There are not many V6 engines that can match its flexibility. Comfort and ergonomics are also modernised and improved. The Colt was the first double-cab to be available with automatic transmission, which I don't recommend if your intention is rough off-road driving, especially with the V6.

NISSAN HARDBODY

In the early eighties Nissan launched the Tracker, a 4x4 derivative of their 4x2 pick-up. The Tracker was very much a conversion, a vehicle that performed reasonably well but fell way behind purpose-built 4x4 pick-ups like the Hilux. In 1989 Nissan's new Sani became the most popular Nissan 4x4, a stationwagon built partly of fibreglass, and based on the newly released Hardbody body and chassis. Hardbodys have part-time four-wheel drive and manual free-wheel front hubs and were offered with two petrol engine options including a 3-litre V6.

All Hardbodys have a solid rear axle on leaf springs and independant front double wishbone torsion bar suspension. In late 1995 the front suspension was given a major revision with the addition of dual front coil springs and shock absorbers designed primarily to improve performance in rough conditions.

The last of the 2,7 diesel engine had the almost unbearable turbo-lag turned out while the latest 3.0 turbo-diesel puts it up front in the battle with the best of the Hiluxes and Colts. The diesel engine is a vast improvement on the old with low down torque and off-road drivability one of the best in its class. The double cab is also one of the roomiest.

TOYOTA HILUX

Once called 'The Workhorse of Africa' the Hilux 4x4 first made its appearance in 1979, 10 years after the first 4x2 Hilux was introduced. This vehicle shared many body components with the one-ton Stout. In 1984 the body was redesigned and with it South Africa's first double-cab configuration met with immediate success. The country's 4x4 leisure market got what it wanted, a loadable workhorse that could carry passengers too.

In 1989 the Hilux became the first diesel 4x4 pick-up on the market and in 1991 the well known Raider models were introduced. In 1998 the Hilux changed what I believe to be fundamental to its success in Africa – the suspension layout. The old model Hilux has simple and very robust leaf spring axle mountings. The solid axles and massive ground clearance are what make it such a formidable off-roader. If you are considering purchasing a vehicle in this class and expect it to work hard in difficult conditions then you cannot do better than the old Hilux. Renowned for reliability, it was built with a 2.2 or 2.4-litre 4-cylinder petrol and a 2.4-litre diesel engines.

The general criticism was that the Hilux's suspension has always been too harsh but could be put down to the fact that the vehicle was designed to carry a load under adverse conditions. In the case of the old Hilux the suspension was not compromised to a great extent and the occupants paid for it by having to endure a back-breaking ride in the rough. Although the Hilux is tough it does not like to be overloaded and can be broken if this is done. In pre-1985 versions the battery support bracket is prone to failure and, although this was improved with later models, it often fails in vehicles used in off-road conditions. A most worthwhile modification to the old Hilux to improve the ride and its off-road performance is Old Man Emu suspension.

The first major mechanical and styling change came with the launch of an all new Hilux in 1998. Its introduction brought fear and dread to die-hard Hilux lovers because real off-roaders know that nothing compares to solid axles when you're off-road. It is true that solid axles offer many advantages off-road and a few disadvantages on-road but the new Hilux is clear proof that only in the most difficult

conditions is a well set up independent front suspension a disadvantage worth noting.

The current Hilux should be compared with vehicles such as the Nissan Hardbody, Isuzu KB and Colt pickups and not be compared with its predecessor. This is because the old Hilux could be forgiven for its hard ride, poor brakes and uncomfortable seating, idiosyncrasies that drivers learned to live with while doting on the vehicle's brilliance off-road.

There is no doubt that the Hilux's popularity has not wained one bit and it remains one of the best in its class. The engine line-up improves the Hilux's appeal, especially the 2,7-litre fuel injected petrol that has good acceleration and is easy to drive off-road. I drove it on dunes and it displayed ample power and torque. The 3-litre diesel is not unlike the old model 2400 petrol in these conditions and often needed several attempts at each obstacle. As a cruising vehicle the 3-litre diesel is underpowered. The KZTE turbo-diesel is without doubt the best engine for the Hilux, although a little pricey but must rate as the best all-round 4x4 pick-up in its class, only the Colt 2,8 coming close.

TOYOTA LAND CRUISER PICK-UP

In 1933 the automotive division of Toyota Automatic Loom Works was established. The origins of the Toyota Land Cruiser began some five years after the Second World War, when US Army Jeeps were a common sight in Japan. These were the only 4x4s available and at the time there was a need for a vehicle a little larger than the Jeep and one that could be built locally as part of the reconstruction programme meant to revitalise Japan's economy. The US Army and the Police Reserve approached Toyota Motor Corporation with a request to design and produce such a vehicle. Toyota used its experience gained during the war when it produced the light scout car, the AK10. In only five months a Jeep-like prototype called the Toyota Jeep was built. Willys quickly pointed out that this name would be an infringement on its trademark, and in the following year it was given a new name – the Toyota Model B-85. Production commenced in 1953 and a year later, after 298 Model B-85s had been produced, so the name Land Cruiser made its mark on the world.

Not surprisingly, it looked very much like an American Jeep. It had a split front windscreen, the only Toyota ever to have one, and was driven by a 6-cylinder 63kW engine and a gearbox that initially had no synchromesh whatsoever, but later was given syncros on the two top ratios only. The 1963 FJ25 model was a short wheelbase machine with a 6-cylinder 236 cubic-inch engine and part time four-wheel drive that could be engaged without stopping. This power plant remained the only engine available until 1968.

Exported from Japan in 1967, the 40 series FJ40 (SWB) and the FJ45 (LWB) and their replacements the FJ42 and FJ47, maintained the strictly military appearance of the earlier Land Cruisers while the 40 series maintained the looks of the earlier machines but came with a choice of hard and soft tops. The hard-top version featured a two-piece tailgate and small windows on the side at the rear. The LWB versions were offered with a pick-up, a soft-top, a canvas top and a cab-chassis options. The early 4-speed transmission was replaced by a 3-speed column shift with a 2-speed transfer gearbox. Between 1960 and 1968 few visual changes appeared, but ongoing mechanical improvements took place. The gear change was moved from the column to the floor and the rear axle diff, which had occupied a position in the middle of the axle, was moved to the position it occupies today. The 15-inch wheel rims were replaced with those measuring 16 inches.

In 1968, the old "135" petrol engine was replaced by a 3 873cc 6-cylinder unit that produced increased power and torque. In 1969 a station wagon version appeared in the form of the FJ55, the predecessor to the modern 60 series station wagons. This machine was the first four-door Cruiser, and was equipped with improved seating, better ventilation and heating and was far more modern in appearance than its predecessors. This vehicle introduced modern materials to the Land Cruiser such as plastic brake and clutch fluid reservoirs and disposable oil filters.

The 1971 range was improved when the engine was fitted with a twin barrel carburettor and the drive train was given Burfield constant

One of the most effective and attractive adaptations of the Land Cruiser pick-up is the FJ-79 double-cab conversion. This one is a Meano conversion.

POLOKWANE 200
NAIROBI 2900
CAIRO 5990
LONDON 9127

With a 180ℓ fuel tank,
the only limits are your own.

With electronic hill-start assist control* and downhill assist control* (in both forward and reverse), it's blatantly obvious that the new Land Cruiser Prado has the off-road capabilities to take you wherever you want to go. But there is yet another remarkable feature; a standard 180ℓ fuel tank, the largest of any 4x4, which allows you to stay there for quite some time. Now, don't you belong outside?

TOYOTA

Prado range: Turbo Diesel; VX Turbo Diesel; VX Petrol. For more information, visit www.toyota.co.za or call 0800 139 111. *VX models only.

velocity joints. Split wheel rims also made their debut. Tyre sizes went from 7.00 X 16 to 7.50 X 16. In 1972 the 3-speed box was replaced by a 4-speed unit and a heater/demister was fitted.

In 1975 perhaps the most significant range of improvements to the already very popular and top selling Land Cruisers were made. A brand new 6-cylinder power plant, the "2F" was introduced. It was a greatly improved 4230cc that produced 96 kW at 3600 rpm and a torque of 274 Nm at 1800 rpm. This was also the year that the first diesel engine was available to the Land Cruiser. The 'H' engine produced 70 kW at 3600 rpm and torque of 216 Nm at 2200 rpm. Diesel equipped vehicles were designated the 'H' series, and so the vehicle was known as the HJ45. Hazard warning flashers and inertia reel seatbelts were added, and some anti-pollution equipment was plumbed into the engines. Brake lining area was increased and fully floating axles were introduced to all models. During the remainder of the 1970s, ongoing modifications appeared. A tubular spare wheel carrier, revised mirrors, a canvas top option for the LWB model, an 84-litre fuel tank, the 'B' series diesel engine, quarter vents and improved seating kept the Land Cruiser up with the times.

In the eighties and nineties the pickup Cruiser was the 75-series, only available in a long wheelbase version in South Africa. Like those before it, it remained an outstanding heavy-duty 4x4. Its design is old fashioned and rugged, very reliable and spare parts are readily available throughout Africa. Suspension is by solid axles and leaf springs. Criticisms still include the long rear overhang that causes heavy loads in the pick-up load box to make the front ride up and cause handling difficulties. There are a few station wagon variants of the FJ40 and FJ75 but these are rare and make excellent safari vehicles. Current Land Cruiser is the FJ95 and although similar in appearance is a different vehicle to the FJ75 in many respects. Wheelbase is longer, front springs are now coil and the load bed is longer. Clearance and angles have been improved marginally and interior comforts while plain have been improved. Engines are the 4,2-litre diesel and 4,5-litre petrol. Both engines are on the thirsty side but are renowned for their reliability. The diesel is just about the only engine on the market still fed by a mechanical fuel pump – ideal for the outback explorer who wants to keep things simple.

Meano Engineering and Baillies Off-Road offer one of the best 4x4 expedition vehicles ever built, based on a Land Cruiser FJ79 pick-up. It is a double cab conversion, a modification together with OME replacement suspension that transforms this Cruiser into an effective, comfortable and extremely spacious expedition vehicle.

LEISURE STATION-WAGONS

ISUZU FRONTIER

The Isuzu Frontier was introduced to South Africa in early 1998 competing in the budget priced station wagon market. The Frontier is a good cruiser, quiet and comfortable and the interior is fairly simple without many frills. Off-road the rear diff lock is a needed feature as the axle travel is fairly small. The Frontier doesn't carry a heavy load well; the rear suspension seems too light for this. Engine choices are the 2,8 turbo-diesel and the 3-litre V6. The diesel is better if you intend taking your Frontier exploring, the V6 if you intend staying close to the cities.

HYUNDAI TERRACAN

Hyundai's heavyweight must rate as the best value off-road station wagon available. For the price of the average double cab here is a comfortable and able city cruiser with perfectly acceptable off-road performance. Sure it's not in the league of a Prado, but at well over a 100K less, this vehicle is really worth a look. It's a much better vehicle than the Santa Fe (that isn't hard) and if the styling isn't your taste the layout may be. Front torsion bar independant suspension, rear solid axle on coils with gas shocks all round. The ride is good, in just about every sphere. It is a bit soft at the back and the front tends to nose-dive a little but the limited-slip rear diff gives it an edge off road. The 2,9-litre turbo-diesel is peppy and not thirsty. Alternatively the petrol engine, a 3,5-litre V6 is typical V6, producing its power at fairly high revs, but still handles well off-road. Best still, it's not expensive.

HYUNDAI

ISUZU TROOPER

The Isuzu Trooper was one of few vehicles to directly compete with the Range Rover when it was released in the early eighties, and there are still a fair number of these older machines around. Suspension was by independent front wishbones and leaf springs and a solid axle at the rear. The current model is an altogether different vehicle. Suspension is now independent at the front with a solid axle and coil springs at the rear. Central locking, electric windows, electric sunroof and all-round disc brakes are standard and for a while it was classed as a top-spec 4x4 competing with the Pajero, Discovery and Prado. The Trooper is equipped with superb seating and is a very comfortable long distance cruiser. It is also very powerful and accelerating and overtaking manoeuvres are a pleasure. The Trooper's most serious handicap emerges when it is taken off-road. When moving over rough ground in low ratio and trying to keep the speed down it is very difficult to control as delicate power applications are awkward due to

GENERAL MOTORS

an over-sensitive accelerator. For the same reason, driving in slippery stuff at low speeds becomes difficult and the Trooper tends to display a lot of unnecessary wheel-spin. Troopers are fitted with automatic free-wheel hubs and part-time four wheel drive. Called the Holden Jackaroo in Australia, the Trooper's looks remain dated.

JEEP CHEROKEE / CHEROKEE SPORT

The Jeep Cherokee, until 2001 was an old-fashioned, basic but good all-rounder. It is a vehicle which excels at nothing, but manages to do everything with a degree of competence which attracts third and fourth time customers year after year. Its weakness is that after a few years of even modest off-road work and long distance touring it feels like a box of loose bolts. The steering soon becomes vague and the handling deteriorates. As a pre-owned purchase expect to spend a bit replacing bushes and having the steering and suspension components tightened or replaced.

The Cherokee Sport is smaller than the previous model and is more of a fashion statement than before. The 2,7 turbo-diesel engine, developed by Mercedes Benz, is one of the most refined and smooth turbo-diesels on the market. Off-road the Cherokee Sport is a good performer but for the clearance problem at the front, between the front wheels, which becomes a real frustration to those taking their Cherokee Sports into really rough terrain. The Sport is a small vehicle and therefore not particularly well suited to extended safaris for more than two people.

GRAND CHEROKEE

The Grand Cherokee is the flagship of the Jeep range and is a top-spec 4x4 crammed with creature comforts. The Grand Cherokee is fitted with an extraordinary traction system. Instead of the ABS brake-managed traction control system found in so many modern 4x4s, the Cherokee uses hydraulics to prevent wheel slip. The result is superb traction and excellent off-road performance. The soft suspension is still solid axles back and front. Clearance is poor so to take advantage of its awesome traction, a suspension lift is necessary.

A Grand Cherokee weakness is its drive-train and build, which are not designed for heavy-duty off road expeditions and not infrequent failures of these components have been reported by those using the Grand for expeditions. In addition, the Grand is a small vehicle and as a family off-roader, extended trips bring space and packing problems. I would therefore not recommend it for this purpose.

The standard spare tyre is a compact type and must not be relied on during back country travel and the petrol model can only run on unleaded fuel, which is not ideal.

LAND ROVER DISCOVERY

In 1989 Land Rover developed a vehicle to compete in the rapidly expanding SUV market, in a segment lying between the Land Rover (Defender) and the now very luxurious Range Rover. This was done 'on-the-cheap'. The Range Rover chassis and drivetrain was used almost unchanged. The body shared components with other Leyland vehicles, such as the rear lights from the Austin Alegro and the door handles from the Morris Marina. It was first offered with the 3500cc V8 or a 2500cc four-cylinder Tdi200 turbo-diesel engine. The interior was all new.

The Discovery joined a range of top-spec leisure vehicles like the Mitsubishi Pajero, Isuzu Trooper and Toyota Land Cruiser GX. Like all these vehicles, off-road ability and on-road comfort trade-offs had taken place. Compared with the others the Discovery was better suited to off-road use, with the associated on-road performance penalties. Interestingly, while it shared the early Range Rover chassis its on-road comfort was far superior but off-road was inferior.

The 1994 face-lift introduced an all-new interior, new light lenses, an uprated 3,9 litre V8 engine and improved on-road manners with the fitting of anti-roll bars to the suspension, a worthwhile improvement.

Unlike the others though, the Discovery is a small, cramped vehicle and the rear springs do not carry a load well. Always a joy to drive, the Discovery sells cheaply secondhand and for the beginner who is happy to spend some time working on the vehicle, the Discovery makes an excellent introduction to the world of off-roading. While it does not offer the reliability of many Japanese competitors it sells for less and is a great all-rounder.

The launch of the Discovery-2 in early 1999 introduced the same wheelbase with a longer and wider body with some new technologies. In addition to HDC (Hill Decent Control) new vehicle management systems namely HPI, EUI, ECM, ACE, ETC and FTC, the details of which go beyond the scope of this book, were introduced. Even without ACE (Active Cornering Enhancement), Land Rover's new stabilising system, it is better than ever on-road. Off-road, however, it is a different story.

ETC (Electronic Traction Control) combined with a centre differential that cannot be locked makes for an off-roader which is difficult to drive and which, when coerced into traversing wheel-lifting terrain, spins its wheels and digs holes into the earth before moving over it, normally in a huge cloud of dust. I could never understand the press's praises of this vehicle and even to this day, I still regard the Discovery-2 as a very poor off-road performer, and I loath driving it. The conclusion was that a well set-up vehicle in the right conditions

Top: Land Rover Discovery 1.
2nd from top: A frustrating vehicle to drive off-road, the Discovery-2 is distinct from earlier models by the long rear overhang, high tail lights, traction control and no centre diff lock. Third down: Discovery Series-3, brilliant off road because the centre diff-lock was put back. Bottom: Handsome as ever, the Discovery-3, (not to be confused with the Series-3) following in the footsteps of the third generation Range Rover, it has full independant suspension all round.

could perform well. On the other hand a poorly set-up vehicle, which was most of them, in any conditions was a nightmare and in some cases were outperformed by 4x2s with rear diff locks. That said, that the auto gearbox models with their viscous centre diff out performed the manual versions by a large margin.

In 2002 a significant change was made to the Discovery when the Series-3 was introduced. The Series-3 is a Discovery-2 with cosmetic changes and most importantly of all; the centre diff-lock put back. At last the Discovery is where it once was, at the top of the off-road ladder, a brilliant performer on rough terrain and an excellent cruiser. This vehicle operates a combination of traction-control and conventional, true four-wheel drive. The traction abilities of this vehicle can only be described as excellent. I still find the Discovery small and a bit cramped and three adults in the back is not a serious option for long trips. The Discovery has a reliability issue that has followed it since it was introduced and while it is one of the best-selling SUVs in the world, it is severely outclassed by all the Japanese and German manufacturers in this department.

In 2004 the Discovery-3 was introduced, not to be confused with the "Series-3". This vehicle, still to be launched at the time of printing, has independant suspension all-round.

RANGE ROVER

This is the vehicle credited with the birth of the now huge 4x4 leisure industry. The Range Rover represented a departure from the norm when it was introduced in 1970, being a completely new vehicle in both design and concept. The idea first came to light as early as 1952 when a truly civilian version of the Land Rover, called the Road Rover, was built but never released. Rover intended to produce a vehicle that would combine the off-road abilities of a Land Rover with saloon-like comfort. Development of the Range Rover began in earnest in 1965 and in less than five years the showrooms were bursting with customers. Range Rovers were displayed with pride at motor shows all over the world and the motoring press announced a triumph for British engineering.

The Range Rover gave birth to the huge market for leisure SUVs by creating a unique mix for the time: An off-roader that was also luxurious, comfortable and most importantly, fashionable. For years the Range Rover lead the pack, and some say it still does. But a comparison between an early model Range Rover and a modern day equivalent reveals how far we have come.

The Range Rover was a combination of a lightweight 3500cc V8 engine, full-time four-wheel drive incorporating three differentials, and long-travel coil spring suspension. It was concluded that coil springs would not only produce a more acceptable ride on bitumen but also offer greater axle articulation to greatly improve traction over rough ground. The alloy 3,500cc V8 engine was a unit bought from General Motors in 1965, lightweight it produced its power at low revs.

Unfortunately, owing to the high torque produced by the V8, no existing Land Rover gearbox was suitable, so a totally new

Top: The last of the Range Rover 'Classics'. This vehicle was used as a test-bed for the many technologies developed for its replacement, such as air suspension and a long wheelbase version. This became the second generation Range Rover. Bottom: The 2002 model, 32 years after its first introduction, is shaped surprisingly like the original vehicle. Once known as the vehicle with the best wheel travel in the business the Range Rover is moving dangerously close to the soft or super-roader category. However it can still be classed as an off-roader with adequate clearance and low gearing.

LAND ROVER SA

transmission had to be designed and built. Full-time four-wheel drive gave the new vehicle the advantage of improved traction, cornering and wet weather handling in all conditions. In the rough the driver could decide at any time to lock the centre differential and prevent slip between the front and rear axles. This made the Range Rover far easier to drive off road than any other 4x4 of the time.

Land Rover made sure that no one was in doubt as to the Range Rover's pedigree – the early models displayed a badge on the tailgate: "Range Rover by Land Rover". The brilliance of the design did not go unnoticed and the vehicle won several engineering and automotive awards. And in 1970 its stylists were recognised as an ambulance derivative was even honoured by the Louvre Museum in Paris.

With the birth of the 4x4 leisure industry advertisers made the claim that there are four types of car: "A luxury car, a performance car, an estate car and an off-road car," and that the Range Rover was all of these. The press responded by asking: what about economy cars? The V8 was thirsty, far more so than the four cylinder Land Rovers in production. The early Range Rover interior was spartan – there was no carpet, vinyl seats and some instrumentation missing. In 1973 when the Mark-2 version was released the interior design was completed.

The Range Rover remained unchallenged for so long that improvements to the design came very slowly. It soon became apparent that this vehicle was very much a status symbol and for almost a decade the changes made were largely cosmetic.

Range Rovers were built in Kenya, Brazil and from 1979 to 1985 South Africa. In most countries quality control was poor and sadly many vehicles earned a reputation for unreliability. Soon after this a series of fatal accidents were documented as a result of catastrophic tyre failures occurring on the now discontinued Michelin 205/16 M+S radials.

Payload is 680kgs and the roof requires supporting if a heavily loaded roof-rack is to be carried as the maximum roof load is just 50kgs. To increase the Range Rover's payload, fit Discovery rear springs, and if that is not enough, an OME suspension kit. The last Classic Range Rover rolled off the Solihull production line in 1996.

In 1994, for the first time in its 24-year history, the Range Rover underwent a major styling change. The brief given to the new vehicle's designers was to create a vehicle that matches if not exceeds its predecessor's off-road ability, improve its driveability, comfort and loadability, while making sure that what is created is unmistakably Range Rover.

The result was a highly complex machine that cost £300-million to develop, once again setting the standard in 4x4 luxury vehicles. Models came with 4-speed automatic or 5-speed manual transmission, and pneumatic cylinder ride-height controllable suspension and three engine variants which include 4.6 and 4.0-litre V8 petrol and a BMW 2.5-litre turbo diesel. Early, second generation Range Rovers suffered reliability problems but after a year or so of production things improved, so if you are considering one for purchase, look for models later than 1998.

The third edition Range Rover was released in 2002 and the vehicle was again a radical departure. All-round independent suspension on a hybrid frame and monocoque chassis with every conceivable luxury puts the Range Rover back where it was, leading the 4x4 fashion world. The big question is: Is it a soft-roader? No, the Range Rover still has adequate clearance and low gearing. In future models I anticipate that the low gearing will be the first to go, followed by the clearance. It is undoubtedly styled for the huge US market. It is smooth, powerful and while awesome to drive does not have the car-like feel of the Cayenne or Taureg. The payback is superior off-road performance, albeit only marginal. A large vehicle can be cumbersome off-road and the independant suspension lifts wheels even in modest axle twisters.

G-Wagen 461-series have the black grille and are the workhorses while the 463-series with the colour-coded squared-off grille are the luxury varients. Some consider the G to be extremely ugly but its engineering was decades ahead of its time. The G may well be the best engineered civilian 4x4 ever produced.

MERCEDES BENZ G-WAGEN

The launch of Puch and Mercedes G-class by Austrian Chancellor Bruno Kriesky took place in 1979. The G was noted as "A technological masterpiece with the aerodynamic drag of Vienna's Holfberg Palace"

Still built only in Austria the Mercedes G is one of the most impressive 4x4s ever made and whenever I see them in action they never fail to impress. Their secret is a long-travel coil spring suspension that gives good articulation while not suffering the body lean that tends to lift weight off opposite wheels on side-slopes. Off-road this translates into easy going over rocks and boulders while at the same time, wheels don't lift when the vehicle is negotiating steep turns on slopes. In addition, the vehicle is so beautifully engineered and built for serious work that from the driver's seat it feels invincible. All pre 1998 G-wagens are underpowered, which often means low first when the ideal gear would be low second, although the vehicle is so good off-road it rarely seems to matter! Early models were regarded as poor performers on sand, due primarily to their underpowered engines.

Among its few weaknesses are its rear springs which must be replaced after 100 000 miles as they are prone to breakage after this and the breakover angle on the 463 LWB models is not particularly high. The 461-series versions have part-time 4WD, the 463-series full-time 4WD and ABS brakes. G-wagens have remarkable transmissions. It is the only 4x4 that I know of where low range can be engaged while the vehicle is still moving and this happens effortlessly. In addition all G's have front and rear hydraulic locking differentials that can be engaged at any time by pulling a long lever out of the floor (461) or pushing a button (463).

The launch of Puch and Mercedes G-klasse into Production by Austrian Chancellor Bruno Kriesky, 1979. The G was noted as "a technological masterpiece with the aerodynamic drag of Vienna's Holfberg Palace"

In 1998 the Gelandewagen was reintroduced to South Africa without much media attention. The model was the 290GD turbo-diesel auto in long and short wheelbase in the 461-series, absent of too many frills, although it did have cruise-control, air-con and electric windows, just enough luxury to make it a pleasure wherever it was driven. The rest of the vehicle was spartan and practical, all the way down to the floor plugs to drain water from the interior after hosing it out after a long safari! I still own one of these vehicles and regard it as the finest 4x4 in the world. The G is no longer made in RHD, production having ceased in 2001. In 2006 an all-new G-Wagen is due for release. It is likely to have a body based on the M-series, a monocoque chassis and suspension and drive train suited to heavy-duty off-road use.

Famous 4x4 explorer, author of several books for Land Rover and my mentor, Tom Sheppard now drives as his personal vehicle a Geländewagen 290GD. It doesn't surprise me one bit.

MITSUBISHI PAJERO LWB

The Pajero was built by Samcor from imported SKD (Semi Knocked Down) kits until about 2000, with a 2,8-litre turbo-diesel or 3,5-litre V6 petrol engines. The Pajero is a dual-purpose vehicle at home in the city and bush. To make comparisons with other vehicles and to arrive at worthwhile conclusions it should be compared with the Land Rover Discovery, Isuzu Trooper and Toyota Land Cruiser Prado. On-road it is level pegging with the Toyota and Isuzu and may even better these for cornering ability and stability. The petrol and diesel engine options

Bellow: The Third generation and best known Pajero that put it on the map as an excellent all-rounder. Right: Styled like the Paris-Dakar race winner, the Pajero, like so many others, has become more luxurious and less well adapted to off-road use.

closely match the Prado's in performance, bettering the old Discovery diesel while similar to the Isuzu's petrol.

Off-road the Pajero is a good performer and is easy to drive. Rear axle articulation is good but at front, where it counts the most, it is very poor. This is why the Pajero is so stable on-road. Even mild off-road obstacles will find the front wheels lifting and spinning.

One of the Pajero's selling points is that it is neither a part-time nor full-time four-wheel drive vehicle as the driver may choose. This is Mitsubishi's 'Super-Select' transmission allowing a choice of two or four-wheel drive for use on-road and four-wheel drive for use off-road including low range gears. Front hubs are automatic and engage as the four-wheel drive lever is used. According to the handbook, disengaging them requires that two-wheel drive be selected and the vehicle reversed a short distance. In reality this is not so as they unlock on their own within a few kilometres after two-wheel drive has been reselected.

The 1998 cosmetic changes did not help the Pajero in any way and the additions look like after-sales add-ons and worse, lowered the clearance.

In 2000 a new Pajero was launched and apart from cosmetic changes this is the vehicle now available. This is a fully imported vehicle and an impressive vehicle in every way. The engines pull smoothly, it eats up the kilometres on long runs and off road, while not outstanding, it is a good performer. For those who want a really comfortable cruiser and a vehicle that will do really well off-road too, consider a LWB Pajero diesel with a full Old Man Emu suspension change. This is a brilliant off-roader and displays remarkable ability.

The Nissan Patrol thankfully has retained the solid axles on coil springs front and back, the best combination for an off-road vehicle.

NISSAN PATROL

The current Patrol is fourth in a generation of Nissan's dual purpose 4x4 station wagons. Since the beginning they have had a reputation for reliability and strength. Early Patrols were called 'Safari' in some countries, suffering a little through lack of ground clearance between the front and rear axles. All have part-time four-wheel drive and the suspension is basic leaf springs all round with live axles.

The second generation Patrol, introduced in 1994, was the biggest vehicle in its class. Coil springs were introduced while the live axles were maintained together with part-time 4WD and a rear axle diff lock was introduced. Its over abundance of chrome and almost grotesque styling found it few friends in the west.

Introduced in 2000 the current Patrol is a refinement in every respect – particularly cosmetically – and now the vehicle has broad appeal. To evaluate its performance it should be compared to the Toyota Land Cruiser GX. Performance is closely matched off-road but

The Nissan Sani was a private venture 4x4 developed in an attempt to produce a luxury 4x4 at a price far below other similar vehicles. The factory closed when import tariffs were eased and vehicles like Discoveries and Pajeros were imported for a similar price. During its fifteen year reign it drew many avid followers and many are still seen plying the remote outback tracks of Southern Africa.

on-road it falls short in a number of ways, the most significant being the ride. The suspension has the tendency to feel a little brittle as if the tyres are over-inflated, although this has been improved with later models. On-road the big petrol engine has plenty of power and hauls this large vehicle along at respectable cruising speeds, performing about half way between the Land Cruiser's 4,5 petrol and 4,2 diesel engines. Seating, ergonomics and space utilisation are an improvement over its predecessor and in terms of extras it is good value. Thankfully Nissan has retained the all-round solid axles and coil springs, an unquestioned advantage off-road.

NISSAN SANI

The Nissan Sani originated in South Africa in 1983 as a result of Chris Holden's dream to build a locally produced affordable four-wheel drive station-wagon. The first vehicles were rather rudimentary, the prototype built in a 3x6-metre garage. In 1986 James Bently joined Holden and together they created what is now a well known marque with a large group of contented followers. The Sani was built by Sani Industries in Pietermaritzburg, KwaZulu Natal where initially production stood at about five units per month. By the late eighties it had reached 25 per month at which time Nissan, on whose chassis the Sani is built, bought a large shareholding in the company and then invested in an entirely new factory.

In 1989 the shape began to change and a new three-door model based on the Hardbody made its debut. Two years later a five-door version was released, powered by Nissan's 3-litre V6 engine. The increased power available to the Sani boosted its sales further. Soon after that, further body styles were introduced, including a double-cab, double-cab Executive and the familiar 5-door Executive.

The original Sani chassis was based on the Nissan Tracker, Nissan's first pick-up-based four-wheel drive. Later Sanis were based on Nissan's four-wheel drive Hardbody pick-up. .

The last model is the third generation Sani, better than earlier models in almost all respects except for off-road performance. Nissan's pick-up range shares many technical details with the Sani station wagon. By far the best Hardbody was released in 2001, refined and a competent off-roader.

The easing of South African import tariffs in the late nineties meant that the Sani became to expensive to build and production stopped.

SSANGYONG MUSSO

Riding heavily on the Mercedes engines installed, the Korean-built SsangYong Musso arrived to challenge the luxury leisure 4x4 market in 1995 and the model, due largely to its competitive price, has done quite well. The Musso is a road vehicle with fair off-road ability. The handling feels limp and awkward and the moment one pulls away the price difference is understood. Normally-aspirated diesel versions are grossly underpowered. The petrol versions are really quite quick and may make a nice tow vehicle. Off-road the Musso is a reasonable performer but is not as good as most of the competition. when considering other top-spec station wagons where it falls short of vehicles like the Discovery, Prado and Pajero. Ground clearance is its biggest problem but can be improved by adjustment of the torsion bars.

MIDDLE: SSANGYONG SA

As with so many vehicles in this class the standard tyres are light-duty and should be changed if adventurous travel is intended. Transmission is part-time four-wheel drive Borg Warner 5-speed manual gearbox and automatic free-wheel front hubs. Mussos are not particularly well made and those that spend a lot of time on gravel roads and rough conditions do not fair well and breakdowns become common. An interesting double-cab derivative has been introduced as the Musso Sport.

TOYOTA CONDOR 4X4

The Condor is a light-duty stationwagon off-roader and has proved itself to be competent off-road as well as a comfortable long distance cruiser. Available with 2,4 petrol and 3.0 diesel engines, the transmission is part-time 4WD with automatic free wheel hubs and a low range transfer gearbox. The chassis is a high-strength ladder frame and suspension is front independent torsion bars and on the rear, leaf springs and a live axle.

TOYOTA SA

The Condor is one of the best value 4x4s on the market. While it cannot be regarded as a serious off-roader many are being used successfully for extended safaris.

TOYOTA LAND CRUISER PRADO

The first generation Prado was a station-wagon development using a Land Cruiser pick-up stlyed cab but the first to reach South Africa was the second generation and best known Prado. It arrived in 1997. The Prado is a luxury station wagon, smaller than the Cruiser 100, with permanent four-wheel drive transmission with lockable centre and rear differentials, independent front coil spring suspension and a solid rear axle on coils. There are two engine options, a 3,4-litre V6 petrol and 3-litre 4-cylinder diesel. If you are looking for a vehicle that will spend 80% of its time on-road then choose the petrol. If you plan to be a little adventurous, go for the diesel. The diesel engine is a beauty, offering good cruising and town driving power but also

The Toyota Land Cruiser Prado like all such SUVs is a compromise between off-roader and everyday town car. The Prado is surely one of the most effective compromises. Its off-road ability is really very good while it is a practical, nice to own vehicle that does just about everything well.

enough low down torque, where the turbo is inoperative, to allow really low engine speeds when moving over rough ground.

Off-road the Prado is as able as any luxury 4x4 on the market and in this category I would place it behind the Discovery Series-3 but superior to the Pajero. Rarely have I ever driven a vehicle more able on dunes than the diesel Prado – put it into low-range fourth and it feels unstoppable and very easy to drive. Until the 2003 face-lift the interior was unexciting and its competitors beat it for seating and appointments. The Prado is not well suited to heavy loads and vehicles built before about May 1998 had rear suspension problems that resulted in easy bottoming of the rear axle, even without a load. This was corrected to some degree on later models. Heavy-duty springs and shocks do well on the Prado and if you intend to use a Prado for heavy loads put them on your 'must have' list.

The 2002 model, the third generation Prado is more than just a styling update: it is an altogether more modern vehicle being quieter, smoother and more refined. It features a host of traction, stability and safety systems which has also improved its off-road ability over the older model, even down to the basic model, the turbo-diesel manual. Engine power of the diesel is a little down over its chief rival the Pajero, on-road performance is on a par and off-road beats it hands down.

TOYOTA LAND CRUISER – 50, 60, 80 and 100 series

I am unable to establish when the first Land Cruiser station-wagon was released but it may have been in 1965. The vehicle shared the chassis of the pick-up but the body was completely different, designed to carry people instead of loads. This was the FJ55. In 1980 the FJ55 was replaced by the series 60. In tune with the growing leisure market in

4x4s, the FJ60 came equipped with luxuries like power steering, cloth seat trim and air-conditioning. There were petrol and diesel engines.

The FJ60 is found working for its keep all over the Third World and have for many years been the most popular choice of many aid organisations. The leaf springs are softer than those found on pickups so passengers get a spongier ride when the going gets rough, but these springs give a superior ride on the tarmac. Heavy steering is power assisted and luxury items such as air conditioning are fitted to many models.

In 1990 a totally new station wagon entered the market – The FJ80. It has coil spring suspension and the redesigned body that so many 4x4 enthusiasts admire today. This was a major improvement in every sense, a fast and comfortable vehicle with improved off-road ability and an outstanding towing vehicle. In the rough the FJ80 is supremely confident, although when things get very rough it can be hard on occupants. At speed it is exceptionally stable with steering feel superior to many. Fuel consumption of the petrol version is quite acceptable up to 120kph from which point it soars rapidly. (At 150kph I measured a staggering 22 litres per 100 kilometres). On the down side there are no jacking points for a high-lift jack and the spare wheel stowage under the load bay is a pain and can create difficulties in the rough. The FJ80 is built with various types of transmission, from the more familiar part-time four-wheel drive on the GX to full-time four-wheel drive with a lockable centre differential on the VX. With some VX models the spare wheel is stowed on the back door. Like the petrol, the 4,2 diesel is fine up to 120kph after which fuel consumption quickly becomes unacceptably high.

Top: The first Land Cruiser stationwagon, the FJ55.
2nd Down: FJ-80 with FJ-60 behind.
3rd Down: FJ100 or more commonly known as the 100-series. This is the GX version, with its solid axles back and front, the most desireable Land Cruiser for the overland explorer.

The 100-series, launched mid 1998, is a development of the 80, retaining the solid axles on coil springs on the GX but going to independent front suspension on the VX and V8. The GX is now aimed at the off-roader who demands the very best in off-road performance. To this end the GX is fitted with front and rear axle diff locks coupled to a full-time four-wheel drive system and a lockable centre diff. However, the centre diff-lock cannot be engaged when in high-range, in my view a significant design oversight. A 45-litre auxiliary fuel tank is also fitted. The Cruiser 100 is a big vehicle in every sense but the balance of on-road comfort and speed coupled with loadability, good range and off-road performance is superb. Its drawback off-road is clearance between the axles and a spare wheel stowage under the load bay. The clearance shortcoming can be corrected by a heavy-duty suspension system and there are several on the market. Engine options with the GX are the familiar 4,5-litre 6-cylinder with fuel injection and the 1HZ 4,2-litre normally aspirated diesel. The diesel is underpowered to the point where cruising can be unpleasant particularly on mountainous

Above: In my opinion, the vehice that put the Land Cruiser in the lead of the heavy-duty off-road luxury station-wagons. The FJ-80 series has been called 'bullet-proof'. It's probably what makes it such a costly secondhand purchase. Right: 2003 model Land Cruiser 100, V8.

roads where a fast overtake is out of the question. Those considering fitting an after-market turbo, be aware that gearing falls short and overheating is often a problem. The refined petrol is the better choice over the truck-like diesel, even when running costs are considered.

The VX and V8 challenge the 4x4 limousine market and tackle the Range Rover and Mercedes M-class head-on. The V8 is every bit as refined as the Range Rover and about as good off-road. However, the VX and V8 are not particularly good load carriers and therefore not very well suited to expedition use. Here the GX is the better choice. The V8 and VX have two of the most outstanding engines of any 4x4, smooth and highly refined. Beyond the V8 is the Lexus, refined to the point where off-road and load carrying performance is mediocre.

VOLKSWAGEN SYNCRO BUS

A four-wheel drive adaptation of the very popular rear-wheel drive minibus is no longer made but second-hand units are available. There are two versions: the standard 'Microbus' and the Caravelle luxury version. Both have a 2.1-litre fuel-injected 4-cylinder engine. Advanced 4WD is permanent using a hydraulic viscous coupling between the front and rear prop-shafts. Suspension is by independent coil springs on all four wheels. Modifications for off-road use include protective plates, a single low gear ratio for off-road work and raised suspension. The Syncro's performance over uneven ground is impressive because of excellent vertical wheel travel and axle differential locks.

The Syncro is seriously disadvantaged when conditions get muddy, because of its small wheels, road tyres which clog very quickly and low ground clearance. The engine is low slung and this is a problem both when wading and when the vehicle is being driven over uneven terrain.

UNUSUAL VEHICLES

BEJING JEEP

Basic, very crude and horrible to drive, this vehicle is a classis example of eastern osterity.

GM HUMMER

Designed in 1979 by American Motors Corp for the US military as a 'High Mobility Multi-purpose Wheeld Vehicles, or HMMWV pronounced Humvee. Over 200 000 have been produced and through warfare the word Humvee has become a household word. Engines include a V10 diesel and full-time four-wheel drive transmission. There are several derivatives including a civilian version. For expedition use it is particularly unpleasant to drive as the wide track does not fit into the avarage dirt or sand track.

UAZ

A marvel of automitive crudity the UAZ is as basic a vehicle as is possible. The UAZ 31512 is the light workhorse, seven seats with a payload of only 100kgs. The UAZ 33035 truck has a payload of only 800kgs. Both are powered by a 2,4-litre, 4-cylinder petrol engine producing 70kW and all-round drum brakes. There are seven derivatives of the 33035. The larger 4x4 trucks make excellent expedition vehicles.

MERCEDES UNIMOG

One of the most desirable 4x4s in the world, the Unimog is the ultimate expedition light truck. There are dozens of derivatives and four wheelbases. Handling of corrugations is terrible and is one of its few weaknesses, and when it bogs down in mud it's very difficult to get out.

UAZ

3. AUXILIARY EQUIPMENT

BODY MOUNTED ACCESSORIES

SUSPENSION MODIFICATIONS

AUXILIARY TANKS

AUXILIARY LIGHTING

GAUGES

ELECTRICS

ROOF RACKS

SNORKELS

MISCELLANEOUS

DON'T BE FOOLED into thinking that without a fully-equipped vehicle you'll not be able to make trips into the wilderness. This chapter will act as a guide through what has become an often confusing shopping experience. Defining which items that are essential and those which are simply nice to have For more on this point of view, read on.

BODY MOUNTED ACCESSORIES

BULL BARS

Bush or bull bars are now commonplace on vehicles from minibus taxis to four-wheelers. They are made of aluminium, mild steel or stainless tubing and are fitted either because the driver wants genuine protection from the possibility of hitting an animal at speed or to look macho around town. Either way, they are useful items when it comes to fitting winches, spotlights and grille guards. In the past it was fashionable to fit overly heavy steel wrap-around tubes designed by retired civil engineers who, during their working lives, designed suspension bridges. Today things are more sensible and most bull-bars sold are lighter in weight and look better too.

Here are some points to consider when selecting a bull-bar:

Top: A-bars protect the radiator from front-on impacts and are handy for mounting additional lights. Bottom: Bars need not be heavy to protect the front of the vehicle. The mounts are more important and must be able to absorb any impacts.

- *Is your vehicle equipped with air bags? If so, only an air-bag compatible bull-bar is acceptable. Non-approved bull-bars may prevent correct deployment of an air bag during a collision and in this case it would be better not to have a bar fitted at all.*
- *Bull-bars designed to ward off serious impact are broad, tall and lean forward, causing whatever it meets to be pushed downward, protecting the windscreen and passengers. This type of bull bar is not necessarily made from very large diameter piping – the strength of its design is its heavy mountings.*
- *Check that the design does not affect the vehicle's approach angle.*
- *Should the upper bar of a bull bar be higher than the bonnet, light from the headlamps will strike the bar and shine back at the driver. This can be very annoying.*
- *If you intend to fit a winch at a later date select a bull bar with an integral winch mount. If you intend to fit spot-lamps ask your supplier for fittings for these.*
- *Take a close look at the mounting points – these are going to absorb any impact, and not the tubing. Thick heavy piping with light mounts make matters worse – if the steel piping has no 'give' or the mounts are weak, a light impact at one end of the bar can push it back along its entire length, and damage the*

Good quality, well engineered branded bull bars such as TJM and ARB are worth the investment as they do a proper job protecting the vehicle, are air-bag compatible and looking as good as they do, enhance the vehicle's resale value

bodywork on the other side of the vehicle. Wrap-around bars are more prone to this.

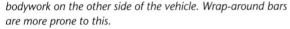

- Painted bull-bars require periodic repainting.
- Alloy A-bars are light and protect the radiator and nothing else. They make good mounts for driving lights.
- A galvanised bull-bar may look less attractive but is a good and cheaper option for vehicles operating in coastal areas.
- Brand new aluminium bull-bars look great but dull over time.
- Powder coating is corrosion and scratch resistant and surfaces also look good. Powder coating differs greatly so shop around for the best quality.
- When adding equipment to a bull-bar avoid interfering with the airflow to the radiator, oil cooler and air conditioner radiator.

SIDE-STEPS/RUNNING BOARDS

Side-steps are often the first items to get damaged on an off-road vehicle. There are two schools of thought: Most after-market side-steps, unless designed by people who actually go off road, are a severe hindrance to off-road driving. Most Excalibur running boards fit into this category. Some are so badly designed that they jut out from the vehicle's side, smearing trousers with mud or dust and do not assist access to any degree. The other thought is that they are damaged first, protecting the more valuable bodywork. I guess both are good points.

Land Rover Defender fold-away steps

Land Rover Defender's fold-away steps are effective and well placed but even they, in their folded position, tend to get bent out of place. They can, however, be easily kicked back into shape.

Fender guards protect the flat bodywork from damage from mechanics, tools, feet (climbing into roof-racks) and general wear and tear. They also look good, particularly these ones made by Proto.

Bumpers and Towing Equipment

Tow-bars, bull bars and bumpers frequently adversely affect a vehicle's ability to traverse uneven ground. Fitment centres, enthusiasts and while less common these days, the manufacturers themselves make this mistake. Keep all such modifications as close to the bodywork and as high as possible to prevent degrading the departure and approach angles. When debogging a vehicle, use the vehicle's towing eyes to attach cables and ropes in preference to towing apparatus which is not designed to withstand the loads that can be created by snatch straps or winches. More information in this regard is in Chapter-6.

Front tow-bars

To make launching a boat easier, fit towing apparatus to the front of your vehicle. Position the tow-bar off-centre to the left. This will allow the driver to see alongside the trailer which will improve directional control. Do not fit the tow bar close to the ground because if it is low, the stern of the boat will be higher, which means the vehicle will have to push the trailer further into the water than would be necessary if the tow hitch was higher and the stern lower. In other words, the boat will float off the trailer in shallower water. And, a low-slung front towing apparatus renders the vehicle useless for off-road use.

SUSPENSION MODIFICATIONS

Most modern 4x4s are equipped with suspensions better suited to road conditions than off-road work. Modifications are often necessary to increase ground clearance and improve payload. Also, vehicles that excel off-road may need softening up for road use. Trouble is, not all spring and shock manufacturers make well-researched products and many a disappointed traveller has cursed the salesman. Bilstein, Old Man Emu and TJM all make high-quality systems but above all, make sure you purchase them from a competent professional who is able to select an appropriate spring/shock combination. Backyard mechanics with limited knowledge are a liability.

Toyota Land Cruiser GX100 fitted with Old Man Emu suspension increases under-body clearance by as much as 50mm. When fitted to leaf spring vehicles it not only increases clearance but improves suspension travel, which in turn improves off-road performance. Beware of going overboard with a higher ride height as the result is compromised stability and safety.

PHOTOGRAPHER UNKNOWN

SUSPENSION
MODIFICATIONS

Heavy-duty springs

When coil springs are exchanged for higher rated units make your selection carefully. Light-duty units will feel similar to those that the manufacturer has fitted but will ensure longer life of the shock absorbers, especially if they are the gas type. Medium rate springs will improve road holding, reduce body roll and improve payload by a small amount. Hard springs will improve off-road handling, on-road adhesion, reduce body roll and are recommended for vehicles with loaded roof-racks. They improve heavy payload handling, stability and safety but may feel harsh on-road. Poorly selected springs often cause instability at speed.

Professional safari operators fit these systems to Land Rover Defenders with good results. The ride is quite a bit better than the standard springs and the axle travel, when combined with gas shocks, is improved.

With leaf spring vehicles such as the old Hilux or Land Cruiser pick-up, the change is even more impressive. The new springs smoothe the on-road ride and at the same time vastly increases the axle articulation due to spring lubrication between the leaves. This improves off-road traction especially over rocks and dune driving. Stick to well known, respected brands such as Bilstein, OME and Dobinsons.

Spring assisters

Coil spring assisters come in the form of helper coil springs that fit inside the existing coils or rubber blocks squeezed between the coils of a spring to restrict its collapse.

Firestone make a highly effective inflatable air spring system, springs that are inflated to suit load and conditions are another option. Once prone to failures the new models are earning a good reputation.

Possible problems caused by suspension modifications

While heavy-duty springs increase ride height the angle at which the prop-shaft universal joints operate is increased, often resulting in accelerated wear or vibrations. Other items to check are the brake hoses. There must be ample length to cope with full axle travel without the risk of stretching the hose. A higher vehicle can mean more body lean, particularly if the springs are poorly matched to the shock absorbers.

Gas shock absorbers

Few vehicles have gas shock absorbers fitted as standard equipment and for a vehicle expected to work long hours off-road they are essential. In the past, few four-wheel drive vehicle manufacturers pay enough attention to shock absorbers.

Working 4x4s need gas shocks. For example, my own Land Rover 110 went through two sets of standard shock absorbers within 30 000 kilometres. Once the second set had worn out, the first being replaced under guarantee, I replaced them with Bilstein shocks. When selling the vehicle after clocking up 130 000 kilometres the shocks were as firm as when I fitted them. Gas shocks often make the ride a little firmer but the real advantage comes when cornering or carrying a load. The difference in my case was a significant improvement in ride even when compared with brand new standard shock absorbers.

Gas shock absorbers are, in my opinion, the first accessory that should be considered for a working 4x4. The improvement in handling and safety are, in many cases, extraordinary. When I hear reports of bad handling when carrying a load, or skittish behaviour on gravel, even with a new vehicle, the answer is so often simple: Fit a set of good quality gas shocks. Not only do they improve the ride, they last two to three times longer than standard shocks.

Torsion bar suspension problems

When fitting gas shocks it is essential that the suspension setup is checked and adjusted if necessary. Not centralising the suspension before fitting gas shocks can cause rapid destruction of the shock absorbers. The reason for this is that when a suspension system, particularly independent wishbone types, are not set in the 'central' position when the vehicle is at rest, the shock absorbers act as bump-stops instead of the rubber bumps designed for the job. The internal components are literally hammered to pieces. Secondly, torsion bars set to increase clearance can create problems when the shock absorbers central or neutral position is altered. In this position the shock absorbers can't work as they should. The resultant poor ride is then blamed on the shock when the real culprit is the backyard mechanic who thought he knew better than the vehicle manufacturer about how the torsion bar should be set.

Thirdly, do not assume that if your vehicle is brand new that the suspension is correctly set up. Many imported vehicles stay lashed down to the bump-stops in crates for months and when they are delivered the suspension has 'sagged' and must be reset. Torsion bar suspension is particularly prone to this.

Why gas?

A shock absorber, simply described, is a metal tube filled with oil through which a piston moves. On the piston is a valve which permits oil to pass through at a limited rate. The tube is connected to the chassis and the piston is connected to the axle. The oil's limited travel damps the movement of the piston and therefore the axle to which it is attached. This prevents oscillation that the springs would create if left undamped. As the piston moves in the cylinder heat is

generated. Heat thins the oil and makes the shock less effective. What is worse, the oil in a hard working shock mixes with air and bubbles are formed. The mixture of hot air and hot oil passes through the valve with ease which eventually causes the shock to soften until the ride is uncomfortable and unpredictable. I have used three brands of gas shocks in the seven 4x4s that I have owned I can highly recommend Bilstein. They are undoubtedly very robust and are my first choice.

Gas shocks are different in that they are pumped with a small quantity of inert gas. This gas cannot mix with the oil and so the main reason why shock-absorbers become soft as they get hot is eliminated. Shock-absorbers on a heavily loaded 4x4 on a rough sand track work almost as hard as shocks on a competition rally car. I know of one Range Rover which after being called to rescue the survivors of an accident in Northern Botswana (that was me in 1987), 'cooked' a gas shock by racing to get to the accident scene. The shock was blackened by heat and destroyed.

Polyester Bushes

Bushes made from hard rubber are fitted in various locations in suspension systems to soften the vibrations generated by the wheels, engine and transmission. In off-road vehicles these bushes are stressed more than in a normal road vehicle and as a result wear out and need periodic replacement. Bushes are located in various places, namely leaf spring shackles, steering dampers, control arms locating the axles, radius arms and steering control arms.

Top: Polyester bushes reduce the rate of wear and permit easier articularion of springs.

The effects of worn bushes can be vague steering, a vehicle that steers itself when driving straight, instability, uncomfortable ride on corrugations, clunks and bangs on rough terrain and clunks when reversing or braking.

A worthwhile option when replacing bushes is to fit polyester units. Polyester is replacing rubber in bushes in industry from shipping to heavy machinery and vehicles are reaping the benefits of the research into new age plastics and graphites. The advantages of polyester are long life and a stiffer suspension which aids stability and safety. A little more vibration is sometimes transmitted to the driver but this is rarely noticeable and they frequently cost less than genuine parts.

AUXILIARY TANKS

Fuel tanks

Easily fitted to some vehicles, these are an effective way of increasing vehicle range in a safe, odour free way.

Jerrycans should be accompanied by a jerry-spout; a pouring spout that makes decanting much easier. I suggest the rigid types.

The position of tanks will vary from vehicle to vehicle. Possible locations are under the front wings, under the seats, in the loading bay as far forward as possible (pick-ups), headers above the existing tank, alongside the chassis rails between chassis and outer body near the doors and on the floor of the loading area. Never install a fuel tank in front of the engine – spillage or leakage can cause a disastrous fire. Switching from one tank to another can be made using either electric solenoid valves or taps, the former being more expensive, or individual fuel pumps. Be aware that electric diesel pumps are notoriously unreliable. It is important to use proper fuel hose when fitting tanks as ordinary hose will soon become brittle and crack. To my horror I have seen 'competent' 4x4 equipment fitters use ordinary plastic water piping in a fuel tank installation. It lasts about a year before breaking up. Industrial hose suppliers sell fuel hose considerably cheaper than auto spares retailers.

Bottom: Fitted to a Land Cruiser FJ-79 this Baillies Off-Road tank carries 170 litres and extends the diesel vehicle's range to a whopping 1500 kms. A similar tank is also made for the Land Cruiser 100.

Carrying fuel

Never use ordinary plastic containers to carry fuel, as they are unreliable and after time the plastic can become brittle and slightly porous, causing fuel to seep out and create a fire risk. Bumping and jolting over rough terrain stresses plastic containers carrying liquid, and the risk of breakage when filled with fuel cannot be over stressed. Steel jerrycans are therefore advised. When purchasing jerrycans look closely at the seal clamp. Some cheap types leak and become a never-ending frustration, so spend a little more and get good ones. Ex-Army jerrycans, if in good condition, are cheaper and can have new rubber

seals fitted and be repainted. (I advise not crossing the border if they are painted military drab)

Diesel is less hazardous to transport than petrol, but if you are carrying diesel in jerrycans once used for petrol, remember that as little as a 2% mix will render it as volatile as pure petrol, so empty the cans completely.

Routing fuel from auxiliary tanks can be done using an electric pump or selector valve. I prefer the selector valve option because of the notorious unreliability of fuel pumps.

Water tanks

Water tanks can be fitted to your vehicle by most safari vehicle supply workshops or can be installed by anyone with some DIY ability and welding skills. Water tanks must be very strong so they don't crack under the vibrations and flexing created when a vehicle moves over rough ground.

The selection of a position in which to fit a water tank will depend on your particular vehicle. The same positions recommended for fitting additional fuel tanks apply to water tanks. However, while fuel should never be carried in front of the engine because of the fire risk, water carried here aids weight distribution and is safe. If a large quantity of water is carried in the front, it is advisable to strengthen the front springs.

There are few things as convenient around a camp as a fixed tap on a vehicle or trailer. The tap used is a Cobra lockable garden tap.

Tanks under the seats in Land Rovers, a position often used to fit fuel tanks, tend to get quite hot and make the water less pleasant to drink, but convenient for washing dishes. The tunnel behind the rear wheel arches in Land Rovers is an ideal position to fit a tank. For easy access, the tap can protrude out of the back of the vehicle and in this position the water remains delightfully cool. In pickups, an obvious position is inside the loading bay as far forward as possible. Carrying water on the roof is not advised for a number of reasons. The tanks get warm, require some effort to fill if a running hose pipe is not available and severely compromise a vehicle's centre of gravity.

Considerations when piping from water tanks:

- *Secure all exterior water taps with small padlocks to prevent theft. I suggest wrapping rubber bands around the locks to prevent them being damaged.*
- *If you have a steel water tank fitted to your vehicle, attach a vehicle tyre valve to the top of the tank, in a position where access is easy. On the output pipe attach a tap and a long hose with a fitting to allow a shower rose to be attached. Now pump in air. The pressure will force water out of the pipe. Do not over-pump or you may split the tank. Test a new system by pumping and monitoring the water pressure. This shower system could also be used to pump fuel to an engine in the event of a fuel pump failure.*

Pioneer plastics make a range of tough, practical plastic water tanks. This one is designed to fit onto a roof rack, which I consider to be a bad idea. To keep the vehicle safe this kind of weight must be kept low down.

AUXILIARY LIGHTING

Original equipment headlights are good for a lot of conditions and masters of none. If you intend to travel at night in the Third World where dogs, chickens, cattle and goats are a constant danger, fit good quality auxiliary lighting to your vehicle.

Driving lights
Driving lights supplement the vehicle's own lighting, giving a moderately broad spread illuminating the road sides and providing penetration ahead.

Fog lamps
Fog lamps are not simply driving lights with an amber filter. What is crucial about a fog light is its spread, not its colour. Genuine fog lamps throw a very broad flat beam that stays low. This prevents glare as the light bounces off the airborne particles and is thrown back into the face of the driver. Amber permits further penetration through the fog, but its primary function is not to increase the driver's visibility but to make the vehicle more visible to other drivers.

Long range
Long Range lights penetrate ahead, the range of a typical quartz-halogen light being three kilometres. Specialist lighting such as the metal-halide 900 000 candle-power units made by KC Hilites are rated at over 18 kilometres. Long range lights are characterised by a prism-less lens. Other excellent examples of quartz-halogen lights are IPF and Cibie.

The Colour of Light
White light is used for seeing and red and amber light is used to be seen. Thus, tail lights are red and driving lights are as close to white as possible. See the chart on the left.

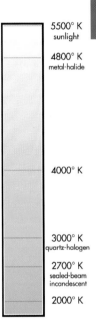

5500° K	sunlight
4800° K	metal-halide
4000° K	
3000° K	quartz-halogen
2700° K	sealed-beam incandescent
2000° K	

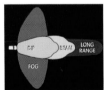

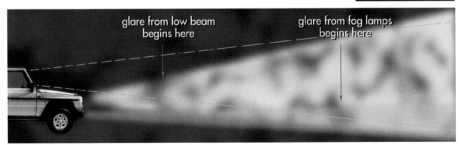

glare from low beam begins here

glare from fog lamps begins here

Metal halide

Metal halide is technology where a special bulb runs at very high voltage. A ballast powers each lamp and these lamps throw light brighter and whiter than all the rest. They are extremely pricey and most systems have a delay as the system charges itself when switching on, an annoyance that is difficult to get used to.

Quartz halogen

Quartz Halogen became standard equipment in most motor vehicles by the end of the seventies, before which incandescent sealed beams were used. Normal wattage ratings range from 50/65 (50 watts dim/ 65 watts high beam) to 100/150. The difference in efficiency between these two extremes is vast and if you are dissatisfied with your vehicle's lights, simply changing the bulb rating may be an economical and effective answer. If you do this make sure that the vehicle's relays and switches can cope with the extra current, otherwise expensive burnout will occur.

Sealed beam

Sealed beams are waterproof and very robust. Incandescent sealed beams are not as white as quartz-halogen and their other disadvantage is that when the filament fails or the lens is damaged, the entire reflector and lens units must be replaced. As a general rule these are no longer fitted to new vehicles.

Fitting auxiliary lights

Auxiliary driving lights must be fitted in conjunction with a relay directly linked to the high/low beam switch, so that they automatically switch off when the headlamps are switched to low beam. Poor performance and unreliability can be avoided with quality connectors and relays and multi-core copper wire with a core diameter of over 3mm.

Having tried a number of makes of long-range driving lamps I have come to the conclusion that Cibie make the best value-for-money light. I suggest pencil-beam driving lights to suppliment the vehicle's headlamps.

Light shields

Light shields protect against flying stones and bushes. White ones that clip over driving lamps are a pain. Why, for decades have light makers made them white, so they have to be removed for the lights to be used? It seems so obvious that clear ones will do the job just as well. However, it's important that the light guards can be removed easily for cleaning. Hinged steel mesh guards are a good alternative but broad-spread slats are not effective against flying stones.

Rear flood lamps

It is also a good idea to have a small floodlight permanently attached to the rear of the vehicle.

- Arrive late at a camp site.
- Hitch up or unhitch a trailer in the dark.
- Perform a tricky reversing manoeuvre.
- Undertake repairs to a second vehicle.
- In addition a 12-volt fluorescent tube with a long cable are ideal for working on a vehicle thanks to their broad, even spread of light.

While a rear flood lamp consumes too much current for use as camp lighting they are indispensible when arriving at a campsite after dark.

GAUGES

Monitoring engine performance while travelling far from home is a good idea. Twice I learnt the hard way. The first occasion was when my oil pump failed in central Botswana on the return leg after two weeks in the bush; and the second was a blocked air filter when a gauge monitoring the exhaust gas temperatures would have prevented a damaged turbo.

Exhaust Gas Thermometer (EGT)

Monitoring the temperature of the exhaust gases (EGT) is highly recommended for all turbo-diesel vehicles. When the exhaust gas temperature exceeds 700°C turbo damage results within a short time. Causes of high EGT are: high fuel-air mixture, blocked air filter and pushing the turbo-diesel too hard. In this way the gauge indicates that damage is being done to the engine. It also indicates if the engine is being driven too hard, for example towing up a long hill on a hot day. Without such a gauge the driver would press on regardless, with the gauge warning the driver, a lighter right foot could prevent engine damage. I highly recommend this gauge, especially if you use your turbo-diesel to tow. I bet, in five out of ten cases, an EGT gauge will prevent a huge repair bill.

Oil pressure gauge

The signal is transmitted to the gauge via either an electrical sender unit or thin copper tubing that carries the oil to the gauge. In general, the latter type is more accurate and reacts faster to pressure changes. The electrical gauge is more common in newer vehicles.

Oil temperature gauge

The signal is transmitted to the gauge via an electrical sender unit. This gauge is an essential item when traversing heavy sand or towing. Know the safe maximum oil temperature for your vehicle and never exceed it. 120°C is the maximum for most vehicles.

Steve's Auto Clinic's EGT fitted to my Mercedes G-Wagen 290 turbo-diesel. I cannot recommend one of these gauges enough. It could so easily save you a huge repair bill.

Above: Some 4x4s are equipped with an inclinometer. It indicates how steeply you are going up or down. They are gimmicks and are more use to the passengers in off-road driving situations. The driver should be concentrating on the terrain, not looking at inclinometers which offer little more than entertainment value.

Voltage meter

This gauge monitors the condition of the battery. Voltage measurements must be taken with the engine turned off and some electrical equipment switched on e.g. park lights. Only when the battery is working can the voltmeter indicate how much more work the battery is capable of doing. This is because it is the voltage drop that determines the condition of a battery. For example, a battery with nothing switched on may indicate 13 volts. If, when lights are turned on, the voltage drops to 10-volts, this indicates a battery in a poor state or one that is old or damaged. If the voltage stays above 12-volts, this can be regarded as normal and the battery in good condition. The higher the load on the battery, the higher the voltage drop will be.

Ammeter

The ammeter measures the flow of current in and out of the battery. Vehicle ammeters have a central indicator that swings to either negative or positive. It is wired to enable a vehicle operator to determine if the load on the battery by electrical equipment is higher or lower than the amount of current the alternator is returning to the battery. For example: If the lights are turned on with no engine running, the indicator will swing to the left, or negative. When the engine is started and the alternator engages, the indicator will swing to the right, or positive. If you find that your ammeter tends to run towards the negative when running electrical equipment, then you need a heavier-duty alternator.

This double battery mount shows a safe way of mounting dual batteries. The positive cables all run along the inside while the negative cables on the outside. This is done so if there is an accident, the likelihood of a short circuit is reduced.

ELECTRICS

Batteries

There are two types of battery applications that concern us: 'Float' and 'Cyclic'. Typical of a float application is an ordinary car battery, where once the vehicle has started the current is replaced quickly as the vehicle drives. Cyclic on the other hand is when a battery is charged and then used with no or little charge being replaced. Such an application is common to the 4x4 scene when a vehicle arrives at a destination with its batteries in a full state of charge. The fridge and lights run through the night and in the morning the battery has lost a significant amount of charge,

An important question to ask when selecting the type of battery is: What is the application, float or cyclic? Running inappropriate applications will shorten a battery's life. If a calcium battery (float application) is used in a cyclic application and the battery is not able to be recharged immediately, the battery will sulfate, causing irreparable damage to the plates. An apparent loss of capacity is noticed and after a short while total failure results. Should a battery designed for a cyclic application be used in a float charge mode the result is stratification of the electrolyte, mossing of the plates and a large amount of active material falling off the plates becoming sediment. This sediment eventually causes an internal battery short-circuit which cannot be reversed.

Battery charge and temperature

A battery's charge is also affected by temperature. A rule of thumb for this is as follows: A battery is rated at 25°C; for every degree below 25° the battery will lose one percent of its capacity. Its life however will be increased (before failure). Also for every one degree above 25°C the battery will gain one percent of its capacity but its life will be reduced.

DUAL BATTERY SPLIT-CHARGING SYSTEMS / BATTERY ISOLATORS

When a freezer or lighting is powered from the vehicle's primary battery, there is a risk that it will be flattened overnight or during an extended stay. Should this happen in the bush the vehicle may have no way of being started. Dual battery split-charge systems solve this problem by enabling a second battery to run the fridge and lighting while the vehicle's primary battery remains unaffected. This second battery must be able to cope with the cyclic nature of the application. Deep-cycle and high-cycle are designed to cope with the larger discharge and recharge cycles than normal vehicle batteries.

Below: The efficient, Mosfet technology Gemini split-charge system monitors the voltage of both batteries and enables circuits to be linked for increased amperage for winching. Undoubtedly one of the better systems on the market.

Current draw and recharge

If you are choosing between an Engel and National Luna and judging it by the current draw then I would say buy any one and focus on the real issue: How is the current going to be put back and how long is it going to take? This is the big question as there are always difficulties experienced with recharging deeply discharged batteries, and there seems to be no cure, just bad, good and better solutions. For more details on selecting, fitting and using freezers, see chapter 8.

Stop fighting about the milliamps better efficiency of one freezer over another and focus on how this current is going to be put back and how long is it going to take. This is the important question.

Charging Deep-Cycle Batteries

Lead-acid batteries, be they float or deep-cycle types, have recharging characteristics which can frustrate the user. Because deep cycle types are used in many off-road applications, I will deal with these alone.

When a deep-cycle battery's charge drops below about 11.8 volts it resists accepting a charge. No matter how much current is fed into such a battery it appears to be lifeless. The reasons are unclear but appear to have something to do with the duration of the charge and less to do with the amount of current.

When the charge is initialised, only a tiny current is accepted. After about four hours (this time varies with the state of discharge) the current accepted suddenly increases and the battery sucks all the current it can be given. In fact it can absorb current so fast that it can damage itself if allowed too much. It is a bit like a horse – if it is fed enough it will eat until it kills itself.

Take a look at the following typical scenario: A battery is used cross country all day. It reaches a point when the engine is shut down for the night and the fridge and some lights are turned on. The following day the vehicle remains stationary. By the morning of the second day, two nights and a day have gone by. The daytime temperatures are high and the fridge has been running about 80% of the time. The operator knows that the battery charge must be getting low but he is not too worried because there is a dual battery split-charge system fitted. He decides to take the vehicle for a short run, mainly to charge the auxiliary battery. The battery voltage, although high enough to keep the freezer working has dropped off the 'high current accepting plateau, ±11,8 volts'. The vehicle is driven for a two hour game drive; plenty of time, so the driver thinks, to recover the battery with the special heavy-duty 100-amp alternator fitted. But, during the two hours the deep-cycle battery has accepted half an amp for the first hour, one amp for 30 minutes and 20 amps for the last 30 minutes – a total charge of 10 and a bit amps. The operator is now under the false impression that he has a fully or almost fully-charged battery. Night falls and on goes the electric lights while the freezer continues to keep

Running cable to the back of the vehicle to additional batteries is an option for pick-ups. It is essential that the cable be fused, as illustrated below, to prevent battery fire in the event of a short-circuit.

its contents frozen. By twelve that night the freezer low-voltage cut-out activates and in the morning everything has thawed. The operator is baffled and curses the battery supplier because he thinks he has been sold a bad battery.

The table below indicates the time required for a deep-cycle Delco battery to receive a measurable current and the usable power of two models of the Delco Voyager. For standard use, discharge is from 100% down to 50% charge. In emergency use, the table indicates usable power from 100% to 0%. A second battery wired in parallel will double the value (excluding reductions due to mismatch due to battery age etc.)

A marine type high-current switch. They are available in two and three-way designs.

Battery recharge solutions:

* *Auto-relay. E.g. Gemeni. More expensive, automatic, efficient.*
* *A great big heavy duty switch. E.g. Marine type switches. Simple inexpensive, reliable, subject to user error or forgetfulness.*
* *Constant voltage chargers. E.g. Engel 12-volt charger. Simple, inexpensive but limited way to split charge batteries.*
* *Diode-based battery isolators. Simple and inexpensive but so inefficient that they are not worth considering.*

Auto-relay split-charging systems

These systems, by far the most complicated, charge all batteries in the circuit and with a monitor unit fitted tell the user the state of each battery down to a fine degree. They do not change the rate of charge and so do not solve the recharge problems discussed. They are fully automated, which is a plus. Their efficiency varies and some are very inefficient. For example one of the better units works like this: Input voltage in this case is 14,1-volts from a Toyota Nipindenza alternator, one of the most efficient. Voltage through transistors and other components drops 0,3 volts. Loss through wiring and connectors, another 0,5 volts. Voltage to the battery is at 13,3 volts. Delco deep-cycle batteries optimum charge voltage is 13,9 volts. Result: the battery is never fully charged and this is a

The Engel 10-amp, 12-volt charger. In short it is an inexpensive way to split-charge a second battery.

TIME REQUIRED FOR A FLAT BATTERY TO ACCEPT A MEASURABLE CHARGE	
ON-CHARGE VOLTAGE	**HOURS**
16 volts	up to 4 hours - check every half hour
14 - 15,9 volts	up to 8 hours - check every half hour
13,9 volts	up to 16 hours - check every half hour

best case scenario! Highly inefficient systems, some of them, deliver about 12,5 volts to the battery. The battery doesn't stand a chance of delivering its rated current.

High-current manual switches

Marine switches are switches able to carry the heavy charging currents produced by alternators running at full revs, sometimes over 100 amps. They connect the batteries in parallel so when the alternator charges the one, so the auxiliary battery gets the same charge. There is little voltage drop, as long as the cables are thick enough and the connectors good. On the down side, if one of the two batteries is bad, it will discharge the other and if the operator forgets to switch the main battery off at night when the freezer is running, he runs the risk of flattening both batteries.

Mount electrical components high up to avoid damage when something like this happens; an over zealous driver trying the impossible.

Constant voltage chargers

The idea behind a 12-volt to 12-volt charger is that no matter what the engine speed, the charge voltage remains constant. A constant rate of charge is very good for the battery and the battery's life is extended. Their downfall is that when the alternator is running at full charge and the battery is in a position to accept such a charge, it will only accept the pre-set current. An example of such a unit is the Engel 10-amp charger.

Diode-based battery isolators

A diode is a component in a circuit that permits current to flow in one direction only. Between two batteries it permits one battery to be charged but not discharged. This sounds ideal but for the inefficiencies of diodes. The voltage drop across a high-current diode is often over a volt. They also tend to permit other current loss, although I am not sure how and why. All I know is not to trust them.

Tips to better battery charging:

- *Use heavy cable, solid-crimped connectors (not soldered).*
- *Make the cables as short as possible. For every one metre of cable length the core diameter must be one millimeter. For example, three metres of cable should have a core diameter of 3mm.*
- *Set the freezer to switch off at no lower than 11.8 volts if you can.*
- *Never put a battery in a trailer without the biggest connector you can find. Don't even consider the tow-hitch connector as the voltage drop is too high. I once measured a trailer battery charge voltage at 12,2 volts. That's the voltage of an almost flat battery!*

Delco Voyager Deep-Cycle and High-Cycle Batteries

Because Delco is the most popular auxiliary battery found in 4x4s, here is some advice for their use.

Features

Delco Voyager are of flooded cell construction, fully sealed and require no topping up. The only maintenance required is cleaning and greasing of the connectors. The built-in hydrometer allows an easy check of the state of charge. The battery is often not suitable for use as a regular vehicle battery as its cold-cranking current is often not high enough to start big diesel engines.

Hydrometer indicator

- *Green: Above 70% charge: Ready for use.*
- *Black/invisible: Between 50%-70%: Recharge if possible.*
- *Red: Below 50%: Recharge immediately.*
- *Yellow/clear: Electrolyte level low. Do not charge.*

Normal charging requirements

Optimum battery life will be obtained if a green hydrometer condition can be maintained and batteries should never be left in a deeply discharged state. Once the state of charge has reached 100%, charging should only be continued for long periods at a reduced rate to prevent long-term electrolyte loss. On-charge voltage should be 13,5-13,8 volts.

Care of batteries

- *Deep-cycle batteries are sometimes suitable for normal vehicle use as well as discharging up to 70% of their capacity.*
- *Keeping a battery cool, keeping it charged and not over draining it are the three most important principles in extending the life of a normal lead-acid or deep-cycle battery.*
- *Overcharging causes grid erosion and can seriously diminish the ability to accept a charge. A current taper with timer or a suitably controlled regulated voltage is the best protection against overcharging.*
- *Do not fast-charge a battery, unless in an emergency, especially if it is a deep-cycle type.*

Storing batteries

Batteries do not store well. When operating a low mileage vehicle or a vehicle that stands for long periods, make sure that the battery is kept in a good state of charge, otherwise it will deteriorate rapidly. Check and top up the electrolyte and recharge every three months – leaving it longer will damage the cells. If necessary store batteries indoors to prevent the electrolyte from freezing as in most cases this destroys the battery. Batteries must be fully charged beforehand and must be disconnected from all loads, however small.

220-volt inverters

Inverting current from 12-volt DC to 220-volt AC is done with an inverter. New technology has made these devices very compact and virtually indestructible. Overload them and they simply shut down or wire them up incorrectly and they simply refuse to work. For one year I used a solar panel to charge a battery which by means of a 200-watt inverter ran an Apple Mac and printer in ambient temperatures of over 40°C. Much of the work on the first edition of this book was done at this time. The inverter became so hot that it could not be touched, yet it operated faultlessly. Current draw reached 10-amps at 12-volts (120-watts).

Quasi-sin-wave inverters are suitable for computers, printers, televisions and hi-fis etc. Sin-wave inverters are required for scientific equipment but are unnecessary for most applications.

A very useful alternative to purchasing 12-volt chargers for cell phones and cameras is a handy low-wattage inverter. This Everpower unit has been with me for well over ten years, still powering laptops and charging my camera batteries. It's compact and inexpensive. Larger inverters, up to 1000-watts have become highly efficient and are suitable for powering light hand tools such as drills and sanders. They are considerably more efficient than the older coil type inverters, which draw large amounts of current as they work.

Portable generators

Despised by me and those who have to put up with the noise of other campers running generators for their TVs, freezers and shavers, all those things we work so hard to get away from. Because alternative power sources are silent, more ecologically friendly and cost no more, I see no place for portable generators in this book – or in fact anywhere where nature-loving people go.

ROOF-RACKS

Roof-racks have evolved from utilitarian galvanised steel frames with wooden slats to alloy silver, grey or black hammer tone powder coating with matching slats. They look better, are lighter and more durable to corrosion. Although alloy racks are lighter they are not as strong as steel and overloading an alloy roof-rack will cause failure long before a similar load would damage a steel rack. The packing and overloading of roof-racks is covered in chapter-8.

I have fitted roof racks to all eight 4x4s I have owned and so roof racks have become part of my everyday life. I have had good ones, troublesome ones, noisy ones and ones that are just right. What follows is some insights info roof racks which will hopefully enable you to select one right for your purposes.

Steel roof racks

If you want the strength of steel and are prepared to pay the price of additional weight, an ideal design is to have a steel rack made and then weld on expanded steel mesh instead of wood. The rack should be galvanised once the entire structure is complete because painted steel requires constant attention to avoid the onset of rust. The expanded mesh needs no maintenance, as does wood, it is comfortable to sleep on and it provides infinite places to attach tie ropes.

There are some disadvantages with steel roof-racks. Metal rubbing against metal, such as the rack and jerrycans causes far more wear than wood rubbing against metal. It is therefore advisable that a piece of ply wood be placed between jerrycans and the metal parts of the roof-rack. No matter how tightly the jerrycans are secured, there will be some movement and with the aid of dust, abrasion will be severe.

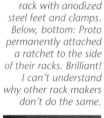

Top: Old-style steel rack with expanded mesh.
Bottom: Alloy rack with wooden slats, an unusual combination

Alloy roof racks

Aluminium is the ideal material from which to make a roof rack but rarely strong enough for the feet, which should be anodized or powder-coated steel. Some aluminium feet are made strong enough but they are generally heavy, unattractive designs. Naked aluminium oxidises and while corrosion is very slow, these racks do not look good for very long. Anodizing is the best, most hard wearing solution.

Foot design

Below, top: Outback's low-profile rack design incorporates an alloy rack with anodized steel feet and clamps.
Below, bottom: Proto permanently attached a ratchet to the side of their racks. Brilliant! I can't understand why other rack makers don't do the same.

One of the most important elements of roof-rack design are the feet. If the feet are too narrow it will cut through the vehicle's roof gutters.

With vehicles designed to twist, such as Land Rover Defenders, full-length feet can damage the roof. Despite the claims by rack manufacturers, this happens! If full-length feet are fitted, the rack must be designed to twist with the vehicle. Most racks cannot do this.

Particularly important are the feet fitted to gutterless roofs. More and more vehicles are being produced with gutterless roofs and this, at first, posed a serious problem for roof rack designers. Some attempts were made to mount racks using riv-nuts. This idea proved a poor solution and breakages and damaged vehicles resulted from heavily-laden racks in rough terrain. The solution is to mount a clamp plate inside the roof onto the part of the roof designed by the vehicle manufacturer for the mounting of a rack. Outback Roof Racks seem to have hit upon an excellent solution and many designs have followed.

Top: Double-Outback racks on a Cruiser Double Cab. Guttered roof on the front, gutterless on the canopy.

Slat design

Slats that run parallel to the length of the vehicle are quieter than those that run across it and those with slats running across require a plate over the windscreen to quieten them. Noise is also generated by grooves, particularly under the rack close to the windscreen. Slats can vibrate and should be rectangular in cross-section. Other shapes can act like a wing and set up vibrations.

Some roof rack designs do not permit the use of ordinary bungie cords. The manufacturers claim that the optional loading eyes are meant to do this and are adequate. I disagree: When you're in the bush who wants to find an eye, get onto the rack, find an accessible attachment point (if there is one), slide the eye along and tighten it

Below: A pratical way of carrying tent poles is in a household PVC drainage pipe with screw-on end caps. It's a bit ugly but saves the time of assembling tent poles each time the tent is pitched.

With just two of us in the vehicle, a simple lightweight frame onto which two spare wheels were bolted was all that was needed for this trip into the westerm Kalahari. Even with a light load such as this, spread the load on the roof gutters as broadly as possible and tighten them so that there is absolutely no movement between the rack and gutter.

just to load a quick bit of firewood? To avoid this frustration slats must have adequate grooves beneath them to allow an ordinary bungie hook to hook.

Weight and load limits

The weight carrying capacity of a roof-rack is usually limited by the capacity of the roof supports themselves, so this aspect should be investigated. Roof-racks which extend beyond the windscreen are a recipe for disaster. The front roof pillars are the weakest, so are the front springs. This kind of rack seems to cause instability at speed.

Did you know that the maximum permissible roof load on a Land Rover Defender is just 75kgs? Most vehicles are around 100-150kgs. A few, like the Mercedes-G, is 200kgs.

The results of overloading a roof rack begin with a cracked windscreen, maybe broken springs, bad handling due to too much weight on the front springs or even a vehicle on its roof! Mounts on gutterless racks are not as strong as those fitted to gutters. Operators of vehicles with gutterless roof-racks must compensate even more, keeping heavy items inside the vehicle.

SNORKELS

If you intend to drive on long stretches of dusty roads or through deep water, an extension to the air intake is highly recommended. The most well known make is the Australian Safari Snorkel. They are available for almost all 4x4s and can either be fitted at home or by off-road outlets, many of which stock them. Benefits are more than just protection from water and dust. The air is cleaner up high and therefore air filters last much longer. The air is also cooler than inside the engine compartment. This clean, cool air will improve engine performance. Fitting a snorkel does mean drilling holes into the body and this is a deterrent to some who want to ensure the resale value of their vehicle. However, engine damage caused by water ingestion is never cheap.

There is some contention as to the effectiveness of a snorkel in dusty conditions. In 2003, during a trip into the Richtersveld shooting one of my 4x4 DVDs I made a simple test. (Images from the video are seen left). Two vehicles, one a Colt and the other a Land Cruiser were used. The Cruiser was fitted with a Safari Snorkel, the Colt has its standard air intake behind a headlight, a common location on many vehicles. Both vehicles were new, with about 7000 kms on both odometers. The drive through the river beds was particularly dusty (see photo). The test was to compare the air cleaners on the last day of the trip.

The results were startling. Each filter was knocked against the front wheel to release dust trapped in them above a white towel lying on the ground. The top three photos (far left) is the snorkel-equipped Land Cruiser. The filter was dusty but still good for thousands of kilometers. There were no stones or sand in the filter bowl. The bottom two photos is the Colt and reveals the dust and sand lying on the white towel. The last frame shows sand being poured from the filter cup. I would estimate the unprotected filter had fifty times more dust imbedded in it than the filter protected by the snorkel.

TAKLA WATERPROOF SEAT COVERS –
TECHNICALLY SUPERIOR
BECAUSE YOU LOVE YOUR KIDS
AND YOUR CAR

 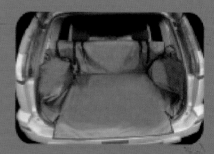

PROTECTIVE COVERAGE
FROM THE INSIDE-OUT

Tel (011) 466-0147 · Tel (011) 466-2510
www.takla.co.za

MISCELLANEOUS

Seat covers and Interior Protection

Seat covers and load-bay linings protect your investment from the wear and tear of bush travel. When a vehicle is loaded and moves damage is caused when the contents rub against the sides of the loading bay. Protection is provided by load-liners and seat covers. I have Takla seat covers fitted in my vehicles for over six years and they are well worth the expense. Because they do not make me sweat any more than the regular cloth seat, I leave them on the seats all of the time, protecting them from my young children's dirty feet and sticky hands. A Takla Load-liner does the same for the load-bay.

Takla seat covers and Loadliners protect the inside of my valuable 4x4.

Melville and Moon make a very attractive seat cover made of canvas. They are very comfortable and look great. I do not believe they are as hard-wearing or as waterproof as the Talka variety.

Protection Plates

The most vulnerable parts of a 4WD vehicle are the fuel tank, sump, and on some vehicles the transfer gearbox where it protrudes below the chassis frame.

Protection plates add weight, tend to collect a lot of mud and grass, and can cause overheating and fires when grass is heated and dried by the exhaust. Universal joint guards also tend to clog up. If you intend to do a lot of driving over rocks or want to go off-road racing, protection plates are a good idea. Otherwise their disadvantages outweigh the advantages.

Below: On a trip through the Kalahari the grass seeds became so severe that our grille nets were inadequate. The seeds were making their way to the radiator underneath because the grille nets did not extend low enough. The solution for a short part of the journey was to attach shade netting across the front of each vehicle. Keeping speeds down meant that the engines stayed cool.

Grille nets

If you intend travelling over grassland, fit a protective net over the radiator grille. This will prevent grass seeds choking the radiator and the resultant overheating. Of the many materials I have experimented with, aluminium mesh works best. The pores are small enough to prevent the passage of seeds while the fine aluminium wire does not greatly restrict air flow. Plastic mesh used to make swimming pool scoops is another alternative, but is less efficient. Grill nets marketed as radiator protectors or seed nets made from regular shade netting are effective but only at slow speeds. Because they restrict the airflow to the radiator it is imperative that they are not used at speeds above about 50kph. I recommend the manufacturers place a large, clear warning on the packaging. Many a time I have seen 4x4s on the open road with these still attached. Do they no realise that engine damage is sure to result?!

Mud flaps

Mud flaps both look good and protect the vehicle and trailer. Manufacturers, all of them, put horrible, feeble flaps that do not do a very good job. Mostly they are too small and when they are a reasonable size, like on a Defender, they are made of material so thin that the rushing air blows them out of the way.

Making your own flaps is easy. Use conveyor belting or heavy rubber matt about 1-1,5 cms thick. Cut it with a Stanley-knife and make some simple aluminium strips as mounts.

Consoles

Additional storage bins are a nice thing to have when on extended trips. A clever and attractive roof console is available and is an effective way of storing passports, two-way radios, CDs, tapes and cash out of harms way. They fit many station-wagons and pick-ups.

Making your own consoles to fit your own vehicle is not difficult. On a centre or dash console stick Velcro down. Then stick Velcro onto your loose articles such as cell phone charger and sunglasses cases. In this way the loose articles stay in one place.

Top: Australian-made roof console, a handy way of keeping valuables out of harm's way. Bottom: A dash console in a Land Cruiser. The Velcro mat is so any items also fitted with Velcro are simply placed on top cannot slide around.

Security

Water tanks and jerrycans should be locked with small padlocks and chained to the roof-rack if a loaded safari equipped vehicle is to be left unattended – day or night. The padlocks should be removed from the jerrycans when driving to prevent sand and vibration from wearing the paint and damaging the locks. External water taps should also be secured by a padlock or have a shut-off valve inside the vehicle, especially in desert regions.

Insurance

Many insurance establishments will not cover vehicles that travel into Third World countries. Make sure that your vehicle is covered and don't get a nasty surprise should something go wrong far from home. Insurances that do cover Third World travel also offer emergency medical evacuation and other services worthwhile to the off-road adventurer. My insurer is Cross Country Insurance, email bruce@ccic.co.za.

Mud flaps made of conveyor belt. The chain is pulled up and locked with a plastic tie to prevent the flap snagging and being ripped off when off-road.

4. WHEELS AND TYRES

TYRE SELECTION

RADIALS, CROSS-PLYS, TUBED AND TUBELESS

SPARE WHEEL LOCATION

WHEEL RIMS

REPAIRING A PUNCTURE

TYRE INDEX TABLES

THE PRESSURE A tyre exerts on the ground and the effect the tread pattern has on the surface over which the vehicle passes will determine the ease and efficiency with which the vehicle will travel. While motor manufacturers go to a great deal of trouble to research what tyre will work best for a particular vehicle, they also determine which tyre will be adequate for the most number of buyers. As a result many 4x4s, particularly luxury station-wagons, are delivered with tyres not well suited to rugged off-road travel.

For best results when selecting tyres ask these questions:

- *Tyres, like vehicles, are a compromise between on-road performance and off-road ability. How much time will the tyres spend off-road?*
- *What kind of off-road terrain is most likely to be encountered? Sand, mud, snow, rocks, etc.*
- *What kind of load will be carried? Exceeding the tyre's load ratings will cause premature failure, blowouts and accidents.*
- *What is the maximum speed that will be attained by the vehicle? Tyres have maximum speed ratings that must not be exceeded.*
- *What kind of ambient temperatures will be encountered? Some East Bloc manufactured tyres will not withstand the heat of an African desert.*

TYRE SELECTION

Typical of a mud tyre is an open, chunky tread designed to clean itself as mud clogs the treads. Self-cleaning only works to a point, and even the best mud tyres eventually clog, particularly if the mud is full of clay.

Mud tyres

A tyre suited to sand or normal road use clogs rapidly and quickly loses traction in mud. The large gaps and open, chunky tread of mud tyres facilitates 'self-cleaning'. As the wheels rotate the mud embedded in the tread is released and thrown out. Heavy treads tend to make more noise than fine treads and this is most noticeable on tar at speed. Purpose built mud tyres do not have good wet road performance, so extra care is needed in these conditions.

Sand tyres

The main feature of a tyre designed for sand is not, as is commonly thought, broad width, but a tread pattern that compresses the sand beneath the tyre instead of penetrating through it – which is what happens when a mud tyre is used on sand. The gaps in the sand tyre tread are narrow and the tread pattern runs longitudinally around the tyre. Good sand tyres flex well when used at low pressures. Sand tyres must also be tough enough to withstand rough tracks and sharp stones of semi-desert regions, since rarely do pure sand conditions last for long before being interrupted by sections of sharp stones and gravel.

Broad tyres

Not all vehicles are designed for very broad tyres. On some vehicles the tyres may rub the steering arms, brake hoses or the chassis when the steering is on full lock. If your vehicle is blessed with good axle articulation oversized tyres may rub against the body when the axles are extended during off-road travel. They also put undue stress on transmissions not designed for the use of big tyres.

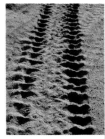

Broad tyres in sand

It's a mistake to think that very wide tyres will automatically be suitable for sand operations. That's due to the belief that it is the tyre's width that affects its penetration. Although this is to a small degree true, almost all of the advantage gained by a tyre's width is counteracted by the fact that broad tyres have a much higher rolling resistance than do narrow tyres. This is due to the tendency of a tyre moving over sand to build up a wall of sand in front of it. The greater the penetration, the deeper the tyre sinks into the sand, and the higher the wall becomes. Eventually the vehicle's progress is halted as the wall becomes higher and higher and the drag overcomes the engine power or traction. Narrow tyres create narrow sand walls, and so have lower rolling resistance.

In the realm of 4x4s, no factor, other than perhaps the driver's skill, affects a vehicle's performance as much as the tyres. And it is not just the tyres themselves that are important, the type of tread or the flex of the sidewall. More significant is the pressure in relation to the terrain being driven.

Broad tyres in mud

I have witnessed occasions when broad tyres have had a distinct disadvantage in mud; and other times (albeit less frequently) when they have been an advantage.

One dry winter on Vaal Dam I was asked to assist a Ford F250 fitted with Yokohama Super Diggers, a common broad tyre well suited to sand. The craft which the Ford was attempting to pull out was a lightweight ski boat with a 30hp motor on the back. Once the tyre treads had clogged the vehicle became useless. My vehicle was fitted with 205X16 radial mud and snow tyres at 2,3-bar. Not only did I extricate his vehicle and boat in tandem, but then proceeded to pull a five-ton yacht up the same slipway.

A self-cleaning mud tyre at work. When mud is full of clay, no matter how good the cleaning properties of a tyre may be it will become clogged and lose traction.

In comparison, consider the case of three Land Rover Defenders fitted with 750X16 Michelin XL mud tyres inflated to 2.5-bar trying to mount a steep muddy slope during a hill-climb. While the Defenders struggled to get up the hill, the Isuzu KB diesel I was driving walked up without so much as the slightest wheel-spin. The Isuzu was fitted with

Continental RVT280s, 265/70R15, a broad general-purpose off-road tyre, also inflated to 2.5-bar.

There seems to be no definite conclusion when is comes to mud tyres and tyre width. What is conclusive though, is that a self-cleaning tyre does make a significant difference to performance in mud, and tyres suited to sand will not have this feature. Tyre pressures are dealt with in depth in the chapter-5, 'Driving'.

Broad tyres in rough country

In rough country, broad tyres are more easily damaged by rocks than narrow tyres. This is the most significant and undisputed disadvantage of broad tyres.

Snow tyres

Generally speaking, mud tyres with reduced pressures work in compacted snow conditions. Virgin, powder snow require huge balloon tyres, that would also be good in sand, at very low pressures.

Rough country tyres

Don't mistake a heavy knobby tread for toughness. The thickness of the sidewalls is of as much importance as the thickness of the tread. Tyres of this type have restrictive speed ratings when they become specialised very-heavy-duty types. If your vehicle is operating under constant off-road conditions where resistance to damage is more important than traction, cross-ply tyres may be worth considering.

In no sphere of tyre operations can designs that look so similar perform so differently. This excellent General SAG general-purpose rough-county tyre is typical of tyres found on more robust 4x4s. However similar looking tyres have proven themselves to be poor performers. This is why word-of-mouth recommendations are so valuable when selecting tyres.

All purpose 4x4 tyres

The vast majority of leisure off-roaders will require a tyre to handle all theatres of operation – sand on the beach or on a safari, mud for the occasional rainy spell that turns the tracks into a slippery mess, and rocks on the family weekend 4x4 outing. No single tyre stands out as being the best for all conditions. The best way to choose a tyre suitable for your needs it to talk to experienced enthusiasts who have been there before.

Summary:

- *Heavy tread far apart: good for mud, mediocre in sand.*
- *Medium tread close together: good in sand, mediocre in mud.*
- *Thick tread: good for sharp rocks, often combined with hard compound rubber which will wear well on rough tracks. Will not flex well – a disadvantage in sand.*
- *Thick sidewall: good for sharp rocks. Good load rating. Less ability to flex in sand. More resistant to damage when at lower pressures due to the strength of sidewall.*

OTHER FEATURES

Speed ratings

The maximum permissible speed is printed on the tyre sidewall. Tyre damage will result if this is exceeded. When a tyre is deflated for reduced penetration, the permissible speed rating no longer applies.

Load ratings

The maximum permissible load is printed on the tyre sidewall. Tyre damage will result if this is exceeded, particularly if high speeds are attained.

High ambient temperatures

Tyre damage due to heat occurs when an under-inflated tyre is run at high speeds. Heat blowouts can occur to inner tubes before the tyre is affected. The result is an inner tube that shreds itself and after such a blow-out it is irreparable. Cheap imported tyres are often totally unsuited to the extreme road temperatures.

Imported or local tyres

Imported tyres generally have softer rubber compound and many do not cope well with local high speed gravel road conditions. Whenever I am consulted as to the best tyre I more often than not recommend a locally manufactured tyre.

Cross-plies

These are constructed by laying strips of fabric over each other at 90° angles, forming a wafer effect. These strips are called plies and the more plies a tyre has the higher its load carrying ability will be, while its flexibility is reduced. They were first used in the 1860s and apart from improvements in the materials used they have changed little in design. When the side wall of a cross-ply expands with deflation, the ground pressure in the middle of the tread decreases. At the same time the ground pressure on the outside of the tyre increases. The lower the inflation pressure the more marked the effect.

When the tread bar of a cross-ply meets the ground it bends. This causes the weaker area of casing behind to distort, allowing the tread bar to move backwards. As the tyre rotates and the tread leaves the ground, it flicks back to its original position. This movement, combined with the distortion of the tread described above, causes trauma to the surface over which the tyre is passing. In sandy conditions, this trauma, exaggerated if the cross-ply is under-inflated, will cause the tyre to dig in. Cross-plies are therefore unsuited to heavy sand conditions.

Cross-plies also have a higher rolling resistance than radials and this will affect fuel consumption. Perhaps the only time that cross-ply tyres could be advantageous is when the vehicle spends most of its time carrying heavy loads at low speeds over hard rocky ground that could cause damage to more expensive radials.

The most common terrain encountered by a 4x4 is corrugations and rough gravel. Tyre failures are common, particularly with luxury station-wagons shod with tyres that puncture easily and are unsuited to the hot, punishing conditions of the outback.

Radials

Radials are superior to cross-plies in almost every respect except price. They offer superior traction, safety and comfort, both on a paved surface and off-road.

Radial tyres are made by laying strips from bead to bead (the bead is the point where the tyre meets the rim). The advantage of this design is that flexing of the sidewall does not affect the tread. They flex independently of each other. So, decreasing pressures will flex the sidewall and tread area, while keeping the tread pressure evenly spread and increasing the tyre's contact area with the ground, thereby decreasing the ground pressure and the tyre's penetration.

Tubes versus tubeless

The question of tubed or tubeless is much debated in four-wheel driving circles.

Tubes versus Tubeless

Tubed tyres can be a problem in sand conditions where sand grains find their way between the valve and rim. Constant chaffing eventually results in damage to the tube. This is not a problem with tubeless tyres.

- *A tubed tyre running at reduced pressures generates more heat and is more prone to damage.*
- *A tubed tyre is often easier to repair in the bush than a tubeless one, because they are easier to remove from the rim and are much easier to re-inflate (tubeless tyres often require a bead expander to do this).*
- *A spike type puncture is easier to repair on a tubeless tyre. If the puncture site can be found, the wheel need not even be removed from the rim. With a more serious puncture or tyre damage they are more difficult to repair than a tubed tyres.*
- *Tubes do not strengthen the tyre or help prevent punctures.*
- *If a tubeless tyre is deflated for use in heavy sand conditions that require excessive throttle, the tyre may move on the rim. The result is total deflation.*
- *Blowouts occur less often to tubeless tyres. In tubed tyres, sudden deflation can be caused by excessive heat that is aggravated by friction between the tyre casing and the tube. This is especially serious if the tyre is under-inflated or overloaded where tyre distortion increases this friction tenfold.*
- *Damage to tyres is common in outback travel. If you use tubeless tyres, carry a suitable tube to enable you to effect a repair should the damage be sufficient to render the tyre useless for tubeless operation. It is very unlikely that you will find the tube of the correct size when you need it and even if you do not intend to go into very remote areas, carry a spare tube.*
- *Blowouts can tear a tube to pieces rendering it useless, so if you use tubed tyres, carry a spare tube.*

An ideal storage place for a spare tube is inside the spare. Whether you are using tubed or tubeless tyres always carry suitable tubes for emergency repairs.

TYRE PRESSURES

The pressure a tyre exerts on the ground is something that can be adjusted – the lower the air pressure in the tyre, the less the ground pressure will be and therefore the less the tyre will penetrate the sand or mud over which it passes. In sand, penetration will halt progress, while in mud and snow this can sometimes be an advantage. Reducing tyre pressure also improves grip, useful in slippery conditions.

Adjusting tyre pressures is therefore a way in which the driver can change the effect his tyre will have on the ground. The key element in deflating tyres for off-road driving is that low pressure increases the length of the tyre footprint (not the width), thus exerting less weight per-square-inch and thereby reducing penetration while lengthening the tread and improving grip. At the same time it means that the sidewall is prone to damage if the vehicle is driven too fast or over unsuitable terrain. Tyre pressures and their effect is covered in detail in chapter-5.

The length of valve stem fitted to tubed heavy duty tyres fitted to a 4x4 must be the short type. Long stems are vulnerable to damage by rocks, grass and undergrowth and are subject to failure, often when the tyre is working hard in a remote location. If you use tubeless tyres, carry a few spare valves with you.

SPARE WHEEL LOCATION

The location of spare wheels carried by 4WD vehicles varies and each position has its advantages and disadvantages.

Inside the vehicle

When fitting tyres with inner tubes it is imperative that once the tyre is inflated it should immediately be deflated and then re-inflated. This will remove twists in the tube. If a twist remains, the tube may split. Evidence of tube failure of this nature can be detected as the tear begins at the point of highest stress, namely the valve. Many tyre fitting workshops do not know this, so you should keep and eye on the fitting operation and make sure that this operation is carried out correctly.

A spare wheel carried inside the vehicle means that you may have to unpack your luggage to get to it. It takes up valuable load space that could be used for more delicate articles. Because it is heavy, it is important that it is well secured.

Under the rear overhang

In almost all under the rear overhang fittings the spare wheel reduces ground clearance. This is particularly serious with vehicles such as the Toyota Land cruiser station wagon. Also, if the vehicle bogs down, a spare wheel makes an excellent base for a jack and a good anchor if it is buried. If the vehicle is bogged it may be impossible to get at the spare if it is located in this position. Most significantly, if it is stolen or falls off, it is unlikely that anyone will notice until it's too late.

On a roof-rack

While only light bulky objects should be carried on the roof, a spare wheel carried here is ideal because it is easily accessible, can be secured well forward to aid weight distribution, and the bowl of the wheel rim can be sat in when game viewing. Spare wheels are usually heavy and it may take two people to lift it onto the roof rack. Keep in mind the average steel rim and tyre will weigh in excess of 35 kgs.

On the rear door and purpose-built spare wheel carriers

A spare wheel carried on the rear door is without doubt convenient but negatively affects weight distribution and on some vehicles not originally designed to have it there, has odd effects on handling. Some door mountings are not strong enough to take the constant vibrations in rough country and eventually break. The Land Rover Defender's rear door is notorious for cracking and so a purpose-built spare wheel carrier must be fitted. If the wheel is attached directly to the door, the hinges and clamps should be periodically tightened and the door jam set so that there is no free play.

Purpose-built wheel carriers are available for a range of vehicles. I have personal experience of the Outback Extreme product and it proved to be a well engineered practical system that carries two spares. Being separate from the rear door they can also be a useful place to carry other equipment such as a spade or jack.

On the bonnet

When the release knob is pulled from inside the vehicle to open the bonnet, the catch often does not release due to its added weight. It is therefore difficult for a single person to open the bonnet if a spare wheel is stowed there. Forward vision is also restricted and safety in a head-on collision is compromised. An advantage of this position is that it offers excellent weight distribution. Removing the wheel and replacing it requires some physical strength and will scratch the bonnet's paintwork.

Purpose-built spare wheel carriers are not only useful for carrying up to two spares, but can be used for attaching other equipment too. For example: firewood, spade and hi-lift jack carriers.

WHEEL RIMS

Magnesium alloy rims

Mag rims are unsuitable for heavy off-road work. The bead, the part of the rim most frequently damaged off-road, is the mag rim's weakness and when damaged they cannot be hammered back into shape as with a steel rim. While mag rims are not useless, steel is the preferred option.

Steel rims

Steel rims are constructed in two parts: a pressed steel centre boss and a rolled circular bed for the tyre. These parts are either riveted or welded together, riveted types being the strongest and

most reliable. Steel rims are sometimes of inferior quality and in some cases severely warped rims are supplied with new vehicles, making perfect balancing impossible.

Damage and repair of steel wheel rims

Common causes of damage are overloading, running with less than the total amount of wheel nuts or driving over rocks, etc. Make sure that wheel studs are clean and lightly oiled otherwise stud nuts can tighten against dirt and rust. Running with loose wheel nuts can cause severe rim distortion which is irreparable.

Slight damage can be easy to repair, e.g. bending of the outer bead. This can be straightened using a shifting spanner and light use of a hammer. Make sure the bead is returned to its original shape and the distortion has not been transferred along the bead. Because wheel rims are made from high grade steel, welding should not be undertaken owing to the possibility of the temper being altered by the heat and resultant weakening of the rim.

There are many worthwhile portable tyre pumps on the market.
Top: Volcano is an inexpensive value for money pump.
Middle: Bushmaster, a very good value pump
Bottom: Thomas pump marketed by TJM. An excellent, high volume pump.

Maintenance of wheel rims

Rust is a bit of a maintenance headache when it comes to wheel rims. Because of the habits of male dogs and the fitting of tyres when the rim bead is unclean, tyres can weld themselves to the rim making them very difficult to remove. It is a good idea to remove each tyre from its rim and then to refit them before going on an extended safari to avoid having to repair a puncture in the bush and spending three hours simply trying to remove the tyre from a rusted rim.

A solution to this problem is hot-dip galvanising although this is not entirely suitable as excess zinc deposits can create small spikes that can cause punctures and zinc deposits on the tyre bead requiring

smoothing with fine glass-paper. Sand blasting and then coating with epoxy paint is the most ideal rust preventative method.

Split rims
Some older vehicles were fitted with split rims of a two part design. This facilitates the removal of the tyre from the rim. It is imperative that the tyre be totally deflated prior to splitting the rim as air pressure remaining in the tyre will cause the rim to split with explosive force which could cause serious injury. Also, when a tube is fitted onto a split rim, a gaiter consisting of a ring of shaped rubber must be inserted between the rim and the tube. Not fitting a gaiter with a tube will result in the tube wearing and eventually rupturing at the joint between the rim halves.

12-volt electric tyre pumps
Electric pumps available vary greatly – some are quick, efficient and costly and others are simple devices more efficient at converting noise into heat than inflating a tyre, but even these use less effort than a hand or foot pump, and they take about the same time.

When selecting a pump, the volume of air pumped is the issue, not the pressure. Look for a high cfm (cubic feet per minute) or lpm (litres per minute). Most imported pumps indicate cfm. Anything under 1cfm is going to be slow. Anything over 1,3 is going to be reasonable. Not many perform better than 2cfm. The pressure rating is not important as long as the pump can reach 4-bar. Note: The volume of air must be measured under pressure. Some pump's specifications look outstanding until they are applied to a half-pumped tyre and then they fall off dramatically.

My pump is unusual in that I have tied two inexpensive Volcano pumps in tandem. I have the benefit of dual redundancy and a fast pump at a low cost. The two pumps however consume over 20-amps so I always run the engine while pumping.

Foot pumps
Electric pumps are fairly reliable, but if they break down they are not easy to repair. It is therefore advisable to carry a foot or hand pump as a backup. Foot pumps are perhaps a little less strenuous to use than hand pumps, but their use in sand can be awkward. They must be placed on a plate or tarpaulin to keep sand from entering the mechanism. Both hand and foot pumps are inexpensive and are easily maintained and repaired.

The best automatic tyre deflators I have used are the Staun Deflators.

Automatic Tyre Deflators
It is a laborious process to go from tyre to tyre to deflate them. Automatic tyre deflators solve this problem and deflate tyres to a pressure preset on each unit. Screw a deflator onto each tyre valve, the valve opens until the preset pressure is reached and then shuts off. The best ones I have used are the Australian Staun Tyre Deflators.

REPAIRING A PUNCTURE

* Electric tyre pump
* Foot tyre pump
* Tubeless repair kit/Tube repair kit combination
* 2x tyre levers
* 2nd spare wheel
* Spare inner-tubes
* Jacks and tools to remove and replace wheels
* Spare valves and valve tool
* Pressure gauge

Carry a second spare wheel and tube

Tyre damage is common off-road. Be prepared to repair it yourself or at the very least have enough tubes, patches and tools so that someone can do it for you.

By carrying a second spare, a puncture need not be repaired immediately. If the second spare is required, this is the time to make a repair. Do not wait until your vehicle is immobile before you make a repair or you may find your vehicle immobilised in a position which makes it difficult for you to work. Change to the spare, drive to a shady place or set up camp and then repair the puncture in a relaxed, unhurried fashion. It may even prove enjoyable and will feel like part of the bushwhacking experience.

Repairing a puncture (tubed)

For punctures that cannot be repaired with the tyre on the rim, follow the instructions under the heading 'Repairing a Puncture (tubeless)' making allowances for the fact that the tyre patch (tube patches do not work on tyres) will be cemented (solution for tubes may not work on tyres and tyre patches) onto the inside of the tyre. Read the literature that comes with the repair kit and follow the tyre removal procedure below.

For punctures that can be repaired without removing the tyre from the rim follow these instructions:

As these plug repair systems differ slightly, read the instructions that came with your kit. Locate the item causing the puncture and draw a circle around it. Do not assume that if you find what seems to be a nail/thorn in your tyre that this is the only cause of the puncture. Look carefully at the entire tyre including the inner and outer sidewalls marking all irregularities. Remove the nail/thorn. Insert the plug into the spiker and apply cement (some systems do not require cement) to the plug. Insert the plug and withdraw the spiker according to kit instructions. Inflate the tyre and splash water over the repair and over any other suspect areas checking for bubbles.

Repairing a puncture (tubeless)

Inspect the tyre and mark any objects which could have caused the puncture. Do not remove the object at this stage. Place the flat under your vehicle and use the jack and the vehicle's weight to break the seal between the tyre bead and the rim. Breaking the bead (separating the tyre from the rim) is the first and often most frustrating task when repairing a puncture in the bush. The problem is that when the tyre is driven over, or crushed using a high-lift jack, the opposite side kicks up. To prevent this, two high-lift jacks placed opposite each other and worked together works well. If you only have a single high-lift, use a bottle jack or similar to prevent the wheel from lifting.

Back On Track make a series of basic puncture repair kits and are available at most 4x4 equipment outlets. For travels into very remote regions it is a good idea to add the extras not found in the standard packs and carry them in a container less easily crushed and damaged.

Once the seal is broken, place the wheel on a ground sheet (it is important to avoid dust) and remove the valve. With a basin of slightly soapy water at hand, wet the tyre levers. Stand on the edge of the tyre and insert the levers between the tyre and the rim. Work your way around the tyre until the bead is over the rim. NOTE: Not all wheel rims are symmetrical. Start with the outside (the side with the valve). If you have difficulty removing the bead, try the other side of the rim. Then with the wheel standing upright, remove the tube where you think the puncture has occurred and mark it. Then remove the rest of the tube, replace the valve and inflate it. The puncture should then become easy to find. Immersing the tube and watching for bubbles is another way of locating the puncture, and may also reveal other defects such as a leaking valve. Mark the puncture and deflate the tube completely.

Repair kits come with a scraper which is then used to roughen around the puncture site after the tube has been dried. Clean away any rubber particles and apply the rubber solution. When it is touch-dry, remove the backing and apply the patch. Rub over the patch with the round end of a screwdriver handle or similar object until you are sure that a good bond has been made. Clean out the inside of the tyre and remove the object that caused the puncture. This is a good time to inspect the outside too, and remove any thorns, stones or nails that may be working their way through the tyre. Dust the tube with talc and fit it inside the tyre with the valve intact. Soap the tyre bead and, with the tyre levers, work your way towards the valve, pushing the tyre over the rim. Be careful not to pinch the tube with the tyre levers.

A flat tyre can happen at the most inconvenient moment. Here, on the banks of the Chobe River in Botswana, a hidden log rolled over and sent a spike through the side wall. The trouble was that we had been watching some very large crocodiles in the very place only minutes before.

The final stage is to inflate the tyre. Roll the wheel looking at both sides checking that the tyre is seated uniformly on the rim. Then deflate the tyre and re-inflate it. If the tube is not correctly aligned it may split when it is run.

Getting a puncture on a steep slope

I have on two occasions needed to replace a wheel while my vehicle was pointing skyward at about 20°. This is no easy task. Preventing the vehicle from rolling off the jack is the first priority.

These are the steps:

- *Wedge all wheels with rocks or chocks.*
- *Anchor the vehicle using its winch cable or a chain to another vehicle. Do not use stretchable rope or a tuggum strap.*
- *The winch cable must be fully stretched before jacking can begin.*
- *Engage low-range first gear and lock all differentials that you can.*
- *Firmly apply the hand-brake.*
- *Remove the spare wheel from the vehicle before jacking.*
- *Have all occupants leave the vehicle before jacking and have them stand to the side. Keep bystanders from walking behind the vehicle.*
- *Make sure the vehicle remains stable as jacking begins and jack slowly.*
- *Only remove the rim once you are confident that the vehicle cannot roll further and fall off the jack.*

Spanset make an excellent tyre extender that can be used with various pumps, to inflate from a spare and comes with a variation of brass connectors to cover all possibilities.

Balancing and rotating

Make sure that all of your tyres (including the spare) are fitted with valve caps. They form a positive seal and keep out mud and dust.

To get optimum mileage out of a set of tyres, the tyres should be periodically rotated. Most radial tyre manufacturers do not advise reversing the direction of rotation, i.e. swapping from side to side. However this is not the case with vehicles equipped with permanent four-wheel drive transmissions, where tyres should be rotated; left front to right back and left back to right front. This should be done every 10 000 – 15 000 kilometres.

Trailblaster is a high-pressure air tank filled with C02. It can pump tyres rapidly and doubles as a fire extinguisher. Only really worth the expense, bulk and weight if repeated tyre inflation becomes a chore.

Balancing should be done every 35 000 kilometres or thereabouts. 4x4s are generally on the heavy side and on some vehicles only when balancing is radically out is the vibration serious enough to be transferred to the driver. If this is left unchecked, premature failure of shock-absorbers and suspension bushes will result.

Make sure the tyre fitment centre does not over-tighten your wheel nuts. If you are concerned that they might, do the final tightening yourself. I always do, unless the fitter is using a torque wrench.

TYRE INDEX TABLES

TYRE WIDTH
ASPECT RATIO
DESIGN (radial)
RIM DIAMETER (inch)
LOAD INDEX
SPEED CATEGORY

SPEED CATEGORY TABLE					
INDEX	MAX KPH	LI	KG	L1	KG
G	90	N	140	T	190
J	100	P	150	U	200
K	110	Q	160	H	210
L	120	R	170	V	240
M	130	S	180	W	270

LOAD INDEX TABLE					
L1	KG	LI	KG	L1	KG
97	710	107	975	118	1320
97	730	108	1000	119	1360
98	750	109	1030	120	1400
99	775	110	1060	121	1450
100	800	111	1090	122	1500
101	825	112	1120	123	1550
102	850	113	1150	124	1600
103	875	114	1180	125	1650
104	900	115	1215	126	1700
105	925	116	1250	127	1750
106	950	117	1285	128	1800

Africa is Dueler country

Introducing the all-new Bridgestone Dueler A/T 694. Tough, rugged and good-looking. Performs faultlessly on or off-road. Designed for the heat of Africa. Long-lasting enough for you to follow your heart and bring you back.

Bridgestone Dueler. Go wild.

DUELER

BRIDGESTONE
Dueler A/T 694

Dueler A/T 694

The Dueler A/T 694 is a true all-terrain tyre for 4x4 and SUV use. A bold tread pattern and rugged sidewalls make it an excellent performer off-road, while retaining a smooth, comfortable ride and solid handling on the tarmac.

BRIDGESTONE
A GRIP ON THE FUTURE

USING FOUR-WHEEL DRIVE TRANSMISSIONS

TYRE PRESSURES

OFF-ROAD DRIVING

4X4 DRIVING SCHOOLS

DRIVING OFF-ROAD IS very different from any other kind of driving. It can be very enjoyable but can also be very frustrating, especially to a beginner who may find him or herself suddenly stuck in conditions that appear at first sight to be easy. Although there are basic rules to follow when driving off-road, the combination of road condition, tyre pressure, type of suspension, driving style and a dozen other factors can have a marked impact on a vehicle's performance. What follows are guidelines to successful off-road driving.

The first time I took a vehicle off-road I got stuck because I did not pay enough attention to where I was going. I was driving slowly over a flat field, when the nose of the vehicle suddenly dropped away and I came to a grinding halt. The front bumper was jammed hard against the opposite side of a metre-deep ditch which had been obscured by tall grass. One front wheel was clawing at thin air and only one of the rear wheels was touching ground. I walked a long way to get help, which came in the form of a cheery old man driving a 4-ton truck and a long chain. As we drove over a rise to my stricken vehicle it came into view looking like a duck feeding in shallow water with its tail feathers in the air.

Driving off-road can be learnt by anyone – it just takes practice. If the vehicle in front of you bogs down and you manage to get through, it does not necessarily mean that you have a better vehicle – it probably means that you are a better driver!

USING 4WD
TRANSMISSIONS

It is safe to say that the majority of 4x4 drivers do not use four-wheel drive as often as they should. There is a misconception that driving in four-wheel drive can damage the transmission. This is true only for driving on dry tarmac in locked-up four-wheel drive, and even then damage is gradual and while it's happening the driver is warned by an unnatural vibration. Don't be scared about using four-wheel drive!

Drive to all four wheels should not only be used when in difficulty but to increase tyre adhesion, even if it appears to be adequate. While researching a book in 1994, I was loaned an Isuzu KB260 for a trip into the Maluti Mountains. After the road ahead was blocked by a swollen river I was forced to about turn and head back. It was getting dark and to make matters worse it started to rain. In two-wheel drive the Isuzu handled fine but I wasn't comfortable because although the surface was firm, occasionally the back would slide out. Then I locked the hubs and engaged four-wheel drive. The Isuzu now drove as if on rails and I felt happy that we were travelling in complete safety. We did not need four-wheel drive but it improved handling so much that we increased our speed from ±50kph to about 80kph. Fuel consumption increased marginally and I calculated that for the 60 kilometres we travelled that evening, at a conservative 5% increase in fuel consumption, I spent an extra 92c on fuel! The increase in fuel costs is so small while the increase in safety so huge.

Driving all four wheels offers better all round safety, handling and improved tyre life on anything but a perfect road surface. So my first bit of advice is: Engage 4x4 not because you need it, but because it's there and safety is everything.

Driving a 4x4 is great fun. No matter what vehicle you drive, as long as it has low gearing and reasonable clearance it can be a source of never ending enjoyment. The driving techniques in this chapter are those that I use and are by no means the 'only' correct techniques. The secret to good off-road driving is to watch others. When a driver clears difficult obstacles with low engine revs and with little or no wheelspin you can bet they are good drivers and are worth watching. Remember, not all experienced drivers are good drivers!

THE BASICS

When Must Four-Wheel Drive be Engaged?

The key is BE PREPARED. Select four-wheel drive BEFORE you encounter difficulties. If you consider that the terrain over which you are about to travel could not be easily traversed in a normal motor car, then engage four-wheel drive. Even if it is just a rough track and the going is easy, engaging four-wheel drive will reduce wear on the transmission by distributing the pounding to all four wheels instead of just two. If you have free-wheel hubs, lock them immediately when you leave the road – you will be able to engage your front wheels from inside the cab at a moment's notice. Do not wait until you need four-wheel drive before engaging.

Holding the Steering Wheel

In almost all off-road situations it is not necessary to fight the vehicle, forcing it to change direction. It is far preferable to let the steering wheel slip through your hands, gently coaxing the vehicle to go in the direction you wish.

Keep your thumbs outside of the steering wheel rim. Steering kickback when hitting an obstacle can jerk the steering wheel around with such force that it can badly bruise a thumb or finger.

Seat belts should be worn although many find that inertia belts are uncomfortable as they tend to tug and pull, locking and unlocking as the vehicle shakes around. Wear seat belts during steep climbs or descents and side-slopes or wherever a roll-over could result. I recommend keeping them off in deep wading situations or any similar situation where there is a risk that a quick evacuation of the vehicle may be necessary.

Inspections

In difficult off-road situations, climbing out to inspect the ground over which you are about to drive can prevent bogging down or vehicle damage. This is especially important when negotiating rocky terrain where transmission damage can result if rocks strike the gearbox or axles and expensive body damage can result. I do not subscribe to the opinion that it's okay for a vehicle designed for off road use to get damaged occasionally.

Avoid Misuse of the Clutch

Engaging the clutch at the wrong moment either to change gear or to prevent a stall can create problems off-road. The beginner should avoid the clutch whenever the vehicle is traversing an obstacle – avoid changing gears and rather let the vehicle stall on a slope than risk a backward slide out of control. Next to hooliganism, misuse of the clutch causes more accidents off-road than anything else.

ENGAGING 4-WHEEL DRIVE AND LOCKING DIFFERENTIALS

Part-time 4-Wheel Drive
Engage 4-wheel drive in conditions where you feel that a 2-wheel drive vehicle may spin a wheel and struggle to get through.

Permanent 4-Wheel Drive (Centre diff lock)
Lock the centre differential if there is any danger that any of the vehicle's wheels will lose traction and spin. Also as a safety measure when travelling at high speed on gravel or wet, oil-slick tar. Lock the centre diff whenever low range is engaged.

'Super-Select' 4-wheel Drive (Mitsubishi)
Engage 4-wheel drive, centre diff unlocked in ALL conditions other than smooth dry tarmac. Locking the centre diff as above.

Rear Axle Differential Lock
Lock the rear axle differential in conditions which are severely undulating, when wheels lift well off the ground.

Many off-road drivers tend to lock the rear diff the moment things become challenging. This robs them of a chance to learn and hone their skills. Just because wheels lift off the ground it doesn't mean that a rear locker is needed. It just means that a rear locker will make it easier. Try your skills, use the push-pull technique (see axles twisters later in this chapter) and try and get through. If you find it is impossible or you feel that the vehicle is being stressed, go right ahead; stop the vehicle, engage rear diff lock and drive through. I recommend this approach because bad driving techniques are easily masked by a locked rear diff.

In flat soft sand axle diff locks can hinder progress due to the understeer they cause. This understeer causes the turn of the front wheels being exaggerated creating a very high rolling resistance of the front wheels, halting progress. Always stop the vehicle before engaging. Failure to do so can wreck the differential.

What makes an off-roader special is the second gear lever. Top: Pajero's second stick selects high and low range, locked 4-wheel drive. Bottom: In the case of 'soft-roaders', the gear lever is often accompanied by another switch. The yellow knob on this Freelander's stick engages Hill-Descent Control.

The Transfer Gearbox
Part of what makes an off-road vehicle special is the transfer gearbox, the second gearbox in which an additional set of gear ratios is available for off-road driving. The transfer gearbox reduces the overall gearing, giving a new set of ratios that are changeable by the gears of the main gearbox. For example, a 5-speed gearbox plus the transfer box provides the vehicle a total of 10 forward gears, and two reverse gears.

Avoid excessive throttle openings when in low-ratio first or second as the high torque loads can destroy differentials and twist off half-shafts. In the case of selectable four-wheel drive vehicles, additional lever/s attached to the transfer gearbox will select four-wheel drive.

Levers on part-time four-wheel drive transmissions:

- Two-wheel drive – high-ratio (normal road driving).
- Four-wheel drive – high-ratio (easy off-road driving and for momentum-critical driving, e.g. sand).
- Four-wheel drive – low-ratio (difficult, slow off-road driving).

Levers on full-time four-wheel drive transmissions:

- Four-wheel drive – high-ratio (normal road driving).
- Four-wheel drive – high-ratio + centre differential lock (easy off-road driving and for momentum-critical driving).
- Four-wheel drive – low-ratio + centre differential lock (difficult off-road driving).
- ABS on/off. (Off-road conditions where engine compression is used to slow the vehicle)

Even for moderate off-road driving it is advisable to lock the centre diff whenever the low-ratios are selected. This will protect the differentials from damage due to excessive torque transmitted when in low-range. The transfer gear lever may have a central position marked "N". In this neutral position no power goes to either prop-shaft. Neutral is used when the engine is being used to drive auxiliary engine driven equipment via power take-offs. It is also the position which should be selected if the vehicle is being towed for long distances.

FREE-WHEEL FRONT HUBS

The sole purpose of free-wheel hubs is to save fuel on the open road. The amount of fuel they save is not measurable under 50 kilometres. Often drivers of part time four-wheel drive vehicles use more fuel than their permanent four-wheel drive counterparts because when the going gets a bit difficult they are often too lazy to stop, get out and lock the hubs and instead battle through in two-wheel drive and use more fuel.

Driving with the hubs locked does not damage the transmission. Some think that they are designed to be unlocked on a tar road. This is untrue. I suggest unlocking them once the long, high-speed tar driving is complete and the gravel and off-road driving lies ahead. In this way the driver will be able to select 4-wheel drive from inside the cab. Then, when the trip is over, and you are on the road to go home, unlock them to get the fuel savings.

ELECTRONIC TRACTION-CONTROL (ETC)

Traction control, fitted to many modern 4x4s, is an electronic traction enhancing system developed to improve traction by taking the energy created by tractionless, spinning wheels, converting it into pulling power which is then transmitted to wheels with good traction by use of the ABS brake system or hydraulics. The driving techniques for vehicles with traction control are not the same as for those without.

In most cases traction control makes the vehicles perform better on slippery ground, the only exception being the Land Rover Discovery Series-2. The reason for this is that Land Rover obviously felt that the centre differential was no longer required as the ETC would handle the wheel spin resulting from no centre diff. In my view they were wrong and in most terrains this vehicle, when fitted with a manual gearbox, under performs most 4x4s and even some 4x2s with axle diff locks. (In the Discovery Series-3 the centre diff has been put back)

Discovery-2, one of the first vehicles with Electronic Traction Control. As an obverser it appeared as if this was a huge learning curve for Land Rover and the entire 4x4 world has reaped the benefits of their experience. Their mistake was the removing of the centre diff. I guess this is the price of being one of the great pioneers of 4x4 technologies as Land Rover continues to be.

The fundamental difference in driver technique is in the use of the accelerator. The technique of easing the throttle during wheel spin will cancel out any effect that ETC may be having. In this case ETC might as well not be there. Should the driver keep the throttle open, a well set up ETC will activate, braking the spinning wheels and transmit power to the wheels with traction. Therefore it is safe to say, if you have a vehicle fitted with ETC and a fully-locked up four-wheel drive system, both techniques will work. Of course the beauty of this is that should the first technique fail, try the second. The best of both worlds!

The Jeep Grand Cherokee fitted with one of the most advanced Electronic Traction Control systems. Working with hydraulics instead of the ABS brakes it has an advantage over many other vehicles, especially in sand.

TYRE PRESSURES

Part of the preparation for driving off-road is the checking and then deflation or inflation of the vehicle's tyres to alter the tyre footprint and thus increase floatation or penetration.

There are few subjects in the world of 4x4s that are under such constant debate. In the four editions of this book, in each edition I have revised my opinions because every time I go out and drive, and watch vehicles perform in varying terrain, my own opinions change. At this time, these are my findings:

Novice off-road drivers frequently underestimate the effect tyre pressure has when a vehicle is off road.

The top tyre print represents a tyre pumped at normal operating pressure. The lower footprint illustrates what happens to the tyre print at half the pressure. It is longer and slightly wider. The increased footprint area means that the pressure on the ground is reduced (Less sinking) while the area of tyre contact is greater. (More traction)

Reducing tyre pressures:

- *When traction is marginal but the surface threatens the tyre tread or sidewall, such as rocks, hard and steep slopes, shallow snow, steep hard sandy inclines and shallow slippery mud, tyre pressures should be reduced by 20% of normal operating pressures.*
- *To reduce the shock effect of tyre impact when driving over rocks, pressures should be reduced by 20%.*
- *To improve comfort, safety and stability of corrugations, depending on the load, pressures should be dropped by 15%.*
- *If conditions require protection, such as on sharp rocks and in conditions where the tyre sidewalls are threatened, then I recommend normal or even 10% higher than normal pressures.*
- *If conditions require floatation tyres should be deflated. On sand tracks where speeds are 40-50 kph drop pressures by 15%.*
- *In thick sand were low range is necessary drop pressures by 50%.*
- *In sand where the vehicle is relying on momentum drop pressures by 60%.*
- *In an emergency situation, to get out of a really difficult jam, drop pressures by 75%. A tubed tyre can safely be reduced to .35 bar and a tubeless tyre to .5 bar. At these pressures drive very carefully or the tyre will come off the rim.*

TYRE PRESSURE SUMMARY	
SURFACE CONDITIONS	**PRESSURE REDUCTION**
Sealed surface	100%
Gravel/Corrugations	10 - 15%
Rocks	10 - 15%
Mud	25%
Sand	50 - 60%
Emergency tubed - tubeless	0.35 bar. - 0.6 bar.

- A vehicle with tubed tyres can be driven more aggressively because the tube serves to hold the tyre on the rim and if the bead is broken, there will be no loss of air. For this reason pressures can be dropped lower than with tubed tyres.
- At any pressure lower than normal, speeds must be kept down to prevent tyre damage, especially if you are using tubed tyres.
- Excessive speed with reduced pressures, with tubeless tyres will quickly wreck the tube and a blowout is likely.

OFF-ROAD DRIVING

STEEP SLOPES

When descending or ascending steep slopes follow the fall line. Avoid tackling slopes at an angle as a slide and roll-over could result. Never try to turn around on a slope that is more than 25°.

Descending a steep slope

The trick is to use the compression of the engine to slow the vehicle down. In doing so all four wheels are braked simultaneously. This eliminates, on all but the most severe slopes, the risk of the wheels locking and a slide resulting.

The golden safety rule for driving, either up or down steep slopes, is under no circumstances engage the clutch. The techniques for descending slopes with a firm base and those with a slippery base differ, as follows:

- Remember the golden rule: if you depress the clutch at the wrong moment you may lose control. No matter what happens, the clutch is not required if the vehicle is moving.
- Engage four-wheel drive, ensure that free-wheel hubs are engaged and lock any differentials that you can lock.
- Select the lowest gear available; low-range first.
- Release the hand-brake and begin the descent.
- As the vehicle begins its descent take your feet off the pedals and place them on the floor. If you're a beginner you may want to tuck your left leg under the seat to prevent the inadvertent use of the clutch.
- On all but the steepest slopes the engine will provide all the braking you need. You will have full control because there is no chance of locking the wheels due to action on the brakes.
- If the vehicle loses traction and starts to slide, steer towards the direction of the slide (downhill) and apply gentle, careful acceleration.
- If engine braking is insufficient, gentle application of the brakes can be made. Do this when the vehicle is moving in a straight line. (so brake before a corner and take the corner under compression only)
- Apply brakes in short sharp jabs to avoid locking the wheels (cadence braking). Be aware that the use of brakes can induce a slide, so take care not to cause a wheel to lock.
- If you are using the brakes they must be released the moment a wheel begins to slide or the vehicle's direction changes due to a slide.
- NEVER change gear during a steep descent without your foot first pressing the brakes. If the clutch is depressed the vehicle will speed down the slope out of control.
- If your engine stalls during the descent because your vehicle has hit an obstacle, start it with the starter motor while in gear and keep your foot well away from the clutch.
- When descending on very slippery ground, the use of the brakes is highly dangerous and can induce a slide from which you may not recover. Low range second is the gear of choice for very slippery descents and descending sand dunes.
- With auto transmissions, use the brakes from the beginning of the slope, control the speed with the brakes and do not let the engine race.

The critical safety issue when climbing or descending steep slopes is not to depress the clutch in the event of traction loss or stalling.

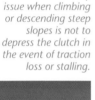

Ascending a steep slope

When confronted with a steep slope to climb the driver must decide: Do I need momentum or control? For example in the case of climbing steep dunes, speed and momentum is the essence whereas climbing a rocky slope, traction is the most important element. A higher gear and speed will provide momentum but if the slope is bumpy this will cause the wheels to bounce, resulting in loss of traction.

The procedure is as follows:

- *Engage four-wheel drive, lock the centre differential and make sure the free-wheel hubs are engaged.*
- *Select a gear that will offer enough torque to get you up, but not too low as to promote wheel spin. Second or third gear low-ratio usually works well.*
- *Select your line. An even, steep slope is better than an axle twister at a flatter angle.*

- *Do not rush the slope. As the vehicle hits the slope at a too high speed energy is absorbed and the result is a vehicle that begins the slope on the rebound. It is at a disadvantage from the beginning. Rather apply firm accelerator the moment after the front wheels begin the climb, and not before.*
- *As the vehicle begins its ascent give a little extra power. The more slippery the surface, the more momentum you will need to get over the top. If the surface is uneven, a lower speed will prevent the wheels from bouncing and leaving the ground, thereby losing traction.*
- *If the vehicle loses traction and wheels start to spin, decelerate very slightly and accelerate again once the wheels grip again.*
- *Decelerate as you crest the slope to avoid hitting an unseen obstacle or go careering over the edge in the wrong gear.*
- *If your attempt fails due to lack of power, select a gear one lower than the gear you first tried. If your attempt failed due to loss of traction, you have two choices – select a higher gear than before and/or, drive the slope with a little more speed. Revise and change your line.*
- *A gear change during the ascent may be needed if not enough momentum can be achieved at the lower section of the slope. A very rapid change down can be attempted but must be done at the place on the slope of minimum traction. e.g. Corrugations.*
- *With auto transmissions, the technique is the same, although a mid-slope gear-change is possible.*

Engine stall on a steep slope

If your engine stalls during a steep ascent the vehicle is in a potentially dangerous situation. The golden rule applies more in this situation than in any other: allow the vehicle to stall and do not try to prevent the stall by depressing the clutch. It is this single act that counts for more off-road accidents than any other.

- *Apply the hand-brake firmly simultaneously holding the vehicle with the foot brake.*
- *Depress the clutch , slowly and cautiously. If safe, engage reverse gear and release the clutch.*
- *If you are unable to engage reverse because the vehicle cannot be held by the brakes alone, have someone pack rocks behind the wheels to secure the vehicle. Once this has been done engage reverse and release the clutch.*
- *Release the hand-brake – slowly.*
- *Start the engine, (only kick the starter otherwise the starter motor will propel the vehicle down the slope) while engaged in reverse with your foot off the clutch, while simultaneously gently releasing the foot brake. The engine will fire and the vehicle will descend safely under engine compression braking. From this point the procedure is described in 'descending slopes' but this time it is done in reverse.*

SIDE SLOPES

When a steep slippery mountain track tilts the vehicle the rear wheels often break away causing a slide. On clay-type mud this can happen without any provocation and is severely exaggerated when one is moving down a slope.

- *Steer towards the direction of the slide.*
- *Accelerate gently.*
- *Do not use brakes as this will increase the slide.*
- *Once the vehicle is straightened up, cadence braking can be used to slow the vehicle.*
- *Side slopes on sand are particularly dangerous because of the danger of roll-over as the lower wheels penetrate the sand increasing the angle. When approaching a slope in thick sand take it at speed under full power, making sure that momentum is maintained.*

MUD DRIVING

A good rule is to walk across the obstacle before you attempt to drive through it. With mud this is rarely done, and this is why four-wheel drive vehicles can easily suffer structural damage while driving in mud. Rocks and logs often lie hidden under the mud and hard mud is often driven through with excessive speed.

Mud driving can be tricky, especially for a vehicle fitted with broad tyres better suited to beach use where the shallow treads quickly clog and sit on the surface without any grip. In most cases mud requires lower than normal tyre pressures.

- Engage 4WD well before you need it and lock differentials. If you have both front and rear axle diff locks, leave the front disengaged unless the conditions are particularly bad – locking both axles causes steering difficulty. Make sure your free-wheel hubs are engaged.
- Select the appropriate gear before tackling the most difficult terrain. For thick, deep mud in a large engined vehicle, third gear low-ratio is suggested. With smaller engined vehicles, select second gear low-range. The lower the gear, the more chance of wheel spin. The higher the gear the more chance of having to change down a gear, which could mean loss of momentum.
- Avoid doing anything suddenly. Keep your actions smooth and your steering wheel dead ahead if possible.
- There are two techniques to be tried: Even and constant power application. Don't accelerate when wheel spin occurs and don't decelerate when the vehicle accelerates. Keep the power application constant. This is often the easiest and most effective technique for beginners.
- Another effective technique is to look for traction. To do this, when wheel spin occurs, decelerate immediately, but delicately. If you take your foot off the accelerator completely your vehicle will slow down too quickly, and when you accelerate again the wheels are likely to spin. It is a balance of accelerating when traction is good and decelerating when wheel spin occurs while also keeping the speed constant.
- If you find that the wheel spin continues and you are slowing down, it means that you are about to get stuck. If you avoid accelerating and continue to decelerate slowly while your wheels are spinning, and you still get stuck, rest assured that although you may have stopped, you will not be deeply bogged down. You would have avoided making unnecessary work for yourself by spinning your wheels and digging yourself in deeper.

Excessive speed is an all too common mistake when driving in mud. However, sometimes wheel spin can be used as an advantage. Here the clogged tread is cleared by a spinning wheel.

Most soft and super-roaders are good performers in mud as long as it doesn't get too deep. Here a Porsche Cayenne plays on a muddy road but its over-abundance of power can be a handicap. Drivers must drive with a gentle right foot to stay out of trouble. Too much boot may result in an uncontrolled slide into a roadside ditch or hollow, the most common way of getting stuck on muddy hilly tracks.

In order to assist the tyres get traction from the sidewalls, try swinging the steering wheel from side to side when the vehicle is moving. This works well if the wheels are spinning in ruts and the consistency of the mud is firm.

When driving in thick mud with broad tyres designed for floatation in sand, spinning will not cause them to dig in as quickly as would narrow mud tyres. Instead, the treads clog with mud and the tyre loses all traction and spins on the top of the mud without driving the vehicle. In this case the best course of action is to drive through the mud at speed, keeping the wheels spinning. In the process the mud clogging the treads is flung out. There is a danger in this situation of damaging the vehicle by going too fast and hitting unseen obstacles hidden under the mud.

Steep mountain slopes in slippery mud

Allowing the wheels on one side of the vehicle to drop into a ditch at the side of a track is one of the most frequent ways in which vehicles bog down in muddy conditions. These ditches often occur on both sides of the track and are caused by water run-off that has eroded deep channels that catch the unwary. Unless your vehicle is fitted with differential locks on the axles, the wheels buried in the ditch will spin and the wheels on the outside will remain stationary. So, if you are travelling on a track that slopes away at its edges, drive slowly and carefully stay in the middle.

Descending slopes in shallow, slippery mud:

- *Use low gear ratios and go slow. Do not be in a hurry. Lock up four-wheel drive even if you do not think you need it. Conditions change very quickly and if you are engaged in four-wheel drive you stand a better chance of handling them.*
- *Steering control is lost when the vehicle's motion exceeds the rotation speed of the wheels. This will occur if you use brakes in the conventional way – so if you need to stop, apply brakes in short, sharp jabs.*

Rocking

This is a method using small wheel rotations (1/4 to 1/2 a wheel turn) to build up momentum when a vehicle is caught between two obstacles. Select low-range second or third gear. Increase the engine revs and release the clutch. The moment before wheel spin occurs, depress the clutch. Your vehicle will roll backwards off the obstacle. As the rear wheels hit the obstacle behind you, the vehicle will bounce forward. Make use of this forward momentum and release the clutch again. Each time the vehicle is rocked back and forwards in this way speed and momentum will increase. At the moment when you feel that enough speed has been built up, release the clutch and accelerate gently. Rocking works particularly well on rocky terrain and often in mud, and will also work in reverse. If attempted in sand however, it usually digs the vehicle in deeper.

SAND DRIVING

Sand driving encompasses dunes, tracks and the beach.

These rules can be applied when driving in sand:

- *Shadows in the morning and evening make driving easier.*
- *Engage 4WD well before you need it and lock up your transmission.*
- *Deflate your tyres according to recommendations earlier in this chapter.*
- *During the heat of the day, especially after long periods without rain, the air gaps between the sand particles will be larger and the sand will have less floatation. During the cooler hours, the sand will be more dense and will support more weight. After rain and in the early morning, moisture will compact the sand and make the going easier.*
- *Select the appropriate gear before tackling the difficult parts. You will need the highest possible gear that will give you enough torque to get through – try high-range first or if the sand is very thick, low-range third. A gear change in thick sand will halt your vehicle as quickly as if you had applied brakes. The lower the gear, the more chance of wheel spin. The higher the gear the greater the chance of having to change gear which could mean the loss of momentum.*
- *Follow other vehicle tracks. This reduces the scars on the landscape which in some desert areas remain visible for decades.*

- If you need to stop, find a firmer patch and do not touch the brakes – simply slow down and let the vehicle come to a halt. Applying brakes will cause a weight shift and a little wall of sand to build up in front of the front wheels – this will make starting off difficult.
- Before starting off, or if you find starting off difficult, reverse a short distance (one metre is often enough) along your own tracks and pull away. This allows momentum to be gained before you reach the wall of sand that was created when your vehicle stopped.
- If you get stuck, try reversing along the same tracks you approached on. The opposite twisting action of the axles in reverse will help give traction. Attempting to leave the tracks may get you stuck. On your second attempt, go through with a little more speed.

Sand dunes

Driving on sand dunes is a particularly delicate conservation issue and should never be undertaken in a thoughtless manner. When driving up and over a dune, check over the top for people, other vehicles and the sharpness of the descent on the other side.

Momentum is the single most important aspect when dune driving and everything a driver does must be geared to maintaining it, no matter how the conditions may vary. When a vehicle is on hard ground between dunes the correct speed and gear ratio for the climb must be established. In most dune conditions I recommend low range third and fourth. While second and third high range is also fine, selecting low range is advisable because if a rapid change-down to second or even first is needed is can be done in a hurry – no need to stop, and change from high to low range.

Correct gear selection in dune driving is crucial. Start off in low second and progress to third and fourth. Avoid changing gear mid-slope as in most cases it will degrade the vehicle's momentum enough to stop it completely. However, all rules have their exceptions.

In 1996 a group of friends in a Hilux and my family in a Land Cruiser went exploring the NamibRand Nature Reserve in Namibia, where we found some exhilarating dune driving. On one particularly long steep climb the Hilux in front balked at the steep dune and came to a halt. After about eight attempts the driver had run out of options and the dune remained unconquered. Approximately two thirds of the way up there was a length of corrugations where the track became a little steeper. The corrugations were created by drivers hitting the accelerator at the base of the gradient increase. Acceleration here simply meant spinning wheels, loss of momentum and the resultant corrugations. I then asked if I could give it a go. On the early part of the slope I realised that flat out in second gear high-range was not going to give me enough momentum to overcome the difficult

patch and hitting the slope with extra speed was not an option. So, when I reached the corrugations, at the moment when my wheels would start to spin, I changed into first gear and powered my way up the final 30 metres to the top. My friend, now in the Land Cruiser, with much more power and momentum at his disposal, did the entire climb in second. In situations like this a gear change may be required and vehicles with more power require less effort to drive. The critical driving technique was not just the gear change, but timing it over the corrugations where the wheels would lose traction anyway.

Rules of dune driving:

- *Deflate tyres before dune driving.*
- *Keep power constant on the slope.*
- *Maintain the momentum of your vehicle.*
- *You must aim to stop at the crest in order to inspect the descent and to engage the correct gear for the descent. The aim is to get your vehicle to stop at the top, even if it means touching the sand under its belly. Ideally its nose should be over the edge and the vehicle lying horizontal pointing slightly downhill.*
- *You will need to decelerate as you near the top and judge it perfectly to get it right. If you stop and are still pointing uphill you will have to reverse back down and try again. Do this once you have checked the gradient and know what you are up against. Once your vehicle is successfully perched at the top, the next step is to dig away the crest that is touching the chassis between the wheels.*
- *Survey the drop and engage the low-range first if it's not too steep and low-range second if it's hair-raising. The higher gear will mean a faster drop but will prevent the sand under the vehicle falling faster than the vehicle. If this happens the vehicle will slide sideways, and that is a very bad idea.*
- *If it does start to slide accelerate firmly. Don't let the slide continue! Slides on dunes turn into a roll-over in an instant. Too much speed going down a dune slope is safer than going too slowly.*

Side slopes on dunes

Never attempt to go sideways when ascending or descending a dune, because if you do the lower wheels will dig in and your vehicle will roll. Loaded roof racks are ill-advised when dune driving, and a conscious effort should be made to keep the vehicle's centre of gravity as low as possible when loading your vehicle. If the track ahead runs for a short distance along the side of a dune where the vehicle may slide, power is the only thing that will prevent the rear wheels from breaking away and the vehicle stopping at a precarious angle. Keep the power on and keep moving. If the back breaks away turn into

the slope (downhill) and keep the power on. Getting stuck on a side slope is often a dangerous situation and the first priority should be to secure the front of the vehicle to prevent it from sliding any further and increasing the angle and the risk of rolling the vehicle.

Sand tracks

When driving on thick sand tracks engage four-wheel drive even if you do not require it. Tyre wear will be reduced and vehicle control will be easier. Fuel consumption will also be improved because, even if you don't realise it, in two-wheel drive wheel spin will occur over the bumpy patches and speed is lost. The proof of this is the effect that a two-wheel drive has on this type of road. The spinning rear wheels cause large waves of sand to be built up and, after a time, driving on these roads is like riding a roller coaster.

When driving along deep sand tracks there is a natural tendency to fight with the steering wheel. This is due to the wheels sliding over the sand with very little feel being transmitted back to the driver as to which way the front wheels are pointing. Deep tracks can be driven without a hand being placed on the steering wheel at all. But don't be fooled by this as I once was, and play a game of chance along the narrow sand tracks in the Kalahari – many 4x4s have come to grief as the front wheels spin out and the vehicle suddenly rolls over.

Don't fight the steering when driving sand tracks. This tendency causes the front wheels to crab, slowing progress and using fuel.

On this type of track the vehicle moves as if it were on rails and the inexperienced driver will tend to fight the steering wheel and most of the time the front wheels will not be pointing in the direction of travel – the front wheels will plough through the sand, absorbing power and consuming excess fuel. Very little steering effort is needed to guide a vehicle in these conditions. Let the vehicle steer itself while holding the wheel firmly enough to catch it if it suddenly swings, gently coaxing the vehicle in the direction you wish to go.

When driving along tracks through thick bush it is important to keep the windows rolled up to eye height. This is done to prevent branches along the edges of bush tracks from whipping into the passing vehicle and causing injury to the occupants' eyes.

Sand tracks that have very high walls are difficult to get out of. To get out of the trough, decelerate lightly, swing the wheel over quite hard and then IMMEDIATELY SWING IT BACK to just off the dead ahead position. If the steering wheel is left in the hard over position, a slide and a roll-over could result. If it works, the vehicle's front wheels will ride over the ridge and the rear wheels will follow. If it does not, centre the steering and try again. If you find it impossible to leave the track, as can sometimes happen, stop the vehicle and try it in reverse. If you are forced to leave the track due to an oncoming vehicle, stop and turn on your headlights. Try the reverse procedure pulling off to the left hand side of the track.

On two occasions I have come across a 4WD vehicle lying in the middle of a sand track on its side. On both occasions the drivers had tried to get out of a deep track. They had swung the wheel hard over and when nothing happened turned it even more. All of a sudden the front wheels hit something solid and the vehicles left the track so sharply that they rolled over.

BEACH DRIVING

Beach and sand driving have obvious similarities, but other important points should be considered when driving on the beach. Make sure you carry a can of Q-20, or a similar water repellent as well as a tyre gauge and pump with you. Drop tyre pressures before venturing onto the beach.

Beach driving recommendations:

- *An outgoing tide is the best time to drive on the beach due to the extra time to dig yourself out should you get into trouble.*
- *Do not underestimate the speed at which the tide comes in – you may lose your vehicle if you do!*
- *Drive as close as possible to the water's edge without getting splashed and you will be driving on the firmest surface.*
- *Beware of shiny wet patches and keep them between you and the surf – they indicate deep patches of sand saturated with water. Areas of pebbles or shells which even under the best lighting conditions are difficult to detect, are treacherous. They are invisible when the sun is low in the sky.*
- *Avoid driving on an unfamiliar beach at night.*
- *Give way to anyone who appears to be having difficulty, and watch out for children.*
- *Too low gear ratios will induce wheel spin unless the driver is very careful about how he applies his right foot.*
- *Use low range. A quick change down is then at hand. Be alert, beach driving can be extremely hazardous to your insurance premiums.*
- *In South Africa, a blanket beach ban has been imposed and vehicles found unlawfully on a beach can be confiscated.*

WADING

Off-road vehicles are often required to forge through deep water. Before doing so, check the vehicle manufacturer's specification data sheet on maximum wading depth, (or the vehicle handbook).

Water is ingested by the engine if the engine stalls and water is sucked up the exhaust pipe or if the water is too deep, the engine intake

can suck water into the combustion chambers. SHOULD THIS HAPPEN DO NOT ATTEMPT TO RESTART THE ENGINE. IN MANY CASES IT IS THE RESTART THAT CAUSES THE SEVERE DAMAGE. Recovery from a drowned engine is covered in chapter-9.

In deep water the engine cooling fan splashes water around the engine bay, so either keep engine revs low, or remove the fan belt. Viscous-coupled cooling fans are ideal because when they hit water the friction slows the fan, reducing the splash. Some vehicles come equipped with bell housing drain holes which allow oil collecting in the bell housing to drain away. These holes must be sealed to prevent water coming into contact with the clutch.

Top: Slow and cautious, the correct technique for wading. Bottom: It's quite a common occurrence that to make a vehicle look great for the camera, advertisers drive the vehicle through water far to quickly. It might look good but it's a bad technique and a lot of it eventually damages the vehicle.

Many years ago (when I was a lot less careful about such things) my vehicle was called upon to extract a yacht from deep water. I was unable to seal the bell housing because of a missing plug but I went ahead regardless and paid a high price. Water entered the bell housing and because the water was very cold, and the engine and gearbox were quite warm, the cooling effect caused water to be sucked into the engine through a leaking rear main bearing oil seal. The water, which was already mixed with fine sand, mixed with the engine oil and wrecked the main bearings. The engine had to be completely rebuilt.

Slow speed is essential and low-range second gear is recommended for most wading conditions. When entering the water do so slowly and avoid creating a splash that will wet electrical components. Drive at a speed that creates a clean bow wave. If you have ever seen a boat moving at speed and then slowing down, you will have noticed the bow wave catching up and pushing the boat from behind. This is exactly what happens to a vehicle in deep water. If you have created a bow wave and lose traction, the bow wave will push your vehicle forward as it catches up. This little push may be just what is needed to get you through a sticky patch, or up a river bank.

The deep hole hidden under the waves can wreck an engine in an instant. Is it worth the risk? This was me circa 1997. I was lucky and the engine was not damaged.

When crossing running water, test the depth and strength of flow before proceeding. If the flow is too powerful to walk against, rest assured that driving through it will be dangerous. Moving water will create more turbulence than still water, so consider this when calculating the depth. Move diagonally across the flow with the water pushing you. Crossing still water is safer but the possibility of deep sediment is more likely.

After wading, bell housing sealing plugs should be removed. Inspect the engine air filters if you think water may have entered the carburettors. Water can contaminate gearbox and axle oils by entering through the breather valves. Because oil floats, it is easy to

remove this water. Allow the vehicle to stand for a while and remove the drain plugs. The water will drain first and when you see oil, stop the draining process. If your engine oil has turned a milky grey colour, water has entered the engine sump. You will need to drain away the oil, flush the engine at least twice with oil or engine flush and then refill with new oil. Universal joints must be pumped with grease after being submerged.

A snorkel is the ultimate engine protection when driving deep water.

Should an engine ingest water into the cylinders it normally stalls before any serious damage is caused. This however is not the case with diesel engines – they are normally destroyed if this happens.

UNEVEN TERRAIN AND OTHER SURFACES

Ridges
When crossing a ridge, stay at right angles to the ridge, passing both wheels on each axle over the obstacle at the same time. Crossing at an angle could result in lifting a wheel off the ground and the loss of traction on that axle.

Troughs
When negotiating a trough, cross at an angle so as to drop only one wheel at a time into the trough. This will always keep at least one wheel from either axle on firm ground. When moving along a series of troughs do so carefully and slowly, otherwise the differential may be grounded if a wheel drops to one side.

While driving in deep water can be fun, it takes a heavy toll on the vehicle. Damaged oil seals, corrosion acceleration are just some of the costs, not to mention the chance of severely damaging the engine should water enter the block. I for one avoid deep water whenever possible.

Axle Twisters
When a series of ruts and troughs follow each other it's often referred to as an axle twister. Driving axle twisters without a rear diff lock

requires a technique called push-and-pull. Some say that to conquer an axle twister a little more momentum is required. I disagree.

During a trip to the Linyanti in 1990, I was confronted by a broad mud flat where the elephants had walked. When they had been there it was wet and their huge footprints made hollows as deep as my knee. All across the flats were thousands of these footprints, now made as hard as rock, baked that way by the October sun. A speed over 3kph would have left my Land Rover in ruins so the push and pull technique was used.

The push and pull technique:

- *Engage full four-wheel drive/lock the centre diff.*
- *Engage low range first or second gear.*
- *Assuming the right wheel enters first, let it drop into the hole. As it bounces upwards apply the accelerator gently.*
- *The left rear will fall into a hole. As this happens the front right wheel may leave the ground. At this time the rear wheels are pushing.*
- *As the front right wheel falls, (this is critical), ease the accelerator. The front wheel, as it strikes the ground must not spin. It will, if it is not spinning, grip. Now the front wheels will pull.*
- *As the front wheels pull, apply gentle accelerator.*
- *The rear wheels will move through the holes, probably one will leave the ground. As it does so, the left front wheel may lift and then fall.*
- *The process of easing the accelerator as the wheel falls begins again.*
- *Using the push and pull technique with too much speed will make it too difficult to apply.*
- *Excessive speed will cause bouncing wheels and traction loss.*
- *A slow methodical approach, hardly audible engine and the suspension working at full capacity is very impressive to watch.*

Above: Driving V-shaped gullies.

V-Shaped gullies

Driving along V-shaped gullies must be done with extreme caution. If one side of the vehicle slides down, and the wheels drop into the gully, there is a very good chance that the vehicle will get stuck. Getting out is also very difficult and digging may not work. One has to lift the lower wheels out of the gully, and to do this without momentum is very tricky. In this situation, differential locks on individual axles help a great deal.

When a V-shaped gully is entered, it should be done at an angle so as not to drop more than one wheel into the trough at a time. Exiting a gully should also be done at an angle so as not to allow both wheels on the same side of the vehicle to drop into the trough. Good axle articulation will assist a vehicle negotiating this type of terrain.

THE DEFINITION OF
OFF-ROAD DRIVING
Many drivers, often
novices, regard the
term 'off-road' driving
as exactly that:
Driving off the road.
The truth is, nothing
could be further
from the truth. Off
road driving means
driving on tracks
and roads where
ordinary vehicles are
unable. Driving over
virgin ground is an
unforgivable crime
to conservationists.
Gladly, the majority of
4x4 enthusiasts agree
with this principle. In
the pristine wilderness
of the NamibRand
Nature Reserve,
pictured right, even
doing a U-turn on
the track is forbidden.
Once a track has been
made in semi-desert
or desert regions
such as this, it takes
decades to fade. The
result of thoughtless
drivers literally going
'off-road' has not only
resulted in numberless
unsightly vehicle
tracks criss-crossing
the landscape but also
many areas once open
to travellers, are now
permanently closed. I
implore you: stay on
existing, well-defined
tracks. If a track is
vague, it may be
trying to mend. Find
a well worn track and
follow that. Let's pay
back the debt we owe
to our beautiful planet
and not drive without
inward thought and
consideration.

Ruts

Deep parallel ruts should be negotiated with one wheel in and one wheel out. If you allow both sides to drop into the rut the chassis may bottom out and progress could be halted. This would mean a great deal of digging to clear the underside of the vehicle to put the vehicle's weight back onto its wheels again.

Rough tracks

Although four-wheel drive may not be needed for traction, it is wise to engage it. This will reduce wear on transmission components and will afford the driver greater control. Avoid the constant use of brake and clutch and rather select a low-ratio gear that will keep the vehicle going at a steady speed. Look well ahead at the track surface and beware of sharp rocks that can tear tyre sidewalls.

Boulders and river beds

Engage 4WD and lock the differentials, even though you may think you do not need it. Select low-range first gear. In this gear, wide throttle openings should be avoided. Beware of the vulnerable parts of your vehicle such as the axle differentials and gearbox casings, especially if they protrude below the chassis frame as in the case of many 4x4 pick-ups. To avoid striking these, make sure that the wheels ride over the higher boulders, clearing the axle and chassis.

Use the rocks around you to reduce departure angles, assist a wheel to climb a step or prevent the vehicle running out of clearance.

Thumbs folded inside the steering wheel rim can get hurt when driving over rocks if the front wheels hit a rock hard and the steering kicks. Keep them on the outside.

Top and middle: Packing rocks to make a descent easier. Bottom: Packing rocks to ease the angle of a rock ledge.

SALT PANS

Driving over salt pans is a nerve-racking experience and to do it successfully will require experience and luck. Don't be fooled by the apparent firmness and dryness of the surface. Underneath lies thick, black, enveloping mud.

Before you venture across the pan, skirt around the edge to find the shortest possible route across. If you have decided to go across test the surface by walking some distance in front of your vehicle. If your feet are breaking through the crust, then do not attempt to drive across, no matter how broad your tyres are. If your feet are stepping on firm ground, then dig a hole about 25cms deep. If the earth is hard and dry, then it may be safe to cross. Unfortunately, there may be areas in front of you that are still soft.

The lower your tyre pressures are, the better your chances of getting through – in theory. In practice is doesn't appear to make

much difference. Engage four-wheel drive, lock differentials and hubs, select low-range third or fourth and proceed fairly slowly. If you rush and the surface breaks you will be a long way from the firmer ground behind you. Follow the direction of other vehicle tracks if they look fresh, and drive parallel to them while making your own tracks. By taking it slowly you can assess the firmness of the surface by how much power you are giving to the wheels. Look down at the wheels to gauge the depth of the tracks you are making.

If the surface breaks and you start sinking, either floor the accelerator or stop. Accelerating may get you through the soft patch, but if not you will be a long way from firm ground when you bog down. By stopping immediately you feel the vehicle sink it will be easier to dig out because of the close proximity of firm ground and suitable anchor points, such as another vehicle. Avoid sudden movements of the steering wheel. Turning will only make matters worse, because your wheels will act as a plough. If you choose to stop, attempt to reverse in your own tracks or try to steer out by making a gentle turn. If your vehicle resists leaving your tracks, straighten the steering wheel and let the vehicle steer itself. If you are making progress and the reverse is getting you out of trouble, all is well. If not, the mud may be so bad that even digging is sometimes pointless. If you have another vehicle with you, which is highly recommended when driving on salt pans, do not waste any time – start the recovery operation without delay. Work fast – your vehicle may be sinking. Watch the recovery vehicle closely – and don't get that stuck too!

Bogging down on a salt pan is a miserable experience. The mud is the worst kind you are likely to find anywhere, and without the aid of another vehicle equipped with a winch it may be days before you get out. Above all, don't take driving over salt pans lightly – they are treacherous. In Botswana vehicles are consumed by the pans almost every year. Do not stop and look at the scenery, no matter how solid the surface appears. Lastly, please consider both the environmental effect your vehicle tracks will have on the pans, and your fellow travellers that will pass after you have departed – in any event, it is far more pleasant and a great deal safer to walk than to drive.

Grasslands

Fit a grille guard to prevent grass seeds from clogging the radiator and causing overheating. Fire may be caused by dry grass wrapping itself around the prop-shaft or exhaust. The grass dries out and ignites, so frequent checks must be made and any grass collecting under the vehicle must be removed immediately. Tall grass also hides ditches, logs, ant hills and rocks, so caution is vital. Remember that your tracks will be clearly visible for some time after driving over grass, so in the interest of conservation use existing tracks if you can.

High speed driving over the flat pan surface is exhilarating but dangerous. A sharp turn can result in a roll-over if the outside wheels dig in even a little.

Unsurfaced roads

Long stretches of unsurfaced roads present their own dangers. Firstly engage four-wheel drive and lock the centre diff if you have one. DO NOT lock the rear diff. If you wish to overtake, check that your outside wheels do not hit the sand that piles up at the edge of the road; it will drag at the wheels on that side of the vehicle and can cause a spin. Secondly, if the road is convex, overtaking or even avoiding oncoming traffic can put your vehicle at a tilt, and this can cause a dangerous slide. If you see an oncoming truck throwing up clouds of dust, take the precaution of either slowing down to a crawl and getting well clear, or alternatively leaving the road and stopping altogether. There are very good reasons for this; for one thing, you will avoid loose stones being thrown up like bullets. For another, there could be another oncoming vehicle overtaking the truck through the dust. I was given this advice by an experienced traveller on the Caprivi road from Kongola to Katima Mulilo when in days past the truck drivers would race each other side-by-side. Only one of the trucks could be seen by oncoming traffic.

Some desert roads are made from a substance called calcrete that appears blinding white in the midday sun, and can be very dangerous. They are particularly prone to the effects of big trucks and storm water,

and after a week of rain can be transformed from a smooth dusty flat that can be covered at 90 kph, to a virtually impassable quagmire.

A driver needs to be very alert when driving on calcrete and driver changes should be regular. Driver concentration can be hard to maintain on long stretches and surface changes are very difficult to see against the blinding white.

If you see a deep rut or trough in front of you and it's too late to stop, apply brakes as hard as you can without locking the wheels. Do this until the very last moment and then, the instant before the front wheels hit, release the brakes. As the foot brakes are released, the vehicle's centre of gravity moves towards the rear and weight is taken off the front wheels. Now the vehicle hits the trough with less than the normal weight on the front axle. Doing this could mean the difference between a broken axle and simply a heavy bump. Swerving and hitting the trough sideways could roll the vehicle.

One more piece of advice: if you are travelling on a busy and dusty road, turn your headlights on and stay visible through the dust.

Corrugations

Corrugations are to be found on all dirt roads that are used by heavy vehicles and are especially bad after rain. They can cause a great deal of damage if driven over too fast. Suspension components are stressed to extreme limits if the vehicle is heavily laden and torsion stresses on the chassis frame can cause cracks in the steel. Corrugations can also cause loss of control, especially with vehicles that are softly sprung. Upon hitting the corrugations, vehicles like these tend to go into a slide, losing traction at the back end. This tendency is dramatically reduced when in four-wheel drive.

Loading a vehicle does tend to dull this tendency, but an overload will have the opposite effect, in which case over-steer increases dramatically. Early Land Rover Discovery and old Range Rover are particularly prone to this. By fitting gas shock-absorbers this tendency is reduced.

Driving at night

If you intend travelling through Third World countries at night, my advice is avoid it at all costs. The dangers cannot be over stressed. Third World countries are generally unfenced, so cattle, goats, chickens and antelope are a constant danger. If you collide with a cow at 80 kph you will be in a lot of trouble! You may wreck your vehicle and if you are lucky enough to get out unhurt, the local tribesman will require compensation. Litigation against owners of animals straying onto public roads in Third World Africa is expensive and time consuming, and in most cases unsuccessful. Trucks without lights are an even bigger danger. They are normally filthy and any reflectors fitted will have a thick layer of dust on them so that when you do see them it may be too late to avoid a collision.

What is more, on dirt roads at night if there is a lot of dust, your visibility will be impaired by the light bouncing back off the dust, making your long range lights useless. I cannot stress this point strongly enough: it is extremely unwise to travel at night in the Third World.

Snow and ice

Even in Southern Africa snow and ice can present a challenge to the off-road driver. During Easter of 1984, I was caught by snow in the Lesotho Highlands, the first time I had had to deal with such a situation. We were descending the mountain at the time, so this made the going even more treacherous. I stayed locked in combat during the entire descent, changing between low-range second and third for over six hours. During this time we covered only 25 kilometres and fuel consumption measured 45 litres per 100 kilometres. My advice is to take extreme care, especially if the area is mountainous. Ice is often invisible and the road surface and tyre adhesion can be very difficult to anticipate. If the ice is thin and the tyres are not gripping, it can be melted by spinning a wheel. This can be tricky in hilly country as the spinning wheels cause the vehicle to slide around without much control. Tyre pressures should be dropped as if driving in slippery mud. Narrow tyres with block treads and hard shoulders are best for snow conditions as they have a better chance of breaking through the snow to grip the surface beneath. Only in virgin powder snow are broad tyres preferable, and in these cases tyre pressures must be dropped to the absolute minimum – to 0.5 bar and speeds kept below 10 kph.

In shallow, slippery snow, tyre pressures should be dropped as if driving on slippery mud: About 50-60% of normal road pressures.

Snow chains are particularly valuable and if only a single set is available, place them on the rear wheels for tricky uphill climbs and on the front wheels when descending steep slopes. When tyre chains are fitted to only the front wheels there is the tendency for the back wheels to slide out, so extreme care should be taken.

- When a vehicle is parked for long periods, lift the windscreen wipers or they will stick to the windscreen otherwise. Do not leave the hand-brake on overnight, as some hand-brakes freeze. Rather park on level ground and engage low range first gear.
- Weather conditions in high altitudes in winter can change very rapidly and it is imperative that when exploring such areas in winter, food and water rations for at least three days should be carried.

Blow-outs

I have experienced four blow-outs while driving at speed in a loaded 4x4. Three occurred on the rear wheels and one on a front. 4x4s tend to have large wheels and tyres and so have a high centre of gravity. The result is that they tend to roll onto their roofs a little easier than normal road cars, especially if the vehicle is carrying a loaded roof rack. Catastrophic tyre and tube failures (blowouts) cause a vehicle to become difficult to control even if the failure occurs on a rear wheel. In such a situation the natural reaction is to stop as quickly as possible, but this is not always the most appropriate course of action. Hitting the brakes with any force in a blow-out situation tends to lead to loss of steering control followed by a slide. If the wheels strike a ridge or trough, even a shallow one, the vehicle can easily roll over. Avoid hitting the brakes. Simply take your feet off the pedals and gently change down one gear ratio. Take your time. Keep the vehicle on the road and away from the camber that will accelerate a slide. Causes of blow-outs range from under-inflation and overload to a twisted inner-tube. See chapter-4 for further insight into preventing blow-outs.

Convoys.
The rule for convoy driving is that you are responsible for the vehicle behind you. It is good manners for the vehicle behind to indicate that a turning ahead has been noted so that the vehicle ahead can proceed. Two flashes of the headlamps is the common method. If you want to attract attention of other convoy members, leave your lights on high beam.

OFF-ROAD DRIVING SCHOOLS

As the 4x4 manufacturers produce more and more vehicles so has another industry sprung up along side it: The 4x4 Information industry, the part of the industry into which this publication falls. Books, magazines, DVD videos, maps, self-guide guided trails and lastly 4x4 training.

The 4x4 driver training industry has been severely criticized for not having a regulatory body to formalise training, set a curriculum and recognising and separating the fly-by-nights from the serious well-experienced schools that provide good, value for money training. On one occasion a 4x4 school in the town of Welcome was set up by a gent who attended a half-day driving school near Johannesburg. This, he felt, was enough to start a business. By all accounts my blind grandmother was a better driver.

It is safe to say, in most countries, the standard of 4x4 training is not high and about 30% of the schools are good, 10% are excellent and the rest are poor, teaching incorrect and sometimes unsafe principles, and accepting wild and hooligan behavior all the while talking about protecting the planet and treading lightly.

I suggest getting word-of-mouth recommendations and treat lightly what you read in magazines. Journalists are often pampered by establishments to write good reports while they in many cases do not have the experience to judge if the techniques are sound and the training good value. Sadly, 4x4 driving schools associated with vehicle manufacturers is no guarantee of quality either.

Over the past four years I have, once a year, done 4x4 driver training at a school called Stoney Ridge in KwaZulu Natal, run by John Rich. John also has a 4x4 book to his credit and is supported by the Mitsubishi division of Daimler Chrysler. As a result of our work together Stoney Ridge is one of the few schools in South Africa I personally endorse. This is not to say it's the only worthwhile school, but I feel that it is the best.

A second school I am happy to endorse is the Goodyear 4x4 Academy high-speed gravel driving course. In my view, in many respects, this training of more value than off-road courses because its primary concern is the improvement of safety on long stretches of gravel found in semi desert regions, where so many lose their lives in unnecessary roll-overs.

To make contact with Stoney Ridge, call 0363 54 7012, email: stoneyridge@futurenet.co.za and the Goodyear Academy at 023 340 4183.

Driving Skills DVD. On DVD and VHS, The consensus among off-roaders worldwide is that this is one of the best 4x4 training videos in the world (This is not my opinion) Almost two hours of training demonstrating how effective the video is for teaching off-road driving. Highly entertaining, shot all over Southern Africa in some beautiful, remote places you'll watch it again and again. Top: The DVD Bottom: The two VHS tapes that make up the two hours of training. Available from www.4xforum. com or by calling 021 852 9984. Also available in most bookstores and wherever good 4x4 equipment is sold.

6. RECOVERY

WINCHES

RECOVERY ACCESSORIES

KINETIC/SNATCH STRAPS

JACKS

SAND LADDERS

ANCHORS

RECOVERY TECHNIQUES

DON'T BE FOOLED into thinking that experienced off-roaders don't get stuck – they get stuck more than anyone! This is because they are keen to try the impossible, are not afraid of ridicule nor are they unfamiliar with the processes of getting a vehicle unstuck. It is important to realise that there is no shame in getting a vehicle stuck. The most important tool required to free a vehicle from a sticky predicament is common sense. I have lost count of the number of times I have come across a bogged vehicle where the driver has taken out his winch or snatch strap without thinking through the problem. Three minutes with a well used spade and a gentle right foot and the vehicle is free. Common sense and a methodical approach often results in little work and a seemingly miraculous escape for the vehicle concerned.

Using recovery gear is more common sense than anything else. Here a trooper cannot move because it has come to rest against a boulder. The high-lift jack was used to move the boulder away from the vehicle while the Jeep used a snatch strap to tug the boulder clear.

Vehicle recovery equipment makes up a large proportion of a typical off-road load. The following covers the equipment that the serious off-roader should carry to free a vehicle or to get it over an obstacle where normal driving has failed:

WINCHES

Novices sometimes think that a winch makes them invincible. The fact is that the winch tends to be an overrated piece of off-road recovery equipment. This is because a winch relies on anchor points, which in so many cases just aren't available when you need them. And even if an anchor can be found, additional equipment such as a high-lift jack and a spade are needed to work in conjunction with a winch to extricate a vehicle. In a situation where there is no anchor, one can be constructed, but in most cases it is easier to use a jack and spade

A rare occasion when a winch was the only way out of a sticky situation. The two Range Rovers are winching over a steep bank. Above the bank the sand was so thick that a moving recovery, such as a pull or snatch, was out of the question. Southern Kalahari.

and dig the vehicle free than to create an anchor and use a winch. In severe cases, both may be needed. So, consider the winch only after you have acquired the other equipment needed to back it up. Once this has been acquired a winch becomes the backup, and not the other way round.

Winches are, however, indispensable for some tasks such as aiding in the recovery of other vehicles and dual vehicle operations where one vehicle can assist another to traverse difficult terrain. Other jobs where a winch is essential are hauling boats up the shores of muddy rivers and for removing obstacles such as fallen trees from the vehicle's path.

WINCH TYPES
Five types of winches are available: electric, hydraulic, engine driven, hub capstan and hand. Hydraulic and electric are either drum (horizontal) or capstan (upright).

Electric drum winches
The most common type of winch is the electric drum winch, manufactured by companies such as Ramsey, Warn and Superwinch. Drum winches with sufficient capacity for vehicle recovery are supplied with steel cable of between 25 and 40 metres which is neatly stored on the drum. They are heavy and require high capacity batteries to drive them (preferably deep-cycle). They overheat quickly in extended use and must frequently be left to cool. They are supplied with a hand held switch with a long extension lead enabling the operator to stand at a safe distance or sit inside the vehicle while winching. The switch allows the winch to wind forward and in reverse.

Capstan winches
These are normally engine driven and often perform superbly when all else fails. Their biggest disadvantage is that they are best operated by two people. This is because a second pair of hands is required to tail off the winch, a procedure like that used for operating the sail winches on large yachts. Only a seasoned expert will operate a capstan winch alone and if this is the case, an emergency engine ignition cut-off switch must be fitted so as to enable the operator, who will not be seated in the cab, to shut down the engine if required. I saw a Series One Land Rover fitted with an original Fairey 3000lb-capacity capstan winch haul 14 vehicles across a stretch of axle-deep liquid sand that no vehicle could traverse. The last and fifteenth vehicle proved too much for the small winch and the worm drive stripped. In the same situation, an 8000lb electric drum type would have overheated by the third or fourth vehicle. The rope for the capstan must be stored elsewhere as there is no provision for storing it on the winch.

Although there are rules and guidelines for vehicle recovery, no two recovery operations are the same. Ingenuity, common sense and a wide range of equipment are needed for most recovery situations. However, safety must be first priority. Don't create campfire stories by being injured by shortsightedness or carelessness.

Capstan winching underway.

Hydraulic winches

Hydraulic power is the most efficient method of powering a winch and those that use it offer immense pulling power. Hydraulic winches require an engine-driven hydraulic pump to run them and until recently they were no more than a dream to the ordinary 4x4 motorist, being fitted to very few non-military vehicles.

Milemarker hydraulic winch is powered by the vehicle's power steering pump. The unit has now made significant inroads and the electric drum winch, particularly those made by Warn, continue to be the most popular.

A range called Milemarker, powered by a standard power-steering hydraulic pump, was for a time available but failed to make their mark here in South Africa. This was due mainly to the lower steering pump pressures in European and Japanese vehicles. When they work, they work superbly. Vehicle warranty problems was another factor against the Milemarker. The winch gearbox has two speed settings, permitting rapid retrieval of the winch cable. Their most significant disadvantage shows itself when the engine stalls and the winch stops working. This could cause difficulty in a situation on a beach with an incoming tide and an engine failure due to water.

Pulling power

A cable guide enables the user to feed winch cable onto the drum without the risk of trapping fingers in the fairlead. A simple, inexpensive tool which few off-roaders appear to carry.

When selecting a drum winch, its rated pulling power represents its pulling strength when the cable is being wound onto the drum itself, not onto layers of cable wound around it. In effect, the smaller the diameter of the drum, the more its pulling power. So, when cable is wound onto a drum and cable is winched in on top of it, the diameter of the drum increases with each layer. For example, a winch rated at 8000 lbs is (theoretically) able to pull 8000lbs on the drum, about 6750lbs with a single layer of cable down, about 5800lbs with two layers of cable down and only about 5150lbs with four layers. For a winch to be useful to extricate a fully laden medium-sized 4x4 from deep mud, a winch of no less than 8000lbs rated pull is required. From this point, a heavier vehicle will require a stronger winch and a lighter vehicle, a lighter-duty winch. (See use of snatch block to increase pulling power).

Hub capstan winches

A hub capstan winch.

Designed specifically for self recovery, hub capstans bolt directly onto the wheel rims and with a cable attached, the capstan winds up the line and hauls the vehicle out as the wheels spin. To overcome the effect of the axle differential, two capstans must be used simultaneously. Hub capstans can pull a vehicle free in both directions, are lightweight, easy to operate, very effective and are inexpensive. Because only a portion of the wheel nuts secure the capstan, it is not necessary to jack up the vehicle to remove them and therefore a single set can be used by a number of common vehicles.

Mounting a winch

There are a few choices when it comes to mounting a winch. The first and easiest option is to purchase a bull bar with integral winch plate and have the entire thing assembled and attached by the supplier. The second option is to make your own. A third option is to buy a winch plate and do the installation yourself. This is most cost effective.

Hand winches

Relatively light and inexpensive and very versatile, hand operated winches are effective for situations where winching in odd directions is required as the winch can be made to pull in any direction required. They can also double as a hoist. Hand winches need physical strength to operate and the pulling power can be sufficient for quite difficult pulling jobs. Some hand winches, such as the Turfor, are a favourite with hardened off-roaders as they are light and although not inexpensive are cheaper than drum winches. The steel cable on Turfor type winches needs to be stowed somewhere on the vehicle but because steel cable does not flex as easily as rope, it must not be kinked or crushed. This can be a problem if stowing it inside a vehicle and cable clamps mounted on a bush-bar or roof-rack are a better alternative. Turfors work by two sets of jaws biting the cable and pulling it through the winch. The cable must be well cared for as damage can cause the cable to slip. Should the cable need replacing, the diameter required by the winch is critical for it to work properly. The snatch block, described below, increases the pulling power of the hand winch and is an essential accessory to all hand winches.

Another option is the removable winch. This illustrates a Warn 9000 winch being temporarily fitted to a rear bumper that has been modified to do the job. Winching backwards is now possible.

Do-It-Yourself winch plate.

Hand winches require brute force. If you are small and travelling alone, think of something else! Must be used with a snatch block.

RECOVERY ACCESSORIES

EQUIPMENT:

- *Spade.*
- *High-lift jack and jacking plate.*
- *Five-metre chain + grab hook.*
- *Tuggum (kinetic) strap.*
- *Safety straps of a length of ski rope .*
- *Two large bow shackles for attaching straps.*
- *Two large D-shackles for attaching chains and straps to vehicles.*
- *Two small D-shackles for linking chain.*
- *Tree protector/ winching strap to attach to an anchor.*
- *Snatch-block to increase winch pulling power or change the direction of a pull.*
- *Sand ladders/PSP to assist self recovery.*
- *Winch (vehicle-mounted or portable, electric, hydraulic or manual).*

- *Gloves.*
- *Air-jack with repair kit.*
- *Q20 or similar.*

SHACKLES

When a link needs to be made between elements in the recovery operation, in most cases a shackle is the most suitable and reliable way to do it. Using the incorrect type of shackle can result in damage to the strap or a failure under stress. When selecting shackles for your recovery tackle don't be tempted to go the cheap route.

Working load markings

Quality shackles are marked with indelible information such as the safe working load, the maker's name and sometimes 45° marks. If there are no markings on the shackle it is probably inferior and cannot be trusted. The safe working load is the important bit of information. Decent sized bow-shackles are 4-3/4 tons. This means that the shackle's breaking load is 5,4 times that much. In the case of a 4-3/4 ton shackle the breaking load is 25,65 tons.

Top: D-shackles. Middle: Clip-shackles are unsafe for recovery use. Bottom: Bow-shackles are the most versatile and useful shackle. The working load must be indicated. Beware of cheap Chinese junk without the maximum load marked.

Important rules when using shackles:

- *When using a shackle for recovery operations, tighten the bolt and then loosen it by a quarter of a turn. This prevents damage to the thread and makes releasing the bolt easier.*
- *When using a shackle for a long-distance tow, hand-tighten the shackle bolt firmly.*
- *Good quality shackles rarely fail – they simply distort so that they are difficult to undo.*
- *Clip-shackles designed to snap closed are unsuitable for vehicle recovery and can fail even in light duty operations.*
- *NEVER use two shackles to join two tuggum straps together. If one strap should break the attached shackles become a deadly missile.*

D-shackles are used in the following ways:

- *Joining sections of chain or attaching a chain to a vehicle.*
- *Attaching a snatch block to a vehicle.*
- *Attaching a chain to anchor/tree strap to the recovery tackle.*

Bow-shackles are used whenever straps need to be connected. The extra width of a bow-shackle prevents the strap from being crushed during maximum stress.

Bow-shackles are used in the following ways:

- *Attaching kinetic straps to chains and anchor straps.*
- *Attaching snatch-blocks to tree straps.*
- *Attaching kinetic straps to vehicles.*
- *Always place the strap over the bow section and the chain or snatch block over the bolt.*

Snatch blocks

A snatch block is a hook or eye attached to a large pulley wheel through which the winch cable runs. A snatch block effectively gears down the pulling power – it doubles the pulling force at half the speed and is used in conditions where the winch power is insufficient for the task.

Using a snatch block has the following advantages:
- *Doubles the pulling power.*
- *Winching from difficult angles.*
- *Overheating of electric winches reduced.*
- *Current draw is reduced and therefore kinder to batteries.*

Double-line pulley or snatch block.

Rings, eyes and tow bars

All off-road vehicles should be fitted with numerous easily accessible towing eyes for vehicle recovery and winching. Factory fitted towing eyes are suitable for light and medium duty towing operations. They are not designed for use with kinetic straps. Therefore when a kinetic strap is used, both towing eyes must be used. The correct alternative is to fit heavy-duty towing attachments. Familiarise yourself with the location of your vehicle's towing eyes before venturing off-road. When a vehicle is stuck in deep mud, it can be difficult to reach towing eyes that are located far beneath the vehicle or low to the ground.

Tow bars should not be used for vehicle recovery. Original vehicle manufacturer tow bars are generally stronger than those fitted by tow bar fitment centres, but as a tow bar should never be used for anything but light-weight towing and recovery operations a tow bar must not be considered as a primary recovery attachment.

Do not attach towing lines to a bush bar or to any part of the vehicle body or steering mechanism. If there are no towing eyes, attach lines to suspension components such as spring shackles, but beware of sharp edges damaging the rope.

Spades/Shovels

Apart from the shovel being the most important recovery tool, it must be designed right – garden spades work, but not nearly as well as those designed for the job.

This is the ideal towing attachment, that can be used for towing and recovery. NEVER attach recovery cable or strap to the ball. It is not designed to carry he load and if it fails the results can be fatal.

When selecting a spade consider the following:
- *Feel the weight. It must not be unnecessarily heavy.*
- *The length should be sufficient to dig under a vehicle.*
- *Fold-away type camp shovels are far too short and make removing material from under a vehicle almost impossible.*

- The blade should be shovel-shaped. A flat blade is far less effective. The blade must not be too big – this adds weight and makes clearing under a vehicle more difficult.
- Fancy materials such as stainless steel are pointless – and, they get lost.
- It should also be painted a bright colour because spades are often left lying in the bush after a recovery operation. Some have illuminous strips on the shaft which is an excellent idea. Many spades are lost at night.
- Find a way of attaching your spade in a convenient place, like on the sides of a roof-rack. Place the shovel on the side near the front of the rack so that the curve of the blade bends around the front corner. In this way it will not be caught by bushes that pass close to the vehicle.

A spade is not a spade when it comes to off-roading. This is a Lasher 4x4 shovel developed in conjunction with the author.

Gloves

Gloves are a major asset to the off-roader and when a recovery operation begins, put on a pair of loose-fitting leather gloves. They help prevent possible injury when handling winch cable, can prevent serious injury when working at the winch and when sand ladders and jacks get hot under the desert sun they are a big help. They are also very useful in preventing blisters when digging and oily hands when jacking.

Anchor straps/Tree protection

When using a tree as an anchor; cable or chain will cut into the bark and this can kill the tree. Also, attaching the hook back onto the cable weakens the cable and will damage it. To protect the tree and cable an anchor strap must be used and with a pair of shackles forms one of the most important components of the recovery kit. They also can be used in a multitude of other ways in all kinds of recovery situations.

The first piece of safety equipment is a pair of inexpensive leather gloves. Make sure thay are not too tight and should come off the hand easily.

Anchor straps are best made from polyester and must have no stretch, so a worn-out kinetic strap should not be used. Purpose-made anchor straps are available from 4x4 equipment outlets.

Chains

An anchor strap is broad non-stretch polyester.

I suggest you carry a length of chain in your recovery kit. Chains are an excellent addition to the complete recovery kit and a length of three metres is sufficient for most jobs. They are particularly useful for attaching straps onto vehicles not well equipped for off-road recovery. An ideal chain is one with an 8000kg breaking strain, electroplated with grab hooks attached to both ends. The chain can be folded back on itself, and the grab hook hooked to any link, thereby shortening the chain to the desired length.

- *Do not shock-load a chain as this weakens the links. Normally a weak link goes undetected until it fails.*
- *Keep away from sharp edges when under load.*
- *Do not let a chain kink. A knot in a chain weakens it dramatically.*
- *To prevent rust, clean the chain in soapy water, allow to dry in the sun and then apply a light coat of Q-20 or similar before storing in a canvas (breathable) bag.*

Chains are not a 'must have' component of a recovery kit, but they are extremely handy. Here they are used to attach a winch cable to both towing eyes of the vehicle being used as an anchor.

Safety straps

The purpose of a safety cord is to prevent a missile being created should anything in the recovery setup break and must be considered whenever a recovery operation is set up. Laying a blanket or towel, or rolling a strap around the cable is quick and easy but not foolproof. I suggest purpose made safety loops. They should last a lifetime because they are only stressed in the event of a breakage. Developed by John Rich of Stoney Ridge and Secure-Tech, many good 4x4 equipment stores sell them.

Tyre chains

Chains linked to form a ladder and wound around each tyre are particularly useful when driving in snow or clay mud. The diamond style of chains are the best. Drive onto the chains attaching the inside chain first. Drive the vehicle five car lengths and then re-tension them if necessary.

A purpose-made safety strap will prevent injury should the kinetic strap or the mount break. Safety straps of some kind are essential for safe recovery operations.

It is a good idea to practice fitting tyre chains before departing because fitting them in ice and snow conditions is messy and awkward without practice. You will need a pair of gloves to fit chains. Do not fit chains to the front tyres alone – driving like this can be very dangerous because the inferior traction on the rear wheels tends to make the vehicle spin at the slightest provocation.

KINETIC/SNATCH STRAPS

Kinetic, snatch or tuggum straps are elasticized towing straps used to extract a vehicle by another vehicle. The tow vehicle moves under power and jerks the vehicle from its bogged predicament. The kinetic strap is the single most innovative invention for the off-roader in the past twenty years.

Selecting a kinetic strap:

- *Don't go the cheap route.*
- *Protective sleeves on the end loops are a good idea especially if they slip, or better, if they can be removed easily for cleaning and replacement.*
- *Breaking strain rating is important but know the weight of your vehicle. When fully loaded, a vehicle may weigh 3000kgs. A breaking load factor of four should be estimated. Therefore: 3000x4=12000kgs minimum breaking strain is required.*
- *A stretch of 20% is sufficient, 30% is better.*
- *Kinetic straps should be more than six metres long. The longer the strap the longer the stretch and the working life. Nine metres is ideal for most applications.*
- *Buy all the attachment accessories you need to avoid having to jury-rig equipment not designed for the job. When breakages occur it is more often attachments that break. Buy the best quality gear.*

A recent Australian magazine tested a range of kinetic straps in the lab and from the results it appears that there is more to selecting a kinetic strap than meets the eye. For example the ARB straps, one of the most respected names in 4WD, came just about dead last, breaking well below the advertised load. Products that did very well were Spanset, and Kaymar. Reliable word-of-mouth recommendations are the way to go. And this doesn't mean the shop salesman.

Tuggum kinetic are unpredictable:

- *The actual stretch is determined by many factors: moisture content of the air, previous pulls and their loads, the time the strap has had to rest, how well the strap was cleaned.*
- *An average strap doing one hard pull stretching to its full capacity needs between 6 and 24 hours to recover (to contract to its original length) Time needed depends on previous work load. A newer strap recovers faster.*
- *When a strap stops recovering fully – to within 90% of its original length it is 'tugged out'. Using it as a kinetic strap and relying on its stretch, which at this point may be as low as 5%, is dangerous. The strap is now good as a pull strap. It can also be used as a winch strap but with the small amount of stretch left in it may not be ideal.*

More facts about kinetic straps:

- *Genuine kinetic straps, those made for the job, are polyamide, not polyester.*
- *The more moisture, the longer the stretch but the breaking strain is decreased.*

- *Cargo carry straps (broad green straps) sometimes sold as kinetic straps are often not suitable and when used, shock-load the vehicle and attachments.*
- *Sand and grit in the webbing accelerates the wear and decreases the breaking strain.*
- *Kinetic straps with a built-in indicator filament (a strip of coloured material is woven along the length of the strap. When it breaks the strap is 'stretched out'). These have been outlawed in most countries because the system is unreliable and must not be trusted.*
- *Kinetic straps cannot be told apart from non-stretch straps unless they are labelled. Novices beware: Using the wrong strap could be disastrous. Only experts in polyamide technology would be able to tell the difference by just looking.*

JACKS

High-Lift

The high-lift jack is one of the most useful off-road tools available, an indispensable and highly versatile device but can only be used if a strong vehicle jacking platform is available. Working four-wheel drive vehicles should have adequate bumpers for this, but unfortunately most modern 4X4s do not. Rear tow bars make good jacking points but on the front end of most vehicles there is nowhere to use the jack. The cure is simple: have your off-road equipment outlet fit them for you. Armed with a spade and a high-lift jack, in most cases, you are better equipped for the unexpected than a vehicle equipped with a spade and a winch.

The high-lift jack, the single most versatile piece of recovery equipment you can buy. But get to know how to use it before you really need it. It can also be highly frustrating and quite dangerous.

The original American-made Hi-Lift has proved itself time and time again to be the best. In most cases high-lift jacks are carried on the outside of the vehicle and dust clings to the oily lifting mechanism, which causes the mechanism to jam. Q-20 or a similar spray lubricant must be used to free the mechanism before it is used. But take care: this can cause the formation of a mixture of dust and oil – a grinding paste which quickly wears the components. The only way to prevent this is for the jack to wear a jack-nappy when in transit.

Air/Balloon jacks

These are large polyurethane bags placed under the vehicle and inflated by exhaust gas to lift the vehicle so that objects which aid traction can be placed under the wheels. Balloon or air jacks have some disadvantages off-road and are not as versatile as the high-lift. They are nevertheless easy to use and do not require much physical strength to operate.

COMPARISONS: HI-LIFT VERSUS AIR-JACK

AIR JACK	HIGH-LIFT JACK
Can be used with almost every vehicle	Can only be used with vehicles fitted with suitable bumpers or add-on jacking points
Does not require jacking plate	Jacking plate required on soft ground
Very easy to use effectively	Requires familiarization in order to use effectively
Safer. A vehicle can fall off an air-jack but it's normally a slow, safe affair. If it's punctured it pops like a balloon and the vehicle falls heavily.	Can be dangerous in many ways as it is unstable and the jacking arm can spring up and injure.
Not suitable for repair work under vehicle	Not suitable for repair work under vehicle
Can be used for 'jack and pack' technique	Can be used for 'jack and pack' technique
Cannot be used for 'jack and push' technique	Ideal for 'jack and push' technique
Not versatile. Some models can also be inflated with tyre pumps.	Extremely versatile can be used for winching, lifting, pushing, clamping and many other less obvious purposes
Subject to puncture by stones, thorns and a hot exhaust. Rendered useless if there is even a small hole in the exhaust system. Can roll over during lift and get punctured	Reliable if kept well lubricated
Dust does not affect operation	Dust jambs the mechanism. Lubrication solves this problem
Reliant on the engine to operate	Independent power source (biceps and back muscles followed by chiropractor)
Small punctures can be repaired	Spare parts readily available. Simple to repair and maintain

Bottle jacks

These are available in a very wide range of lifting capacities from one to 15 tons and over. Bottle jacks tend to be rather tall so before you set off on your safari, simulate a puncture by releasing the air out of one of the rear and one of the front wheels and make sure that the jack fits under the axle now that the tyre is flat. Bottle jacks must be upright to work and periodically need topping up with hydraulic fluid. To jack up a fully loaded 4x4 you will need one with at least a five-ton capacity.

Upright screw-thread and scissor jacks

These are sometimes supplied with a vehicle as standard jacking equipment. Those that resemble bottle jacks are worthwhile although a little tedious to operate. Some designs are intended to work on one specific vehicle only. The screw threads must be kept clean and well oiled to prevent jamming by dirt and dust. Unlike a hydraulic jack they function at any angle, which is useful when using the jack to straighten bent bodywork.

Scissor jacks are generally unsuitable for off-road use, as they jam easily as dirt clogs the threads and are unreliable and break in heavy duty use.

Jacking plates

When using a jack, other than a balloon jack, on soft ground a plate is needed to prevent it from sinking while the vehicle is being raised. A steel or thick wooden plate approximately one foot square, preferably with lugs attached to its surface to prevent the jack from slipping sideways, is ideal. A heavy wooden laminated bread board with large wood screws to act as lugs is easy to make and works well. An even cheaper jacking plate can be made from two square 16mm pine boards. Laminate them together with a waterproof wood glue, making sure that the grains run perpendicular to each other. As a last resort the spare wheel makes a very effective, if cumbersome, jacking plate. Jacking plates such as the one illustrated are available at 4x4 stores. For me, I just take along a heavy 50cm pine plank.

When using a regular bottle jack a wood block about 45mm thick can be very useful as a jacking plate, and also for when the bottle jack is used in awkward predicaments, for example when the maximum stretch of the jack is not sufficient. It is also very useful when the bottle jack is used to aid vehicle recovery.

Above: A jack nappy protects the jacking mechanism from dust, which when mixed with the lubricating oil turns it into a grinding paste. They are made short and long or an old inner-tube can be made to cover the shaft.

Below: An effective recovery kit should include kinetic strap, anchor strap/tree protector, pull strap, snatch block, bow shackles and gloves.

SAND LADDERS

Sand ladders/traction aids are purpose made articles that are placed under the wheels to aid traction. They are made from plastic, rubber, steel or alloy. The generic term, 'sand ladders' can be confusing as they are designed to work in mud, sand and wherever a vehicle can bog down. Some work, others don't.

PSP (perforated steel plate)
Perforated steel plate (sometimes made from aluminium) was developed by the British in the second world war when they were used to assist vehicles in the mud and to build runways on slippery ground. They are bulky, heavy and awkward to use. They are highly effective in sand and all types of mud. Grip is often superior.

Trac-mats
Flexible sand ladders, called Trac-mats are more effective than traditional rigid types in most situations. Each section of the track is pressed with sharp projections that increases grip and they work in clay mud as well as in sand. Being flexible they tend to mould into the ground. Less digging is required to lay them and they do not kick up and damage the vehicle as sometimes happens with rigid types. However they have a higher tendency to 'shoot' under the vehicle as power is applied. They are also more compact, easy to stow and in most respects more versatile than rigid ladders.

Rubber mats

Lengths of rubber mat normally used as industrial flooring are being sold as debogging aids with various names. They are cheaper than metal, fairly effective in sand but utterly useless in mud. Rubber does not grip on rubber when wet.

Plastic sand ladders are a budget alternative. They work reasonably in sand but not particularly well in clay mud.

Plastic 'ladders'

In an attempt to bring sand ladders at a budget price various plastic alternatives have been introduced. A rigid type (illustrated) and clip-together plastic strips are available. Both options perform reasonably when dry but not as well when wet. In mud their performance is not good. The rigid types are effective in preventing a vehicle from sinking and are quite useful. Both must be well anchored to be effective.

Steel ladders

Many off-road workshops fabricate simple steel ladders as traction aids. They are cheaper than PSP or Trac-mats but most seem to suffer in the same way – when they get muddy tyres lose their grip. Some designs interlink for bridge building. Word of mouth recommendations are advised for these individual designs.

Bridging ladders by Proto, Stellenbosch are one of the best rigid multipurpose ladders available anywhere.

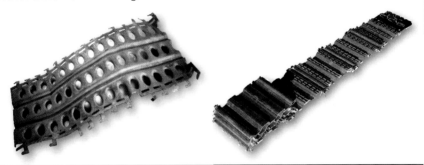

COMPARISON: PSP PLATE VERSUS TRAC-MATS	
PSP (Rigid)	**TRAC-MATS (Flexible)**
Bulky to transport. Steel is particularly heavy.	*Folds up and easier to transport.*
Must be periodically flipped over so that a bend does not set in.	*Do not distort easily.*
On uneven ground plates tend to kick up and hit the vehicle.	*Excellent for uneven ground as the flexible tracks conform to the shape of the ground.*
Versatile in that they can be used as a short bridge when strapped together.	*Cannot be used as a bridge.*
PSP plates are shorter than tank tracks.	*Added length aids recovery.*
PSP hold a firm grip in the ground.	*Higher tendency to 'shoot' from under the wheels.*

RECOVERY TECHNIQUES

Vehicle recovery is more about common sense and using your equipment smartly. Should your initial attempts fail, stop, have something cool to drink and try to analyse why the vehicle cannot be freed.

The golden rules of vehicle recovery:

- *Stop spinning your wheels the moment it appears you are stuck. Trying too hard only makes things more difficult. Every unnecessary rotation of the wheels digs the vehicle in deeper.*
- *Are the tyre pressures right for the conditions? If not, change them.*
- *Establish if any part of the vehicle's weight is resting on anything other than the wheels. If so jack up the vehicle and correct this first.*
- *Take a close look at all four wheels and establish which one is halting progress. Work on this wheel first.*
- *Take a second look at each wheel. Any other wheels that do not have a clear path ahead of them must be worked on next.*
- *Do not be tempted to try to drive out after a half-hearted attempt to de-bog a vehicle. Failure means that all the work done the first time will have to be redone.*
- *Use all the resources at your disposal. These include all areas behind or in front of the wheels that are firm (push the vehicle in that direction), a slight slope (gravity can be a major ally).*
- *Look out for things that will hinder progress. These include a slight slope (gravity can also be an enemy), front and rear wheels dropping into a ditch simultaneously (arrange things so that wheels drop alternately).*
- *Adapt your equipment to be used in more ways than meets the eye.*
- *Never use a tow ball with a winch or snatch strap. Should it break it will become a lethal missile.*

Using a spade

Using a spade to dig out a vehicle may appear like common sense, but there is more to it when in the field. Bear in mind that in 90% of all recovery operations some digging or clearing of the path in front of the vehicle should be undertaken. In many cases a little digging is all that is needed.

So often, especially in sand, a little digging is all that is needed.

On the beach

Assuming that the tyres have been deflated to the required pressure, bogging on the beach can easily be overcome with a little digging, as long as the driver hasn't got the vehicle in so deep that the axle is buried and the vehicle has grounded. Once the vehicle has stopped, dig out a good measure of sand from all four wheels and attempt to reverse out. If this fails and a kinetic strap or winch is to be used, always clear a path with your spade.

Over-extended axles

Over-extending the vehicle's wheel articulation, creating a situation where a wheel has no weight on it, is a common way of getting bogged. The most common practice is to place material under the spinning wheels. This is far less effective than digging under the wheel in the opposite corner which has the most weight on it. By doing so you are reducing the required axle articulation. In effect you are placing the vehicle's own weight on the wheels that are airborne and spinning.

Hung-up

When a vehicle attempts to traverse uneven terrain and exceeds its break-over angle and the chassis between the front and rear axles touches the ground the vehicle has 'grounded' or is 'hung up'. This is very much an unforgivable situation because the cautious driver should have had someone marshalling the obstacle from the outside who could warn of impending disaster. The recovery procedure is to dig away the ground from under the vehicle or to raise the vehicle with a high-lift jack and place material under the wheels. Do not climb under a vehicle supported only by a high-lift jack.

The tyre pressure gauge is one of the most important recovery tools you own. The very first thing to do once a vehicle is bogged, is to check the tyre pressures and drop them if they are too hard for the conditions. Do remember though, dropping the tyre pressures will also reduce the clearance.

Direct pull

One vehicle pulling another using a non-stretch rope or chain will require good traction to be able to exert a meaningful pull. A four-wheel drive will easily spin its wheels on firm gravel or sand even if pulling a vehicle that is only lightly bogged. When attempting a direct pull, always look for an advantage, like a slope or a surface where the wheels will get a better grip. Be careful that the recovery vehicle does not bog down while attempting the recovery.

Winching with a double-line pulley and a strap draped over the line as a safety device. The snatch block halves the pulling speed while doubling the pulling force.

SAFETY STRAPS

Purpose made safety loops are a relatively new addition to the range of 4x4 recovery equipment. They are used to arrest the cable or strap in the event that it, or the mount on the vehicle, breaks. They are attached by looping themselves over themselves. No shackles are used. The pictures on the left illustrate how they are used. These loops are so effective that no other items need to be draped over the cable. A set of two loops is required.

THE USE OF WINCHES

The first safety rule when using a winch is that a single individual must be put in charge of the winch. This person will be the ONLY one to use the switch – and the ONLY one handling the recovery of the winch cable once the winching operation is complete. This is done to prevent anyone losing fingers – a common injury when the cable handler lets someone else operate the switch.

Winches are potentially hazardous. Study these key points:

- *Before winching have everyone stand well clear. The slingshot effect caused by a cable break under load can cause serious injury.*
- *Wear gloves when handling winch cable and use a cable guide when feeding in loose cable.*
- *The winch cable should be cared for and wound neatly on the drum under tension.*
- *Always have five turns of cable wound around the drum before winching. Less than five turns could mean the cable clamp on the drum coming undone.*

Bottom: Make sure that there is at least five turns around the drum before winching. Damaged cable is the best reason for wearing gloves.

- *Be aware of the condition of the winch cable. Damage, as illustrated on the left, severely reduces the breaking strain of the cable. Damaged cable is also the best reason for wearing leather gloves.*
- *Never stand in the 'V' of a winching layout under tension.*
- *If you are not in control of the recovery operation, avoid stepping over a strap or cable after it has been attached, even when it appears to be lying harmlessly on the ground.*
- *Never hook a winch cable around an object and then back on itself. This is a common cause of cable breakages among the inexperienced. Anchor straps are used to prevent this.*
- *When a winch gets hot, let it rest.*
- *Ensure that the winch cable does not bunch on one side.*
- *Look after the winch cable and pack it tightly on the drum when finished.*
- *NEVER have one person hold the switch and another feed in cable. This is the single most common cause of injury during vehicle recoveries.*

ANCHORS

Natural anchors

Natural anchors are anything that you find suitable to attach a cable to – trees, rocks and signposts (signposts on gravel roads are unreliable and pull out of the ground very easily) If you are going to use a tree as an anchor, protect the tree by using a tree-strap to prevent the steel cable from cutting into the bark as this can kill a healthy tree. Attach the strap as close to the ground as possible.

A recovery rig with multiple stakes. The more bits of chain, different sized shackles and lengths of strap you have, the easier it is to construct a complex rig.

The strength of an anchor depends on how badly the vehicle is bogged and how much preparation is made before winching begins. Assess the strength of the anchor first – if it appears weak, then pre-preparation to the vehicle will need to be extensive. If the anchor is fool-proof, little or no preparation may be needed, and if winching fails nothing is lost and some digging and clearing can be done.

Have someone monitor the condition of an anchor during recovery. If it appears to be loosened by the winching, then halt the process before it is weakened further because even a weak anchor is better than no anchor at all. To put less stress on the anchor more clearing around the wheels and jacking must be done before further winching.

Man-made anchors

If there is no anchor to which a winch cable can be attached, a man-made anchor can be created. No made-made anchor of any reliability can be made without a lot of effort.

Anchor construction tools:

* *Heavy hammer*
* *Iron standard/s or purpose designed stakes*
* *Danforth boat anchor*
* *Chain, shackles and anchor strap*

Creating an anchor:

* *Drive steel stakes into the ground at 45° and about two metres apart and then attach the cable to the stakes as close to the ground as possible. Create 'Vs' between the top and bottom of each stake.*
* *Danforth-type boat anchors also work well if the ground is soft. This is because the harder the pull, the deeper they drive into the mud – in theory. The angle of pull must be as close to the ground as possible. The Danforth is bulky and overly heavy for expedition use.*
* *A long length of chain run along the ground secured with ten or more long tent pegs. The more difficult the winching operation,*

the more tent pegs will be required. This man-made anchor takes little effort and if the vehicle is not deeply bogged it is a quick and effective way of creating a light-duty anchor.

- *As a last resort a spare wheel can be buried either horizontally or vertically, which is the more conventional but less effective way. The winch cable is passed through the middle of the wheel and attached to a steel bar. After burying the spare wheel, dig out from under the vehicle making sure that no earth is supporting the vehicle's weight. This is a last resort because burying the wheel is very hard work and despite perseverance it is often a waste of time.*

When attaching the winch hook, make sure the bend is toward the ground. In the event of breakage, if attached in this way, it tends to shoot downwards into the ground and not up, potentially hitting someone.

Remember: the harder the effort put into an anchor, the better its effectiveness. Before using your man-made anchor, which under most conditions will be suitable only for a light-weight pull, dig out channels in front of all four wheels to allow easier forward movement. Do not be in too much of a hurry when preparing the anchor or digging out earth from under the vehicle. If you try to winch before you are absolutely ready, you may fail – and have to go through the entire process again.

RELEASING A VACUUM

Mud can sometimes be the most difficult stuff. When it is particularly thick it creates a vacuum under a vehicle and no matter how much winching and heaving, the vehicle just won't move. When this occurs the vehicle's progress is halted as much by the lack of traction as by the vacuum. Here a combination of high-lift jack and winch is required.

Place the jack about a metre in front of the bogged vehicle and lift up the jacking step to shoulder height. Run the winch cable over the jacking step to the anchor. Tilt the jack away from the vehicle and take up the tension. Now, with someone supporting the jack, begin winching in. As the cable is retrieved the jack is pulled upright, simultaneously pulling the vehicle forward and up, releasing the vacuum. Repeat this as many times as required.

USING HUB CAPSTAN WINCHES

It is easier to run the cable from the anchor to the vehicle, and not the other way. The cable is guided through a groove in the capstan and secured with a knot or buckle. If you are using rope then it should be wound around the capstan at least five times, crossing over itself. The direction of wind and the gear selected (forward or reverse) will determine the direction of pull. Hub capstans on both wheels on the same axle must be used simultaneously as the axle differential will not allow winching on a single hub. Because rear half-shafts and differentials are generally stronger than those in front, it is

recommended that the rear wheels are used for pulling. Using hub capstans can damage the vehicle if the cables are allowed to get too short when the wheels are pulled together by the narrowing angles between the two lines.

USING A SNATCH BLOCK

The snatch block is a heavy-duty single-line pulley. It is used to increase the pulling power of the winch or change the direction of pull.

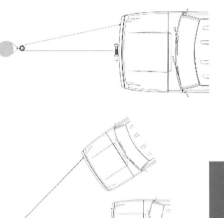

Self-Recovery

During self recovery the snatch block is attached to the anchor. Run the cable from the bogged vehicle through the pulley and back to the vehicle where the cable is then attached. This is where dual towing eyes are very useful. Normal winching at half retrieval speed and double the pulling force is then performed.

Two-vehicle recovery

During two-vehicle recovery where the free vehicle's winch is used, attach the snatch block to the bogged vehicle. Run the cable from the winching vehicle through the snatch block and back to the vehicle where the cable is then attached to a towing eye. If your winch is rated at or under 6000 lbs pulling power, then it is very likely that one day your winch will be under-powered for a job and a snatch block will be necessary.

If you have a winch fitted you will be in a good position to help another vehicle that has bogged down.

To prepare for winching:

- *If the area is slippery, anchor the winch-equipped vehicle by chaining it to a tree, a second vehicle or by digging holes into which the front wheels will be driven.*
- *The line of the winch cable should follow the route that the bogged vehicle will move along when it is pulled out. If the winch is pulling from an angle, the winch cable will gather on the one side of the drum.*
- *Clear a path in front of the wheels of the bogged vehicle and remove any obstacles in its path.*
- *Once the stricken vehicle is attached to the winch cable and the cable is pulled taut, everyone should stand well clear.*

- By opening the bonnet during the winching operation, the windscreen will be protected from damage should anything break.
- The winching vehicle should have its engine running to keep the battery charged and the operator's foot should be on the brake.
- The driver of the bogged vehicle should engage low-range second and gently release the clutch as the winch takes up tension, rotating the wheels slowly to assist the winch. Avoid spinning the wheels.
- When the vehicle is free, drive clear of the obstacle. Avoid driving over the winch cable.
- Where an anchor point is not in front of the bogged vehicle, or in the case of lack of space in front of a bogged vehicle in which to allow the winch equipped vehicle access, the snatch block is used to change the direction of pull.

Using a snatch block to pull a vehicle over an obstacle

If you wish to drive through very deep mud or climb a slippery slope and you suspect that your vehicle will not be able to do it without some assistance from the vehicle accompanying you, the use of a snatch block to change the direction of pull may be the solution. Attach the snatch block to an anchor on the other side of the obstacle. Run the winch cable from one vehicle, through the snatch block and back again to the second vehicle. As the second vehicle reverses on terra-firma it will pull the first up and over the obstacle. Now with one vehicle through, it can use the cable and pull the second vehicle directly towards it over the obstacle. No matter how easy the pull, always have a competent person at the wheel of the vehicle being pulled as in the event of equipment failure the driver must know how to stop the vehicle safely.

The winch cable is passed through the snatch block and is then returned and attached to a towing eye on the vehicle.

USING KINETIC STRAPS

Kinetic or tuggum straps are dangerous but highly effective. Because of the immense loads that a kinetic strap can store and release, breakages of the strap or mounting points during this kind of recovery can injure or kill. So often kinetic recoveries are done without a lot of thought as to what the consequences might be in the event of the failure of one component or other.

The pulling vehicle must be similar in size and weight to the vehicle being pulled.

Important rules for using kinetic straps:

- *Do not use the snatch strap if the vehicle is badly bogged i.e. with its weight resting on its chassis. Use a jack and spade to put the weight back onto the wheels first.*
- *The pulling vehicle must be similar in size and weight to the vehicle being pulled.*
- *The pulling vehicle must run in a straight line. Do not attempt to pull at an angle of more than 10°.*
- *Use bow-shackles to attach the snatch strap to the vehicles.*
- *Always use safety loops on both ends.*
- *Do not compromise on the security of attachment points. Use both tow eyes if the vehicle is fitted with them.*

Attach the kinetic strap to the front or back of the bogged vehicle. Consider first which will be the most effortless direction of travel.

Then follow this procedure:

- *Manoeuvre the recovery vehicle to the bogged vehicle and stop at a point no less than half the total length of the snatch strap.*
- *Attach the snatch strap to the bogged vehicle, making sure that there are no knots in the strap.*
- *Lay a blanket over the strap or attach a safety line (ski rope is ideal). In the case of the strap breaking the weight of the blanket will rapidly absorb the energy of the broken strap.*
- *With a go-ahead signal from the driver of the bogged vehicle, the recovery vehicle moves off at normal take-off speed in first gear. Accelerate very gently and keep the speed constant. As the pull of the rope is felt, try to maintain a constant speed and continue to accelerate very gently – it is not engine power and torque that are doing the work, but the vehicle's momentum and energy being transferred through the elasticity of the strap.*

Unfortunately, if the bogged vehicle is badly stuck, something will break. If it is an attachment it becomes dangerous to both bystanders and drivers.

Double kinetic-straps used together.

Having the towing vehicle move off with excessive speed does not increase the pulling force. However, doubling the length of the strap together with a higher speed does have the desired result. To do this a joint must be made linking the two straps. UNDER NO CIRCUMSTANCES join two straps together with shackles. Should one strap break the shackles become a deadly missile.

Never use shackles to join two kinetic straps together. Omitting the stick or grass will result in an undoable knot.

To make a safe join:

- *Pass the loop of strap A through the loop of strap B.*
- *Take the end of strap B and pass it through the loop of strap A*
- *Place a stick or even a thick bunch of grass in the new loop made. This is so that the knot cannot over-tighten.*

Safe use, care and maintenance of snatch straps

Never have a light vehicle try to 'snatch' a heavy vehicle that is deeply bogged. It may recoil and hit the bogged vehicle.

Case history: A Suzuki Jeep attempted to snatch a Land Rover Defender. The Suzuki took off at full speed from a distance of only about a metre from the Land Rover (which was the incorrect procedure anyway), The Suzuki came to the end of the stretchability of the strap and instead of the Land Rover moving forward the Suzuki recoiled and smashed into the Land Rover. Both vehicles, and the Suzuki driver, needed to be repaired.

Never have a heavy vehicle try to 'snatch' a light vehicle that is deeply bogged.

Case history: The SADF in northern Namibia some years ago used a military snatch strap, normally used to free armoured vehicles weighing up to 20 tons, on a deeply bogged Land Rover and an armoured troop-carrier was used as the tow vehicle. Instead of the snatch strap breaking, the Land Rover's chassis was torn from both axles, which remained firmly stuck in the mud.

Clean nylon straps with washing-up liquid after use. Dirt abrades fibres and speeds deterioration. Beware of detergents attacking the nylon. With extended use their stretchability deteriorates and they quickly become dangerous.

Measure the static length before use. Write it down. When the length of the strap has increased by 10% of its original length, it is no longer suitable for snatch operations. However, it still has many uses; long distance towing, extra long tree protector etc.

USING A HIGH-LIFT JACK

There are few bogging down situations that cannot be overcome with a high-lift jack, a spade and a strong back. The high-lift jack is without doubt the most valuable piece of equipment that an off-roader can carry. The jack discussed here is the American standard brick red-coloured unit that has been around for many decades. Although there are competitive jacks on the market, the 'old favourite' is virtually unbreakable and as long as it is kept well lubricated it is reliable. Unfortunately, more and more 'off-road' vehicles are being introduced with fancy curved plastic bumpers – impractical for bush work because of the absence of points where a high-lift jack can be used. There are cases where a vehicle has bogged down so completely that jacking has been the only way out.

A typical high-lift jack point added to a vehicle.

The jacking mechanism is used in the following way:

To lift a vehicle:

- *Stand the jack under the jacking point and push the operating lever (small L-shaped lever on top of the lifting mechanism) down.*
- *Raise the jacking arm to the upright position to hoist the entire mechanism up the shaft so that the jacking foot is positioned under the jacking point of the vehicle.*
- *Adjust the jacking foot position exactly. Once this is done pull the arm down, thereby lifting and firmly locating the foot under the vehicle jacking point. Should the position need changing, lift the arm and readjust. Once satisfied with the foot's position, lower the arm once again all the way down until the lifting pin enters the perforations in the upright shaft or 'ladder'. It will click into place.*
- *Lift the arm to the upright position until a click is heard.*
- *Pull the operating lever into the upper position. It will click into place. The jacking foot will be held at that height. The vehicle is ready to be lifted.*
- *Hold the lifting arm with both hands. Gripping it firmly, pull it down once again until the pin locates and clicks into place. Lift the arm to the upright position and the second lifting pin will locate itself. Continue until the vehicle's wheel/s are off the ground.*

To lower a vehicle:

- *Raise the jacking arm to the upright position.*
- *Push the operating lever down.*
- *Gripping the arm with both hands, lower the lever so as to release the lifting pin. At this point the vehicle's weight is in your hands. If you do not have a good grip and your weight is pressing down on*

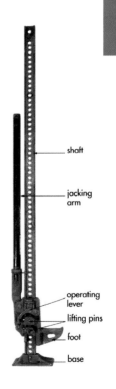

shaft

jacking arm

operating lever

lifting pins

foot

base

Top: An ARB jack adaptor. Bottom: A unit designed not only to work as a jack adaptor for jacking points but also to enable a wheel rim to be jacked. While this is a good idea in principle, jacking a wheel can damage the rim.

the arm it can shoot up and cause injury. Have bystanders stand well clear.

- *From this point jack the vehicle down by lifting and lowering the arm to its full extent.*

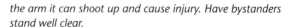

High-lift jacks can be dangerous.

- *When lifting or lowering a vehicle, hold the jacking arm firmly and with both hands. If released at the halfway point while under load it will shoot upwards with great force. It can smash teeth, cause concussion and the upward movement can release the lifting pin, causing the arm to drop by itself, starting an auto-jacking sequence which rapidly lowers the vehicle onto the ground. Once this auto-jacking has started it is too dangerous to try and stop it running its full course. Holding the jacking arm firmly is especially important when lowering a vehicle.*

- *When the jack is left unattended and under load, the jacking arm must ALWAYS be left in the upright position, clipped to the upright with the supplied wire clip. In any other position the jack poses a threat to anyone close to it.*

- *High-lift jacks are unstable. Never climb under a vehicle that is supported only by a high-lift jack. If you need to dig under the vehicle, do what you can before you jack it up.*

The following situations demonstrate how the high-lift jack can be used to extricate a vehicle:

Jack and push

Imagine that your vehicle is stuck on soft ground with the axles grounded on a ridge; or you have dropped into a gully and two or more wheels are off the ground and spinning. If the ground is soft, place the jack on its broad base and jack up the vehicle, high enough so that the one set of wheels is higher than the ridge on which the axle has been caught. Now push the vehicle sideways. The vehicle will pivot on the jack and land on the ground with the wheels on the ridge, thereby clearing the axle from the obstacle. In some situations you may need to do the same with the both front and rear axles.

Spare tyres attached to the tailgate may have to be removed or swung clear as the falling jack may catch on them and damage the vehicle bodywork. If they are removed from a separate wheel carrying frame, the frame can be closed and used to protect the rear of the vehicle from the jack during this operation. Unlike the air jack, the high-lift jack is perfect for this technique but beware that vehicle body damage can result if carried out carelessly. Whatever you do, practice with the high lift before you need it!

Jack and pack

Quite often the ground under the jack is soft and slushy and in these cases the jack and push method is not effective – the vehicle topples off the jack, the wheels dig into the mud or sand and the vehicle settles back onto its chassis. In this situation the best course of action is to jack up the wheels that are dug in the most deeply. Once this has been done find something to place under them – sand ladders, Trac-mats, carpets, rocks, branches or logs – in fact anything lying around (in wet mud, grass seems to make matters worse). Lie items in the direction of travel so that the wheels can gain some momentum as they ride over them. If all four wheels are deeply dug in, this must be done to all wheels.

In soft ground, jacking the vehicle up and then packing firmer items (rocks, sand ladders, dry earth etc.) under the wheels for better traction is the most common self-recovery technique. Wet grass doesn't help but just about anything else does.

Before attempting to drive out think about the gear ratio to use. Should you use a gear ratio that is too low, the result may be wheelspin, and you may not only undo all your hard work but still have a bogged vehicle. Select the highest gear you think may work – try to remember the gear ratio that was getting you through difficulties beforehand, because once off the mats or logs you must be able to keep moving without a gear change. Selecting this gear ratio is critical and for each vehicle and for each situation it differs. The vehicle is then lowered and with everyone pushing, the clutch is let out gently with acceleration as smooth as possible. Avoid wheel spin.

High-lift winch

The high-lift jack can also be used as a hand winch. Heavy manila rope must be used (the stretch of nylon rope renders it ineffective).

Proceed as follows:

- *Remove the steel foot from the jack by sliding out the pin.*
- *Lay a length of rope from the bottom of the jack to the bogged vehicle. Do not attach it to the jack.*
- *Attach a cable or rope to the top of the jack and then onto the anchor.*
- *Position the lifting foot of the jack at its lowest position.*
- *Join a short length of chain to make a loop. Lay this loop across the rope at the bottom of the jack. Pass your hand through the loop and underneath the rope. Grip the chain and pull it through so that the chain loops around and grabs the rope.*
- *Using a D-shackle, attach the end of the chain you are holding to the hole in the base of the jacking foot.*

The jack is used as if lifting a vehicle. As the rope is pulled taut, the chain grips the rope. When the jack is at its highest point, slacken the rope and chain, slide the jack back down to its lowest position, slide

An air-jack is not as versatile as a high-lift but is can be used on vehicles without adaptation. The best air-jack on the market today is without doubt the Takla Air Jack.

the rope through the chain, and begin jacking again. Although it is a time consuming process, it is often successful when conventional winching techniques have failed.

Care of a high-lift jack

The 'old favourite' is criticized by its competitors for jamming under load. It's a valid criticism and to prevent this the lifting mechanism must be clean and well lubricated. Have a can of Q-20 handy and at the first sign of slicking, give it a good spray. Despite this it remains, in my opinion, the best high-lifter on the market. If the jack is carried on the outside of a vehicle, some method of preventing the mechanism being clogged by dust should be devised such as the jack-nappy, a washable nylon sleeve that covers the mechanism.

USING AIR JACKS

The jack and pack technique is the same as with the high-lift jack. The jack and push technique is different. Unlike a high-lift, two people are needed to operate an air jack.

Air bag techniques:

- The air jack must be slid under the vehicle with none of it protruding. In the field this is often very difficult. If the jack has part of itself protruding it will bend and bulge as it is inflated. This can burst the bag and topple when the vehicle's weight is on it.
- Place rubber floor mats between the bag and the vehicle. Be careful of protrusions, stones and thorns puncturing the bag.
- Close the valve on the bag.
- Insert the inflator into the exhaust pipe and rev the engine.
- A vehicle will become very unstable during jacking.
- If there is a hole in the exhaust system, pack it away and try something else.
- If you just push the vehicle off the jack there is every likelihood that the bag will get punctured. Instead deflate the bag as the vehicle is pushed.
- Over-inflating the bag produces the most hideous bang. It's probably dangerous. The best bags are fitted with pressure release valves.

USING SAND LADDERS

An experienced driver will call for a sand ladder before too much digging is required. If the vehicle has been allowed to dig itself in to the extent that the vehicle's weight is resting on the axles or chassis, a great deal of digging and jacking will be required. Do not dig a little and then attempt to drive out. This is a waste of time – if the attempt

is unsuccessful the entire digging effort will have been wasted because the spinning wheels will replace the sand you have removed. Dig until you are sure that more digging would be a waste of time.

Dig channels in front of the wheels that appear to have the least traction and lie the ladders in front of them. If in doubt as to the wheels under which to lay the ladders, select the front wheels, since once the vehicle gets moving the rear wheels will also get the benefit of the extra traction (assuming you are driving out forward).

If in sand with the rear wheels sunken and the front wheels remaining clear, place the ladders under the rear wheels. Dig out a channel in front of the other wheels too, so they do not have to roll over any ridges of sand that may have built up in front of them. In very deep sand the sand ladders may get buried when the vehicle drives over them, so mark the position of the ladders with a spade.

Unfortunately for those doing the pushing, this may mean a bit of a walk, as it is important for the vehicle to be driven to firmer ground before it is stopped. The sand ladders will have to be dug up and carried. Attaching a rope to tow them out is not wise as the extra drag can cause the vehicle to bog down again.

This 4x4 Recovery DVD is part of a series of six videos. The DVD version also features the 45-minute bonus video '4x4 Vehicle Equipment', all about equipping the ultimate expedition 4x4.

RECOVERY DVD VIDEO

To complement this chapter I have made a one-hour 4x4 Recovery DVD/VHS video. It covers just about all the elements in this chapter. Video is such a good tool for 4x4 training but off-road, nothing is ever the same each time we go out. This is much in evidence in the video as not all the recovery techniques work first time, even with the 'experts'. Highly entertaining, often funny and highly informative, it will have you glued to your seat.

Available from www.4xforum.com or by calling 021 852 9984. Also available in most bookstores and wherever good 4x4 equipment is sold.

One of the most difficult and challenging recovery operations is when a vehicle is caught on a side slope as in these two photographs. It is imperative that the uppermost part of the vehicle is secured to prevent the angle from increasing, otherwise the vehicle may free itself by rolling down the slope. The recovery of the Land Rover is mentioned in the DVD featured on the previous page.

7. TRAILERS AND TOWING

TRAILERS VERSUS ROOF-RACKS

TOWING EQUIPMENT

TRAILER DESIGN

TOWING ON-ROAD

TOWING OFF-ROAD

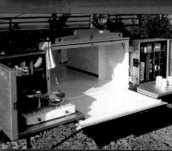

The step to buying and towing a trailer on outback trips is a big one. Many find success in pulling a trailer while a similar number use a trailer for one trip, get back home and sell it.

While trailers are a practical alternative to roof racks for carrying bulky safari equipment on overland trips they are also over-used. By this I mean that a trailer offers so much extra space, that the space is used because it's there, not because it's needed.

The off-road trailer market blossomed in the nineties and at one time there were over sixty off-road trailer manufacturers in South Africa, more I reckon than any other country in the world.

One of the problems with trailer manufacturers is that because their products are becoming so complex (freezer battery systems, water tanks and plumbing, etc.) the designers have to be experts in so many fields, which most are not. Often the result is a great trailer built by mechanical engineers with a poor electrical installation designed by the same engineers who do not know enough about the auxiliary installations, so much of their development is by trial and error, often at the expense of the buyer.

An off-road trailer is not just a trailer with big wheels. Many designs have failed, and the failure has been paid for first by the user in the middle of the bush with a broken axle and then the manufacturers who, after a number of similar failures, had to pick up the pieces to rebuild their businesses. The most well known example of this was the debacle with Rubex rubber torsion axles. After three manufacturers fitted these axles and found that the axles broke after off-road use, they stopped using them. It cost some of them a fortune. Then along comes a manufacturer entering the off-road trailer market with an off-road caravan. It was fitted with a heavy-duty example of the same axle. Despite warnings they went ahead. Axles broke all over the country. Then my book and some magazines reported the events. We were threatened with lawsuits and some magazines wrote apologies, in my view changing the truth to lies to appease the complainant.

South Africa has some very good trailers, and while the caravan, in my view, hasn't been fixed, the trailers and accessories are among the world's best with only a few poor quality products remaining. This chapter will hopefully assist you in making the decision to either buy or not buy a trailer, or when selecting a trailer choosing one that will be a practical addition to your off-road excursion experience.

TRAILERS VERSUS ROOF RACKS

Off-road trailers must be designed and built to withstand extended outback travel: Sand, mud, rocks, ridges, troughs and axle-cracking corrugations.

Trailers – their advantages over roof racks are:

- *Easier to load and unload, especially heavy items such as full jerry cans.*
- *Payload is significantly higher than a roof rack.*
- *Trailers do not negatively effect the vehicle's centre of gravity.*
- *Extra equipment can be loaded onto the trailer lid which can also be used as a work surface.*
- *Packing and unpacking is often quicker than a vehicle.*
- *Built-in kitchens help take the chore out of camp cooking.*
- *Heavy items carried in the trailer can be left at 'base' while game driving and exploring.*

Their disadvantages over roof racks are:

- *More difficult to tow over loose and uneven surfaces.*
- *Experience is required when driving off-road and reversing.*
- *Trailers can be a severe hindrance in any terrain where traction is a problem.*
- *A poorly loaded trailer can cause instability when cornering and braking.*
- *A trailer adds wear and tear to the towing vehicle, exaggerated when the trailer is badly loaded or when towed by inexperienced drivers.*

TOWING EQUIPMENT

Tow hitches

Beware of tow bars fitted by independent fitment centres. Four-wheel drive vehicles often stress their tow bars in excess of what would be considered normal towing operations.

Ideas about tow-bars:

- *Towing off-road stresses a tow bar far more than ordinary towing.*
- *Tow bars are sometimes used for vehicle recovery, although this is very unsafe and ill-advised.*
- *Off-road trailers are bigger and heavier than the average family man's little 'Venter'.*

- When considering a tow bar; if the one being offered looks similar in strength to those fitted to a normal road car then it is not strong enough for your 4x4.
- Broken tow hitches occurring in the wilderness are not uncommon and depending where the breakage occurs, it can be difficult to repair without welding equipment.
- The standard 50mm tow ball is rated to pull a trailer with a mass of no more than 3500kg. This rating is calculated for towing on a paved surface not over rocks or in heavy sand.
- Maximum permissible weight on a standard 50mm tow ball is 150 kgs. This is often exceeded when towing off-road.
- When calculating how much weight the vehicle can carry after the trailer is hitched up, double the tow hitch weight and deduct that from the vehicle's carrying capacity.

Ideal vehicle – trailer combinations

- Long wheelbase combined with short rear wheel-to-tow ball distance makes for a stable tow vehicle.
- Short rear wheel-to-tow ball distance with long trailer tow hitch to axle distance improves stability.
- Trailer's vertical C of G must be less than 40% of the trailer's tow hitch to axle distance.
- Short vehicle wheelbase or short rear wheel-to-tow ball distance combined with long trailer tow hitch to axle distance make for easier reversing.
- Vehicle tow ball height must equal trailer tow hitch height when trailer chassis is horizontal. Essential when towing twin-axle trailers.
- Mud flaps must be fitted to the rear of the tow vehicle to prevent damage caused by flying stones.

TRAILER DESIGN

One of the best trailers around: The Conqueror Safari Trailer.

During the years I have received a great deal of conflicting feedback from many trailer manufacturers over what I have written. Nevertheless I must report it as I see it. These are my opinions and are based on what I have heard through the bush telegraph about trailers; what makes them good, and what breaks when they break. My own experience of trailers amounts to towing large yachts, horse boxes and travelling with people who dote on their trailers. I do not own an off-road trailer and have no desire to. I would rather drive a bigger vehicle or carry less.

Suspension and chassis

The type of suspension is critical to the success of an off-road trailer. Trailers tend to bounce around a great deal so it must be built to withstand severe punishment. Suspension types range from torsion bar to leaf spring. Rubber torsion bar suspension is not an option, no matter how "heavy-duty" the axles is claimed to be. They all eventually fail in off-road use.

Leaf springs fitted with shock absorbers are the strongest and appear to work the best. Check where the springs mount onto the chassis – this is where breakage occurs and it must be reinforced. The chassis should be a rigid steel frame, steel tube or heavy channeling, extending all the way to the rear spring shackles. Springs mounted directly onto a stiffened load box are rarely strong enough. Breakages also occur at the joint between the A-frame and the load box and this should be reinforced.

Axle breakages often occur not because the axle is not strong enough but because the mounts aren't. Should the mount slip or break the axles shifts and the wheels no longer run true. This creates a build up of heat in the bearing which eventually ceases. When this occurs the hub shaft snaps from the overload. The failure is due to inadequate strength in the mount and not the axle's ability to carry a load.

Shock absorbers need to be fitted to leaf spring-sprung trailers. I recommend their use for two reasons; shock absorbers reduce bounce and reduce shock loads to the axle. Vertical wheel travel is of little importance in trailer design but the ability of the axle to absorb shock and not bounce is.

Desert Wolf's axle location design is probably the best: A radius arm locating the axle independently from the spring. Nothing, not even spring failure, will cause the axle to run off true.

Tow hitch

The tow hitch is a critical component and badly designed ones break! The trailers's tow hitch must be attached with high-tensile steel bolts. Mild steel bolts are not strong enough. Check your trailer's bolts and change them if they are mild steel. Light-duty tow hitches welded onto the chassis draw-bar, which is the cheap way to build them, are not strong enough and many have failed in the bush.

Wheels and tyres

To improve stability on bush tracks the wheel track should closely match that of the towing vehicle's. To avoid having to carry spares specifically for the trailer and to allow its wheels and tyres to be interchangeable with the vehicle's, they need to have interchangeable wheel rims with identical tyre diameters. However, trailers with wheels that have a larger diameter than the vehicle's will pull better through sand. If you can carry a spare specifically for your trailer, fit

Key to the strength of the draw bar is the trailer coupling. The type seen below attached with high-tensile bolts is recommended. Welded couplings are not strong enough for heavy off-road work.

over-sized wheels and tyres on the trailer. These tyres can then be deflated to pressures below that of the vehicle and the trailer will cause far less drag.

Rust protection

Most trailers are stored outdoors and therefore are prone to rapid decay by corrosion and a trailer cover is a good idea. A stainless steel body is only necessary if you intend to use your trailer extensively on the beach. Galvanized mild steel is an excellent alternative and is almost as good, easier to repair and cheaper. For use inland, sealer-protected mild steel is fine if the trailer is stored under cover. Trailer components that seem to deteriorate first are attachments such as hinges and clamps. These should be stainless steel and attached with stainless bolts. When looking at the many South African off-road trailers, most manufacturers have placed rust prevention high on their priority list.

Clever idea. Desert Wolf run the cables inside the chassis channel keeping them away from flying stones that can cut clean through electric cable.

Stability at speed

Stability depends more on weight distribution in the trailer and in the towing vehicle than on trailer design. There is no simple way of testing a trailer's stability at high speed other than to tow it yourself. Weight distribution is critical to stability. If you have deflated trailer tyres to assist progress through sand, this will cause instability when you get back on the road. Remember to reinflate your trailer tyres.

Length

The distance from the tow ball to the trailer axle will determine ease of use. The shorter the distance the better it will handle off-road but the penalty comes with reversing and on-road stability. The longer the tow ball to trailer axle distance the easier it will tow in all conditions other than severe off road.

Over-run brakes

Many off-road trailer manufacturers omit over-run brakes or offer them as an option. This is because in very heavy dust conditions brake drums tend to fill up with sand which wears out the shoes. This only occurs in excessive dust conditions. If the wheels are as large as the vehicle's, which they should be, the same dust problems occur to the vehicle brakes as well. If dust does become a problem simply remove the shoes from the drums and lock the brakes open at the tow arm, an hour's job for both wheels. As for me, I would rather take the safe route and the unlikely risk of troublesome brakes than drive at 120kph with a ton of unbraked load behind me.

Another argument against the fitting of brakes is that when driving over uneven terrain the brakes engage and disengage as the trailer bumps around. All over-run brake systems are fitted with a locking device on the tow arm. This is a hinged piece of steel that wraps around the arm to prevent the brakes from activating when reversing. This must be engaged when driving over uneven ground where speeds are low and over-run brakes are no longer required.

Trailers need to be dust-proof. Some less well-designed trailers are not, which is another reason to select a well respected brand.

Trailer manufacturers may place a weight restriction plate stating 750-kgs on a trailer capable of carrying a ton or more, because with a stated payload of over 750 kilograms the trailer must, by law, be equipped with a braking system. The choice is yours; are you prepared to take a risk and tow such a large mass without a braking system? Under normal driving conditions you may not realise the risk, but do an emergency stop and it could mean the difference between stopping clean or rolling your vehicle.

Jockey wheel
This wheel supports the nose of the trailer when standing alone. Because off-road trailers are often left parked on uneven ground, the longer the jockey wheel the better. It must be able to be removed completely and stored on the trailer when driving off-road. If it is simply raised, it is vulnerable to damage off-road.

Echo is one of the pioneers of off-road trailers and build a range of unusual and sometimes highly practical designs. They also build highly customised trailers for their clientele.

Trailer-top racks and tents
A tent on a trailer is a excellent, practical idea because the tent need not be taken down when going on a grame drive. The trouble is that unless the trailer has side access doors you are unable to get to the trailer's contents once the tent is erected. A tent does raise the trailer's centre of gravity and those with raised tent platforms tend to be a bit top-heavy.

Auxiliary equipment
A vast range of equipment can be specified when ordering a trailer as most manufacturers build to order. Articles fitted range from built-in water tanks with camp showers, dual battery systems linked to the vehicle, fridge/freezer units and simpler items like jerry can and gas tank racks.

In chapter-8, I discuss in detail why it is a bad idea to locate a freezer in a trailer and why it's even a worse idea to fit a battery in a trailer. Briefly, the long cables and trailer connector cannot take the current and the system works at very low efficiency. Freezers and batteries must remain in the vehicle. However, a series of power

points and a fluorescent light fitted inside the lid and connected to the vehicle electrics is very handy.

Consider that the more you fit into your trailer, the heavier it will become and the more difficult it will be to handle in the bush.

Storage systems

Weight distribution in a trailer is very important. Some trailer designs have all the jerry can brackets and water tanks fitted behind the axle which can cause low trailer hitch to total weight ratio. This in turn can cause instability, especially when climbing steep hills, where the trailer lifts the rear of the towing vehicle. I have seen a Pajero battling to get up Sani Pass, which is normally effortless for a 4x4, because its traction was seriously compromised by the badly packed trailer behind it. Consider carefully where the optional extras you choose for your trailer are fitted. Nose-cones storage boxes and boxes on the mudguards are very handy and must be dust-proof and lockable. Jerry can mounts on a trailer must be low down to keep centre-of-gravity low. Trailers are ideal for carrying spare fuel.

Portable power units are made by a number of manufacturers. For vehicles without split charge systems or with trailers with freezers but no batteries, this type of power source can work well.

If your vehicle carries its spare wheel on the tailgate make sure that it can be swung free with the trailer hitched on. Spare wheels carried here can make hitching awkward and any boxes, clamps or other attachments above the tow arm can make matters worse. Another reason for limiting attachments on the towing arm is that anything that could obstruct the wheel carrier from being opened can also hit the spare wheel when driving through a dip, when the trailer lifts and the vehicle drops. The option of removing the spare wheel carrier and placing it on the trailer is an alternative, but remember that the vehicle needs to carry a spare when the trailer is left at 'base camp'.

Practicality

When judging if a trailer is suitable, open and close all of the boxes and the lid. Pretend you are at your camping site and you need to find something in the trailer. Many trailers are fitted with a tailgate – a very useful feature as you can pack travelling items such as the day's lunch or a tool box at the back which can be easily accessed when travelling. Other features include cubby holes, exterior boxes or interior compartments, some of which are cleverly designed and some impractical for reasons such as a narrow aperture which become frustrating when packing and unpacking. Some trailers fitted with tailgates require that the roof be opened in order to open the tailgate. That is bad enough but some go even further in poor design – to open the tailgate the lid must first be opened. But in order to support the open lid the tailgate must be closed. Draw your own conclusions!

Summary

Assuming that you have decided that a trailer is the way to go, look for a lightweight trailer with a good sturdy chassis frame, a heavy axle (2,5-ton) on leaf springs and a minimum of weighty gadgetry. The three best off-road trailers made in South Africa are without doubt Desert Wolf, Conqueror and Echo. All three are made by people experienced in the off-road world and all have enviable reputations.

TOWING – ON-ROAD

The most important safety considerations when it comes to towing on-road is straight-line stability, oscillation or weave and stability in a turn. Factors which affect these are as obvious as trailer hitch weight and trailer weight to vehicle weight ratio as well as items which are seemingly inconsequential such as the spring rates of the towing vehicle and trailer centre-of-gravity.

In this section we illustrate causes and effects of vehicles and trailers in an attempt to improve safety. I give credit here to Tom Sheppard's outstanding book, 'The Land Rover Experience', published by Land Rover, from where much of this information and many of the analogies are taken.

TRAILER DYNAMICS

Straight-line stability

Consider a trailer being towed on an undeviating course by a vehicle moving in a straight line. Here the only force acting on the trailer is via the tow hitch and as a result the trailer moves in a straight line. Now consider a gust of wind or undulations in the road surface (supposing that the vehicle is unaffected), the trailer now acts under a new force – sideways. The trailer's tyres will as a result be at an angle, albeit small, to the direction of motion. As a result an opposite side force is exerted by the tyres bringing the trailer behind the vehicle again. Understanding this simple principle is required as we go further.

Oscillation - decaying or increasing

Let us distinguish between decaying or increasing oscillation and how it relates to towing. Consider an ordinary school ruler with a hole in one end. With the ruler swinging on a pencil pushed through the hole, properties governing oscillation can be demonstrated. With the pencil stationary, the ruler hangs straight down by the force of gravity or in our scenario a vehicle moving on an undeviating course. Take the bottom of the ruler and pull it sideways and release it, keeping the pencil stationary. The ruler exhibits decaying oscillation at it swings back a few times quickly coming to rest, demonstrating straight line stability as described above. Now, take the pencil and simulate a vehicle moving over an uneven road surface by moving it sideways as the ruler is pulled sideways and released. If the frequency of the movement of the pencil matches the frequency of the swing, increasing oscillation takes place. This will happen as you instinctively try to match the phase of the ruler swing, trying to make the ruler swing as high as possible.

Whiplash effect

Again let us use the school ruler to demonstrate whiplash. This time hold the ruler in a horizontal plane with your forefinger and thumb over the hole. Flick your wrist to the right and left. As you do so, the ruler trails the wrist movement and then overshoots.

Applying what we have learnt

With all these analogies it can be seen that an incorrect combination of hand and wrist action, ruler weight and thumb grip can produce varying effects. Getting these combinations right, the action of the ruler is very much as described. This in turn demonstrates that the varied actions of the ruler (trailer) and the wrist (towing vehicle) result is varying degrees of decaying oscillation, increasing oscillation and whiplash. Understanding these principles will assist in improving performance and safety.

Centre of gravity (C of G)

A trailer's C of G exists in the horizontal and vertical plane. Both have an effect on the trailer's stability. To demonstrate C of G in the horizontal plane consider a round bottle (trailer) laid on its side and spun. It will spin around its centre of gravity. Grab the bottle by one end while it is spinning. Instead of spinning around its C of G it will now spin around the end where it is held (trailer hitch). Energy is transferred to this end and will exert a reactive lateral force (the bottle will attempt to rotate and spin simultaneously) on your hand (tow hitch). It is necessary therefore to consider the position on the trailer's

C of G and its associated lateral force acting on the vehicle thereby affecting stability. An operator can control this C of G by packing sensibly and making sure that the trailer's C of G is at an optimum – which lies 10 – 20 cms in front of the axle.

C of G in front of the axle

With the trailer's C of G ahead of the axle, as the towing vehicle swings the trailer exerts a force on the vehicle that reduces yaw and as a result the oscillation begins to decay. On the other hand, trailer's C of G in front of the axle degrades cornering stability. When the C of G is too far forward it can provoke a slide and roll-over in a turn as a result of the same forces in place in our rotating bottle example.

C of G behind axle

With the trailer's C of G behind the axle the result of vehicle swing creates a force that amplifies yaw and begins what can become increasing oscillation.

Towing on-road – Summary

- *All stability problems are amplified as the trailer gets heavier. Once the trailer's weight exceeds 70% of that of the towing vehicle you are entering the critical zone with regard to stability and safety. The onus is on you to take extra care.*
- *Estimate the trailer's C of G at 10 – 20 cms ahead of the axle.*
- *Concentrate heavier articles over the axle thereby reducing inertia and improving stability.*
- *Remember to keep the tow ball greased and replace the grease in very dusty conditions because grease + dust = grinding paste.*
- *Take extra care in tight bends – the forward trailer C of G tries to push the vehicle's tail around the corner faster. A break-away can result.*

TOWING OFF ROAD

A vehicle's ability on slippery ground is degraded significantly when pulling a trailer. The forces exerted by a trailer off-road are similar to those on-road but are amplified. Instability and control problems can manifest themselves at very low speeds.

Off-road towing points to be considered

- *Disconnect the jockey wheel and stow it before the ground gets rough.*

- *Disengage the over-run brakes by sliding the lock over the towing arm, preventing it from retracting and engaging the brakes. When driving, allowance rarely needs be made for the trailer's ground clearance as in most cases it exceeds the vehicle's. However, a trailer will reduce manoeuvrability off-road and off-road trailers are frequently damaged by trees, stumps and bushes that the tow vehicle runs past.*
- *Make allowances for the additional weight when braking and descending steep slopes by braking gently and changing to low gears timeously.*

Descending steep slippery slopes with a heavy trailer behind you is one of the most difficult off-road manoeuvres and should be done with extreme caution. The loss of steering control experienced in such conditions is exacerbated by the trailer. As the driver tries to direct the vehicle from the front, the trailer acts on the tail, steering it anyway it feels. In this predicament jack-knifing can occur and no amount of expert action on the part of the driver seems to be able to stop it. If gentle acceleration fails to pull the trailer straight or if acceleration is too risky in terms of losing control of the vehicle, then the only way out may be to disconnect the trailer and to manhandle it down the slope on the end of a winch cable.

Back view of a 7-pin towing:

1. *Left-hand indicator*
2. *Power point.*
3. *Earth*
4. *Right-hand indicator.*
5. *Right-hand tail light.*
6. *Stop lights.*
7. *Left-hand tail light and number plate.*
- *Protect with a fuse of no more than 30 amps.*

8. ON THE TRAIL

VEHICLE PACKING

PORTABLE REFRIGERATION

BUSH CAMPING

SOLAR RECHARGING

WATER AND SURVIVAL

PACKING LISTS

CONVERSION TABLES

While many 4x4 owners enjoy their vehicles for the fun they can have driving off-road, many enjoy them more for their ability to take them to destinations far from crowds and on occasion far from other 4x4 owners. This chapter deals with this aspect of 4x4s.

VEHICLE PACKING

Efficient use of load space makes all the difference on an extended safari holiday. The speed at which a vehicle can be unpacked and repacked, the ease of finding equipment and having everything in its rightful place is one of the pleasures of off-road adventuring.

Primary containers must not be too big so as to be difficult to load and off load. Popular boxes are Wolff Packs (top), blue trommels (middle) and camera-style alloy (bottom). All can be customised to personal needs.

CONTAINERS

Large containers required to hold kitchen equipment, vehicle spares, tools, food, lighting or general camping equipment should be designed to do the job so that camping does not become a chore. For example, a single box containing kitchenware and food will be too awkward to pack and too heavy to load. A series of smaller containers are more practical and, if designed to fit efficiently onto a vehicle, while remaining accessible, can remain in the vehicle for the entire safari.

Containers, whether steel, plastic or cloth should have flat sides for ease of packing and lids must be dust-proof. A good example is the Wolff pack or the smaller Gumo boxes. They can be made dust proof with strips of foam stuck into the lids. They are ideal for carrying breakable items such as torches, lamps and stoves, vulnerable items such as matches, fuel bottles and fire-lighters, and items which you hope you will not need such as tools and spares which can then be loaded in the far reaches of the load bay and forgotten.

All containers, especially those made from metal, should be lined with closed-cell high density foam to prevent damage to the contents. Even tools, because of rubbing and chaffing, steel-on-steel will soon produce iron filings.

Military containers are ideal for safari use because they are built to withstand abuse, but, because of the sensitivity of Third World road blocks, they MUST be repainted, preferably white. Items such as military heavy-duty canvas bags or tarpaulins should be dyed black or blue.

Tying articles down inside the vehicle is also advisable if overland travel is anticipated. When a vehicle rides over an obstacle and drops down the other side, it seems to fall faster than the load inside it. The result is that when the vehicle rebounds and is coming back up, its load crashes down. The result is noise and breakages. Tie down strips are the answer.

- *A basin has many uses such as bathing, washing clothes and dishes, draining oil and collecting water.*
- *A cast iron pot, or poitjie, can be used to cook almost anything and cooking in this way improves the flavour of canned meats and dried vegetables.*
- *A small fold-away spade can be used for digging trenches around tents threatened by water, making a safe place to light a camp fire and for ablutions.*

- *A large piece of plastic or canvas sheet/tarpaulin with eyes at each corner is a very useful item. It can be used for shade when strung between trees or vehicles, as a ground sheet for pitching tents on thorny ground, or for working under a vehicle, wrapping up sleeping bags on cold nights and collecting rainwater.*
- *Make a protective canvas sleeve for the braai grid and stow it on the roof.*
- *Pots should be designed to fit into one another to save packing space.*
- *Although non-stick frying pans tend to get damaged on safari consider how inexpensive a small lightweight non-stick pan is. They do away with a major cleaning headache and are cheap enough to replace every couple of years.*

Top: A roller- drawer system such as the Outback, makes a practical base from which to customise the load bay of a station-wagon or double-cab. Middle: Front Runner make a similar unit but this one enables traditional storage boxes such as the Wolff-packs to be used. Its advantage is that unlike drawers, they can be removed, used around the camp and then put back and slid away. They also cost less. Bottom: The Allu-Cab custom pick-up packing system. An elegant and practical solution for a pick-up.

Packing Systems

A packing system is one of my favourite accessories. It transforms the inside of a vehicle and is not only great for extended trips; it's great as an everyday practical accessory. The best packing systems are over-engineered because through time and shaking, poorly built units begin to rattle. Roller drawers are also excellent for security as they can be locked. Roller drawers designed for standard boxes such as Wolff packs are also available. They are less expensive but no less practical.

Items to help with roadblocks or border posts

Items for low-key bribes are ball-point pens, cigarettes, T-shirts, pair of tackies. Have a few of them visible when approaching road blocks – soldiers manning road blocks may ask for a smoke. Obliging them aids with negotiations. In the Third World these are often worth more than money and if items are offered as a gift they are less likely to be construed as a bribe.

Food containers

The rattling and bouncing created when a vehicle travels on dirt roads and over rough ground will take its toll on inadequate food containers. Hard plastic is a better choice than glass. Brittle plastic bottles such as those commonly used for cooking oil quickly develop cracks and the flip top lids pop open, creating a horrible mess. Small flexible plastic Tupperware type containers are ideal for storing most foodstuffs as well as condiments such as spices, mayonnaise, vinegar, oil, sauces and food leftovers.

Fresh foods such as onions, carrots, potatoes, cabbage and gem squash will stay fresh for some time as long as they are protected from being crushed. Eggs stay fresh for weeks but should be well packed. On a 10-day safari into the Kalahari we broke all of our eggs into a Tupperware container and simply poured them out as needed. After days of very rough conditions (In a series-3 Land Rover), of the 36 eggs, only one yolk had broken.

Containers for safari should also consist of what I call, 'convenience containers', those that carry items needed on the road or at a single overnight stop en route. Camp Master make a range of exceptionally well designed articles such as this combo cooler picnic bag and this modular bag used as a first aid kit.

Your kitchen should include a wooden spoon, cooking pots, an egg lift, a sharp cutting knife, a chopping board and sealable containers for salads and fresh foods. Shrink wrapped meat lasts very much longer than unwrapped meat even if it is not refrigerated.

Packing a roof-rack

As an important safety measure, roof-racks must be considered as light-duty bulky gear carriers and all the heavier equipment must be carried inside the vehicle. This will keep the centre of gravity as low as possible. Heavy roof-racks are dangerous. Keep heavier articles as far forward as you can so as to lessen the load on the rear axle and distribute the weight evenly.

One of the best methods of tying items onto a roof-rack is with a hammock spread over the load held down with a number of elastic tie-downs. Bungie cords or rubber straps made from inner tube rubber, with heavy wire hooks attached at the ends, also make excellent tie-downs that will not perish in the sun. Secutex make an excellent net used for tying down on racks.

A roof rack bag, waterproof and dust-proof as the good ones are, is the best way of carrying matresses and sleeping bags.

When packing jerrycans on a roof-rack make a broad rubber band from old inner tubes and wrap each can with the band. This prevents metal-to-metal contact that results in excessive static built up and damage to the cans. Purpose made jerrycan brackets are made for most roof racks and are practical and inexpensive. Don't overload the roof and regret it when your vehicle rolls!

Roof-Top Tents

To me the most significant benefit of a roof-top tent is that mattresses, sleeping bags and pillows remain in the tent. The space saving can even be enough to sway a decision from buying a roof-rack over a trailer. Unless it is housed in a hard case, the convenience of a roof-top tent comes when erecting it, less when packing it away. When they are covered by a waterproof polyurethane bag, packing it away can be a tiresome chore and sometimes more time consuming than a regular dome tent. It is also quite strenuous to pack away because it is normally done while trying to balance standing on one of the rear tyres.

When choosing a roof-top tent look for sturdy construction. Those built with very light poles, for example, move around a lot in windy weather and because the tent is held aloft, is more susceptible to wind. Manufacturers are trying to make their products lighter but few have succeeded because these light-weight products don't last. Poly bags tend to fill with air and balloon once the vehicle reaches about 80 kph so they need to be strapped down to reduce drag.

Roof-racks are meant for carrying lighter bulky loads such as mattresses, chairs and tables. A roof-top tent adds considerable weight, often 35-40kgs on the rack, reducing how many additional items that can be safely carried.

    Eezi Awn's new tent has elastic ties fitted inside the tent to assist packing away. With the alloy case it is extremely quick and easy. A disadvantage of a rigid housing is that they are more difficult to get in and out of because of the lip of the case. Before you purchase a tent be sure to climb all the way in and out and have the entire family do the same. Disappointments come when the tent is taken on a safari and only then is it realised that they are difficult to climb out of or are too small. Select the widest available. Two smallish people often find the narrow tents cramped. Rigid cases also fill up with water. Drain holes do not come standard with some makes – they need to be modified, or perhaps ask your supplier to do it for you. The holes need to be capped to prevent dust ingest when the tent case is closed.

COMPARISON: ROOF-TOP VERSUS GROUND TENTS

Roof-top tent	Ground tent - bow style 3-man
Secure from wild animals, to a point. A rapid evacuation from the area is not possible.	Less secure from wild animals although they are not a real danger, more a perceived one.
Secure from insects and scorpions. Security from mosquitos depends on tent quality.	Keeping the flap zipped up is more important. Security from mosquitos depends on tent quality.
Even the large ones can only sleep two adults, and even then it's cramped. Leave the bags in the vehicle.	Tents advertised as 3-man bow tents can easily accommodate three adults and their bags.
Takes a shorter time to erect, perhaps 20%. Easy to unpack, a real pain to pack up and return to its cover.	Quicker to pack away, perhaps by 20%. Easy to pitch and pack.
Must be collapsed and packed away fully before the vehicle can be moved, for a game drive etc.	Self-standing.
If the ground is not level, the vehicle can be made level with rocks etc.	If there is no level ground or it's covered with rocks, too bad!
You have to be a bit of a contortionist to get dressed and undressed in a roof top tent.	You can almost stand up.
If you move around a lot, the vehicle rocks to and fro. Warmer.	The ground can be very hard and cold.
The mattress and sleeping bags can be left inside as the tent is folded away, saving space in the vehicle. A huge advantage.	Tent must be emptied when packed away.
Heavy. Reduces remaining weight permitted on roof. Lifts the centre of gravity.	In comparison, lightweight and can be carried anywhere.

PORTABLE REFRIGERATION

Being able to keep foodstuffs and beverages cold on a safari is a real luxury. Once you have used a fridge or freezer on safari you will never be able to do without one.

There are three types: Compressor, heat-exchange and thermo-electric cooler. All have advantages and disadvantages.

Tie down slats and eyes developed for aircraft are now available at most 4x4 equipment outlets. They are ideal for strapping down freezers and heavy loads.

Compressor fridges

The best compressor freezers run on both 12-volt and 220-volt without an additional power supply. Because they are controlled by an adjustable thermostat, current draw is very efficient maintaining the fridge and its contents at a temperature controlled by a knob. Some designs have a thermometer. The colder the setting, the higher the current consumption both in attaining the desired temperature and maintaining it. Space utilization varies from efficient to down right bulky.

Thermo-electric coolers

Thermo-electric coolers run on the Peltier principle that if a current is passed through a special metal element it becomes cold and if the current direction is reversed the element gets hot. So thermo-electric can also be used to warm up food. Apart from a small fan, thermo-electric fridges are solid state and very quiet but will not freeze and are slow to cool when compared to compressor fridges.

They run off 12-volts and are not thermostat-controlled, meaning that they are inefficient in terms of current consumption. Get one if you will be satisfied with only running it when the engine is running, drinks that are cool and not cold and no chance of freezing anything.

Heat Exchange Freezers

Powered by LP gas and by 12-volts and 220-volts, heat-exchange fridges are inefficient when run off 12-volts, fairly efficient off 220-volts and highly efficient running on gas or paraffin.

The versatility of power source means that in situations where they remain in one location for a long period when battery charging is not possible or practical, they keep working. In a vehicle they must, for safety reasons, work off 12-volts. However, when in a moving vehicle or trailer under electric power they do lose some efficiency and depending on outside influences, may not freeze. When set up in a fixed location they must be levelled, the flame centred under the chimney tube and the regulator set to the manufacturer's specified pressure. A yearly service of the heat-exchange mechanism should include cleaning soot from the chimney tube, shake the fridge around and inverting it for 24 hours.

Top: Engel 80-litre, a highly efficient fridge/freezer. Middle: Very popular 40-litre Engel, a compact and very robust unit. I have used two of them for five years without problems. Bottom: This National Luna unit is the only one if its kind (at present) to have separate controls for the freezer (43/44 litres) and fridge (29/40 litres). There are two models and both are space and current-efficient and work brilliantly.

Selecting a compressor fridge/freezer

Engel and National Luna currently make the best portable fridge/freezers anywhere. There are other makes but do yourself a favour and get one of these. Some makes are appallingly inefficient. I have found that some products, particularly those that are imported, don't perform to their own specifications under real outdoor hot, humid conditions, inside a vehicle.

My advice is dismiss them and look for solid word-of-mouth recommendations. Secondly, as mentioned in chapter-3, I believe that it's more about how the current is put back into the battery than how much is taken out, because these two compressor freezers are so similar in their current consumption.

Because compressor freezers are by far the favourite for the 4x4 operator, I will confine my discussion to this type.

- Compact and efficient space utilization because space is a vehicle is always at a premium.
- Record of reliability.
- Spare parts supply and easy service backup.
- Stainless looks better in the shop but deteriorates rapidly and before long looks shabby in the vehicle.
- External thermometer is nice but not essential.
- A combination freezer and fridge is really practical.
- Buy new. Old designs are far less efficient as new technologies have improved designs significantly over the past five years.
- Removable baskets improve ease of packing.
- Low-voltage cut-out prevents a battery voltage from dropping to a level which could cause damage. Even a deep-cycle battery can be damaged in this way.
- Tie-down handles ensure that the unit can be well secured which is essential for travel in rough country.
- A slide out tray attachment is really worth it.

In comparison with heat-exchange fridges, compressor fridges cool down very much faster. Because current draw only becomes efficient once the fridge has cooled and is simply maintaining a temperature. It is important that the fridge be run for some time before the engine is switched off and battery charging ceases, otherwise the compressor will run for a long period draining the battery to reach operating temperature.

Unlike heat-exchange types, they do not need to be levelled to work efficiently and are therefore more suitable for use in a vehicle. Compressor fridges are virtually maintenance free.

SETTING UP

Don't waste any space if you can help it. Here, I removed the plastic trim from the rear door and found a useful place to strap a fire grid, gas cooker and cooking plate.

Inadequate wiring caused by a combination of cheap connectors and thin cabling are the most common causes of problems with freezer installations.

When the compressor starts up, the current draw, albeit only for a second or two, can soar to 15 amps. Use the best quality connectors you can find.

The following calculation can be used to determine the cable core thickness when wiring up a freezer. Divide the length by 1000, for example, if the cable length is 3 metres (3000mm) then the minimum cable core thickness is 3mm and if the length is 4 metres then a 4mm cable is required, and so on. This will ensure adequate current flow along the length of cable, no matter how long it is.

Dual battery split-charging systems

To prevent over-discharge of the vehicle's battery when the freezer runs at night it is essential to have a second battery and a charging system to split the two batteries. This is covered in chapter-3.

Calculating electric current draw

Calculating the consumption of a compressor freezer is difficult in that although current draw with many modern freezers is approximately 3,5 amps, it is interrupted by a thermostat. So, current draw reduces significantly after the operating temperature is reached. Current draw is now dependent on thermostat setting, quality of insulation, outside temperature and how many times the fridge is opened.

Having an electric freezer mounted in a trailer is a bad idea. The current loss along the long distance renders it inefficient, unless powered through a separate heavy duty connector. A battery in the trailer is an even worse idea. For the same reason it can't receive a full charge. And, when you go for a game drive, the battery is not reaping the charging benefits of the engine running.

Preparation: (particularly important for heat-exchange types)

- *Cool down everything in your household fridge before packing the vehicle freezer.*
- *Remove the plastic cling wrap around canned beverages, otherwise the plastic will inhibit air flow and reduce cooling efficiency.*
- *Liquid is better stored in metal containers as plastic does not conduct heat well.*
- *Over-filling the freezer will have a detrimental effect on the cooling efficiency.*
- *Have a clasp to keep the lid tightly closed to prevent it bouncing open.*
- *By keeping the amount of time the freezer is opened limited, the freezer will consume less current and the contents have a better chance of remaining frozen.*

I do not advise fitting freezers or batteries in a trailer because:

- *Current loss occurs along the long cable and plug.*
- *Do not have a battery in the trailer and expect the charge current to pass from the vehicle through the tow hitch electrical socket. A separate socket with 6mm core cable is needed or the battery will never receive a proper charge.*
- *When you go on a game drive the battery will not be recharged, wasting valuable engine charging time.*
- *The contents of a trailer are shaken about far more than those in a vehicle. Freezers that ride in trailers over long periods can suffer ruptured piping due to vibration.*
- *Heat exchange freezers can be fitted in a trailer and in some respects is an advantage. They can be levelled and remain unmoved during an extended stay, running from gas bottles in the trailer.*

For enjoyable, trouble-free car

Venturing into the great outdoors has never been easier or more convenient with Makro's incredible range of branded 4x4 and Campmaster camping gear.

ng, make Makro your first stop!

From the groundbraking Wilderness Trailer to the latest innovations in camping equipment and 4x4 accessories, this range is manufactured to the highest quality control specifications.

SOLAR RECHARGING

There have been significant advancements in solar technology in the past ten years and at last solar recharging is a practical and non cost-prohibitive method of charging batteries in the bush.

The reason solar has earned a bad reputation is because so many products are sold that simply do not live up to the claims made by those who sell them and the ignorant buyer who gets taken for a ride so easily.

Consider the following:

- *Do you want a solar system to lengthen your stay in a camping spot without having to start the engine to charge the batteries?*
- *Do you want to add 25% on your time there, double your time or stay indefinitely?*
- *If you want to add 25% to your time, you need to supplement 25% of your power consumption.*
- *If you want to double your time there, then you require 50% of the current drawn to be replaced.*
- *If you want to stay indefinitely, then your solar system must recover more than 100% of the current drawn.*

My experience with solar power was when I wrote my first book, in 1991 when I lived in the Okavango. Today I still use the panel I used then and it has been with me on countless trips. It supplies enough current so I can double the length of my stay in one place.

A simple exercise

For example if you are running a 40-litre Engel and two lights, you need to measure the average current consumption over a 24 hour period. If that's too much stress to measure then try this: How long can you stay at one place without charging batteries? Let's say it's three days drawing current from one, 100 amp battery. This means that over one day 33,3 amps is consumed (100 divided by three days). To add one more day you need to add 33,3 amps to the battery and you must do it within three days.

Let's say you want to double your stay. If your consumption is 33,3 amps per day, then you must put back half of that, 16.65 amps in each 24-hour period. In effect you are halving the current consumption and doubling your stay. In the same way, if you want to stay indefinitely your system must replace 101% of the current drawn – a little over 33,3 amps each 24-hours.

The solar experts will probably baulk at this and what I am about to write, because it is too simplistic. I say, "So what?" It's my experience that solar experts are the opposite – too technical and often make claims that are relevant in the laboratory but are meaningless to 4x4 drivers like you and I who are looking for a simple solution to a technical problem. They may say, "There is no simple solution". Nonsense.

Outrageous claims

Let's take a 60-watt cell. This is a common medium-sized solar panel. 60-watts means that at the point that the sun is at its highest, and at the moment when it is shining directly at the panel it will, on a good day, when the panel is brand new, produce 60-watts, if you're lucky. 60-watts translates into 5-amps at 12-volts. The time that panel will spend delivering 5-amps, if it gets there at all is probably, on average, never. It will more than likely top out at 4,5 amps. All the other time the current delivered will be less, far less.

The angle at which the sun strikes a panel reduces the output current significantly, even if it's just a couple of degrees. So, a 60-watt panel is actually a 28.5-watt panel. Why? With eight hours of sunlight, the first and last two hours the oblique angle means that the panel is only running at an average of 15 watts. That means that for four hours out of the eight it produces just 1.25 amps-per-hour, a total of 5 amps. For the other four hours it produces an average of 3.5 amps per hour, totalling 14 amps. Add this to the 5 amps and the panel is producing 19 amps. That means that with just one 60 watt panel, that delivers 228 watts. Over the eight hours of sunlight the panel delivers 28.5 watts, replacing over half of the current I use over a 24-hour period. So you see with this example based on what happens at my campsite on a sunny day, this surely gives you comfort that with

a simple solar set-up such as I have, solar recharging is possible without spending a fortune. Fact is that I have worked a 60-watt Solarex crystalline panel for over twelve years and have had much joy and success with it.

Types of solar panels

Solar experts will talk about crystalline and amorphous panels and the advantages of both as well as voltage regulators and other devices. I will leave the details of these to them. For most 4x4 users this is not of any real consequence. What does matter is the amount of current they will generate in the environment in which we play and the cost-per watt.

Strapped to a roof rack, placed on the ground, leaned against a tree or bush with a few wires run down to a regulator and onto the battery system. As long as the meat stays frozen and the drinks are icy, that's all that really matters. My advice: Keep it simple.

Powerfilm is a flexible range of solar panels. While not as efficient as rigid panels, Powerfilm is robust and ideal for use in the bush.

Solar panels and their performance claims:

- *Look for panels with good low-light claims.*
- *Ratings must be measured above 13,8-volts. Some panels boasting high yields boost their figures by lowering the voltage to 12-volts or lower. Don't be fooled; a 12-volt battery at 12-volts is a flat battery!*
- *Look at the ratio of current per cost. E.g. For every unit of currency spent I get X units of current (amps or watts).*
- *Beware of cheap Chinese trash. So many badly made panels stop working soon after delivery as they are unable to take the vibrations from being mounted on a vehicle.*

Sanyo's massive 180-watt HIT panel. Actually its not that big at 1,44x0.81metres, it easily slides under the average roof-rack. In full sunlight this baby delivers a massive 15 amps. In realistic terms though, during a sunny day, it will probably replenish ±40 amps. That's enough for most campers to stay in one place indefinitely.

Solar panels come in rigid and flexible types. Flexible units are more robust and practical for 4x4 use, but they are costly and inefficient for their size. Rigid panels are almost twice as efficient size for size, but are bulky and must be loaded flat on a roof rack and tied down very firmly. If they flex, even a little bit, they will break.

The cables must be heavy multi-core copper. Hand joins, bad connectors and thin cables will severely reduce efficiency. This is VERY important. There are advanced electronics that help the solar panel deliver more current more efficiently, but these are a nice to have and not a must have. For years I have run heavy cable from the panel, via a diode, to the battery. I can measure the battery voltage and can measure the current the panel is delivering. Without fancy electronics I achieve much. With it I could achieve more, true, but do I really want it? It is better to spend the money on heavy cables and the best connectors you can find. I should add, if your solar system has the potential to over-charge your batteries, a regulator is essential.

I have recently been playing with some Sanyo HIT solar systems marketed by Off-road Mega World. I am particularly impressed with the low-light capability of these panels and their efficiency for their size. Low light ability means that when the sun is not shining directly at the panel, it still delivers good current.

Made from rubber thong and plastic clips, a simple roof net can be constructed and built into pick-ups and stationwagons. It is perfect for the storage of light bulky items such as speeping bags, blankets and pillows. Ask your 4x4 equipment outlet for the components.

BUSH CAMPING

Sleeping inside the vehicle

Mosquito netting cut to size and attached to the windows with Velcro will allow the windows to be opened at night. If the vehicle has to be emptied, all foodstuffs must be stored in very strong boxes (preferably steel) to resist attempts by animals such as hyena gaining access.

Sleeping on the vehicle's roof-rack, whether in a tent or in the open, is ideal because being well away from the ground is a safe refuge from snakes and scorpions. Still my preferred way of sleeping in the bush is in the open on a roof-rack – except for attacks by mosquitoes, which can be dealt with by constructing a simple mosquito net which covers the part of the body that is exposed. Alternatively, burning mosquito coils all night helps a bit. (Inadvisable in malaria regions.)

Camp cooking ideas:

- *LP Gas is the most common fuel used on the safari although it is less efficient than many other fuels. The convenience of gas and the wide range of accessories is its biggest advantage.*
- *Alternatives such as multi-fuel stoves are smaller, lighter and more fuel-efficient.*
- *Cast iron pots are very useful on safari. I find that three legged iron pots are awkward to pack and are less versatile than flat-bottomed types. We have used a flat-bottomed pot with great success in baking bread, rolls of meat, potatoes and even chocolate cakes on an ordinary wood fire.*
- *Camp baking can be done in steel bread ovens or in cast-iron pots. Build the fire in a shallow hollow on a flat rock. Before cooking remove ALL coals from the rock and position the pot on the rock, placing hot coals around, without too many of them touching the pot. Then place a few hot coals on the lid. Rotate the pot from time to time. No need to purchase a bread oven as this versatile pot does everything.*

Cooking grids are dirty and difficult to pack. Many types are available with covers and have fold-away handles.

Lighting fires with wet wood

If you find your matches wet and you don't have a lighter, use a magnifying glass from a penknife or a lens from a binocular to burn dry grass. Dry grass is better for lighting fires than newspaper, but start with only a small clump otherwise the fire will be smothered and will smoke excessively. If all the wood is wet and smokes instead of burning, line the base of your fire with tin foil. This insulates the fire from the damp ground and the heat reflected by the foil accelerates the burning.

Keeping warm at night

If you don't have a hot water bottle take a rounded rock, about 25cms in diameter and place it next to the camp fire with one side of it over the coals. Rotate it periodically during the evening. Fifteen minutes before retiring wrap it in a towel. Do not let the rock get too hot otherwise you may scorch the towel. Place this warm bundle inside your sleeping bag. It will provide a substantial amount of heat for most of the night. However, do not rely on finding suitable rocks in desert and semi-desert regions. Parts of the Kalahari, for example, are completely without rocks.

Camp lighting

Some lamps are noisy and others are quiet. Some give a very blue light, and others nothing much more than a warm, golden glow. The colour temperature of a light source, be it blue or gold, differs greatly, and although not always apparent to the eye, affects the eye's ability to compensate to darkness when the light is extinguished. Briefly, the bluer the light, the slower the eyes will compensate. After being exposed to bright gas or fluorescent lights, the eyes will take a very long time to compensate, while the effects of low intensity electric light, LEDs or fire light may only take a minute to disappear.

In order from blue to red, the list of camp lights is as follows: fluorescent; high pressure paraffin/gas; electric incandescent; paraffin/candle/firelight, red LEDs.

The light intensity, or brightness, will also affect the eyes' ability to compensate. Ideally, the light source should be a low intensity warm light. It should also be quiet. If using LP gas lighting, as most campers do, run it at half power. The light will be warmer and therefore kinder to the eyes. It's very much quieter and is far more fuel efficient. At first, running lights at half power will appear dull but you will be surprised how well your eyes will compensate.

Awnings

Awnings permanently attached to the side of a vehicle are what I call 'instant' awnings. They are a convenient way of creating shade in an instant. If you, like me, like to stop on a lonely road, drink something icy and simply stare at the surroundings during a break for lunch, then an instant awning is a real luxury. They come in the less expensive roll-up variety and in the enclosed tube like the Ezi-Awn.

Candles

The warm glow of a candle is impractical in the bush unless it can be protected from the wind. The Bush-Lite candle lantern does just that. A single candle lasts all night and the lantern can also accommodate a mosquito pad.

Cooking equipment that fits into one another is a typical way where lots of space can be saved.

Torches

The torch market has stagnated in recent years with every camper that uses a high quality flashlight using a Maglite. As good as a Maglite is they have not changed their design in a significant way in about twenty years. Meanwhile other manufacturers are making better engineered and better performing torches at about the same price. I have four Maglites, the only one still in regular use is the Mag Charger. I have not used the others for years.

Feather-weight alloy tables are available. Heavy steel ones are now a thing of the past. This one is available from Makro, and many other camping stores.

The reason for my sharing this with you is that there are better torches out there. Go find them!

In 1999 I was introduced to Streamlight, a range of brilliant torches, some with LED options, which is a low-current option perfect for close work, map reading, and as a night light for children.

Camp comode. This idea was born when I made a film and a friend, almost jokingly, explained how he had converted an ordinary camp chair into a comode. Someone saw the film and developed the product.

Fire Extinguishers

Motorists who carry fire extinguishers rarely use them. Rather they use them when helping out fellow motorists who do not have one and suddenly have a need for one. There is no substitute should you have a fire. To the off-roader, when travelling over grasslands, fire is always a serious risk. Grass tends to get caught around the exhaust, it dries out, smoulders and eventually ignites. Once the grass ignites, it burns so fiercely that even with an extinguisher, extensive damage can result. Many vehicles have been lost in this way and I know of a brand new Nissan Sani, on its first trip out, that caught alight in the grasslands of the Makgadikgadi Pans in Botswana. After all the precious drinking water had been used in an unsuccessful attempt to put out the blaze, they were left without food, clothes and water with a 70-kilometre walk to the nearest town ahead of them. Although the vehicle was destroyed, the two men escaped with their lives.

Many vehicles are prone to this danger. I also know of a Land Rover Series-3, Mercedes Geländewagen, and a Nissan Sani and Patrol that have been lost in this way. Every vehicle must carry their own, easy-to-reach, fire extinguisher.

Fire Extinguishers ideas:

- *Dry powder extinguishers are suitable for vehicle fire applications. Carry one of at least 2kg.*
- *CO2 Extinguishers are more potent and heavier. They can also be used for pumping tyres. (See Trailblaster in Chapter-4)*
- *Neglecting and failing to service fire extinguishers is common. Let's not be caught napping with a fire that destroys our vehicle.*

Insect repellents

Insect repellents come in many different forms. Mosquito coils are very effective as long as there is no wind. What is more, they work even better if burnt close to the source of light. Spray-on and stick repellents such as Peaceful Sleep and Tabard are best applied to ankles and socks as well as to exposed skin. This will prevent ticks from crawling up the leg. Repellent lotions are also available, and all of these products are toxic. Contact with sensitive skin, on the lips and eyelids will cause irritation. Some repellents may cause a skin reaction with certain people and if a new brand is taken on safari it is advisable to test it on the skin before departure. Mosi Wipes, wet-wipes impregnated with repellent, work very well.

Other less orthodox methods of discouraging mosquitoes are found in repellent arm bands, repellent bars and vitamin B12 which perhaps is the most unusual. I am assured that a course of vitamin B12, started two weeks before departure and continued during exposure, makes mosquitoes think twice about biting. Arm bands impregnated with insecticide are also effective and if worn around the ankles would also be very effective against ticks.

Refuse and ablutions

Some conservationists abroad advise burying rubbish. In Africa this is contrary to all proper thinking. Animals, namely baboons, jackal and hyena dig it up and spread it around. Burn it or take it with you. To aid in the processing of refuse and to make it easier to carry,

A plastic folding basin. What a brilliant idea for saving space!

Ideas for handling refuse:

- *Use paper plates and burn them in the camp fire.*
- *Do not burn plastic – it melts down but still constitutes litter. Put the small bits into cans, burn them and then toss them into the refuse bag, Burnt tins don't smell.*

- Use bleach-free toilet paper and if possible burn it before burying it. Dig a hole as deep as possible – at least 30 cms.
- Use a four pound hammer and a wooden block (or the jacking plate from your high-lift) to crush beer, soft drink and food cans. This will reduce the bulk of your rubbish.
- Carry some large sized heavy duty plastic bin bags in your safari kit. Rubbish in bags strapped to a roof-rack will prevent smells inside the vehicle and can be easily discarded when a town is reached.

SAFARI CLOTHING

Perhaps the single most important item in the safari wardrobe is a good hat. Wide brimmed hats are better than caps as they keep the sun off the neck as well as the face. Like the hat, other clothing should be chosen to protect the body against the elements and to blend in with the surroundings.

Daytime:

Camouflage against animals is not dependant on colour, since most animals are colour-blind. Interrupted patterns that break up the human shape work best. Even bright blue and red cannot be seen by animals – in fact, pure blues are better than any other colour for

animal camouflage. Long baggy trousers are the best protection against snakes and are most comfortable when walking through tall grass.

Night time
Never underestimate how low temperatures can fall during darkness. Wherever and whenever you go on safari, take along a warm jersey and a wind cheater.

Footwear
If you intend to walk, wear boots or tackies. Sandals and flip-flops are totally inadequate – they allow grass to cut the feet and are no protection against biting insects or snakes. At night, boots or tackies are also recommended, as snakes and scorpions are largely nocturnal.

First aid
You will need a basic kit for emergencies or to tide you over until medical help is found. This is something to discuss with your family doctor. You should also mention drugs that will be carried to combat common illnesses; diarrhoea, vomiting and allergies as well as the carrying of needles and syringes should an injection be required in a situation where sterility is dubious.

A first aid kit should include:
- *Analgesic ear drops.*
- *Antihistamine ointment and oral preparation.*
- *Anti-inflammatory gel.*
- *Anti-emetic preparation.*
- *Antiseptic concentrate, ointment or powder.*
- *Cotton wool.*
- *Crepe bandages; large and small.*
- *Gauze swabs.*
- *Paracetamol for fever or pain.*
- *Paracetamol plus codeine for stronger/adult analgesia.*
- *Rehydration powder or tablets.*
- *Scissors.*
- *Sling and splints.*
- *Sticking plaster and wound closure strips.*
- *Thermometer.*

Snake bite kits
The value of a snake bite kit in the bush is questionable. Seldom is the small amount of antivenom carried in a kit sufficient to help the patient in any way. More importantly, due to the toxicity of antivenom,

it should only be administered by a medically qualified person in a situation where appropriate action can be taken to counteract the severe life-threatening allergic reactions which can occur.

Stings and bites – First Aid
The effects of stings and bites from insects, scorpions and snakes can be partially relieved with the use of a suction device called Aspivenin. The kit consists of a special syringe and a range of suction nozzles of varying sizes. If applied immediately after a bite or sting, the Aspivenin will suck a quantity of poison, relieving pain and reducing swelling.

Phutsi fly
This annoying insect is found throughout Southern Africa and is particularly prevalent during the wet months. It lays its eggs in damp clothing that has been hung out to dry. Then, when the clothes are worn the eggs hatch and the worms burrow into the skin causing severe irritation. Spread a liberal layer of Vaseline jelly over the infected area and cover with a sticking plaster to starve the worms of air. To prevent Phutsi Fly, all washed clothing must be ironed.

Thorns and narrow bush tracks
It's a good idea to keep water in blue cans and fuel in yellow, green or red. Plastic makes the best material to carry water as it rarely causes an unpleasant taste. Don't carry fuel in plastic cans: You may get them mixed up.

Keep windows wound up at least to eye-height when travelling along narrow bush tracks. The dangers of eyes and faces being spiked by thorns is then kept to a minimum.

WATER AND SURVIVAL

Do not underestimate the importance of water and the maintenance of proper water intake by the members of your group of travellers. In May 1998 I got a vehicle bogged down on Sowa Pan. Two of us were travelling in a single vehicle. The day before I had spent about three hours in the sun shooting pictures and by evening I realised that I was dehydrated. I began a program of drinking large amounts of water over a prolonged period. By the time we got bogged down the following day I thought I had recovered. After 30-minutes in the scorching heat on Sowa Pan the symptoms returned in a form which spelt danger. Initial symptoms of dehydration is a headache and tiredness. Advanced dehydration comes in the form of nausea, light-headedness while sweating seems to stop. It can also be accompanied by a rise in body temperature probably because the body's cooling mechanism is failing.

This is what happened to me. It was our last day before our return leg and we had only 15-litres of water remaining. The heat

was intolerable, the sun and white surface of the pan unbearable and our vehicle, which had overheated, was deep in a mire of thick black mud. Already dehydrated, with not enough water, miles from nowhere and with an immobile vehicle – it was a scary situation. Knowing the dangers of crossing the pans and having got myself into this predicament I wanted to turn around and give myself a swift kick in the backside for my foolishness. I decided that we should have one attempt to get the vehicle out but that our preparation would be thorough. If the recovery attempt failed we would construct a shelter and rest until nightfall. Having donned a long sleeve cotton shirt and long trousers for protection we began to work. One hour later, with rests every five minutes, we made our first attempt and succeeded. Things could have been much worse.

Simply screwed onto a gas tank, Front-Runner's water heater is so simple yet effective, it makes you think, "Now why didn't someone think of this before?".

Carrying water

Water consumption should be calculated at no less than six litres per person per day in summer, and four litres per person per day in winter. This includes washing and drinking. Additional water requirements must also be catered for.

These are:

- *Vehicle requirements: radiator refills, windscreen washing, cracked pipes and leaks.*
- *Tyre repairs: soap and water is needed for lubricating tyre levers.*
- *Evaporation and spillage.*

On extended trips, water stored in a translucent container will eventually turn green. Black, light-proof plastic containers are therefore best for water storage.

Water cans with a plastic tap at the base are very convenient, but because the taps are easily broken, remember to remove the tap and replace it with a plug when travelling. I prefer heavy plastic water cans with handles. I decant water from these cans into a smaller insulated water container with a small tap at its base. This keeps the water easily accessible and cool at the same time. The light weight of the small container also means that it can be moved around with ease.

A water bladder by Front Runner. Bladders are more versatile than cans as they can be folded away when empty. This one is designed to lie on the floor in front of the back seat.

Steel water cans can give the water a metallic taste and rust can make the water undrinkable. If you wish to carry water in steel jerry cans, paint them white to avoid possible confusion with fuel cans. The white surface will also help to keep the water cooler.

Wine bags (the silver bags found inside 5-litre boxed wine) make excellent water carriers. When frozen solid and then placed in a cooler-box, they make excellent space and weight savers – when they thaw, you have 5 litres of drinking water, and when empty they can be folded up and put away.

Water carried in goat skin or canvas cooler bags is a way to keep water cool for drinking but the substantial water lost due to evaporation must be taken into account. Although hanging a cooler bag on the front of the vehicle cools the water very quickly, the bag must not simply be hung on the string handle as the abrasion caused by a rocking vehicle quickly damages the bag and the string handle soon breaks.

Be sure to disinfect water bottles once they are more than a year old by filling with water and adding a teaspoon of chlorine. Leave for a couple of days and then rinse thoroughly.

Vehicle water tanks

The golden rule when carrying water is: never carry all of your water in one container. Should a fitted tank split while travelling and all the water run out, you may find yourself in a situation where you are left with no water at all. A second container inside the vehicle must be regarded as your emergency supply and should not be decanted into the vehicle's auxiliary tank. The fitting of auxiliary water tanks is covered in chapter-3.

Camp showers

Portable camping showers consist of a heavy duty plastic bag, black on the one side, transparent on the other. A short hose, tap and rose are attached to the bottom. It is filled with water and left in the sun with the clear side exposed. After about three hours, it is ready to

give a delightful hot shower. Left in the midday sun for five hours it will produce water hot enough for a cup of tea, although this is not recommended by the manufacturers. These showers hold between 10 and 15 litres, are inexpensive and are available in most camping stores. Alternatively, use the cooler times of the day to view game and enjoy your surroundings, and during the midday heat when all the animals are resting in shady places, enjoy a cold shower. Electric showers are another option

Washing clothes

For very long trips into the wilderness a bucket with a sealed lid is useful. Put in the soiled clothes, a tablespoon of washing powder and hot or cold water. Now drive for a while over some rough ground. The harder your suspension, the cleaner your washing will be. The bucket is also useful for many other camp duties.

Jerry can brackets are made in single and double sizes.

Sound Systems

The owner of an overland vehicle has an additional responsibility with regard to sound systems. To be out in the bush is a luxury few are fortunate enough to experience. It is a very special place. To the lover of the great outdoors there are few things more irritating than when some inconsiderate philistine – who obviously does not appreciate his surroundings – insists on playing his music so loud that every living thing for miles around can hear. The whole experience is spoiled, and the din is hardly conducive to attracting wildlife.

WATER PURIFICATION

Chlor-Floc

This is perhaps the best tested chemical field purification system available and is called 'Syn. Aquacure' in Britain. Its name is derived from what it does; 'Floc', means flocculation: the removal of debris, and 'Chlor', means that it chlorinates the water. Ingredients in each tablet cause the sediment to coagulate and separate. This sediment can be removed by pouring the water through a cloth strainer. No special equipment is necessary and purification can even be done by making a hole in the ground next to a raw water source.

Fitted to the side of a double-cab, a fold-down table makes a useful place to make a roadside meal or boil a cuppa tea in camp. This one is made of plywood with an aluminium frame.

Filtration

Unless filtered through ultra fine membrane filters, filtering without chemical purification will not make the water drinkable. It will only serve to make it more pleasant to look at, since harmful bacteria and viruses will pass through all but the finest of filters. Filtration should take place before purifying with iodine or chlorine, and afterwards when using Chlor-Floc. A cloth filtration bag available at camping stores will make the job easier.

Iodine and chlorine
In an emergency Iodine is very useful to the traveller for purifying water because it is readily available in most towns. It is also available at mission hospitals and clinics. Chlorine tablets are available as a water purification agent, but like iodine, are rendered inactive by pollutants in the water. It is therefore necessary to filter the water through gauze or cloth before the chlorine or iodine is added. Beware of overdosing – iodine and chlorine are poisonous in high quantities.

It is far better to equip yourself with one of the better suited water purification systems available from most camping stores. Good examples are Chlor-Floc purifiers and Katadyn water pumps.

Filter pumps
I have had first-hand experience of Katadyn water filter pumps. These devices require no chemical additives whatsoever, and although expensive, are unequalled in their efficiency and ultimate safety – in fact they are so safe that the source water can be ridden with typhoid, dysentery, cholera and the purified water leaves the pump crystal clear and ready to drink. Not only is the water cleared of harmful bacteria and viruses but of pesticides, herbicides and harmful chemicals as well. In some models the water produced is pharmaceutically sterile. There are many makes of filter pumps now being used as standard issue to the Red Cross throughout the world.

Filter pumps work in this way: the inlet pipe is lowered into the source and the water is first filtered through an open cell foam filter housed in a wire cage, thereby preventing the ingestion of

To mount a gas tank on a roof rack (which is a good idea since they are bulky things) a special bracket is needed.
Top: A common unit.
Below: The Proto low-profile clamp, a design copied by Front Runner. Low profile clamps are desirable if low underground parking lots are a frequent problem.

Boiling water will kill many, but not all of the bugs in water that could make you or your family ill. Because there are many hardy viruses that will not be killed, additional purification methods should be used, especially if the water is taken from areas close to human habitation. If boiling is the only method used it is vital that the water be boiled for a minimum of 12 minutes.

If anybody in your family or group has a problem with privacy when using the toilet or washing in the bush then purpose made cubicles such as this one are available.

large particles. Then the water is pumped under pressure through a special ceramic filter. Even if you think you may never need it, buy a purification kit or filter pump and stow it in your vehicle. Be prepared for the unexpected.

WILD ANIMALS

Before you set up camp, look closely at the area you are considering. Game tracks look like people tracks – flattened paths that snake their way through the bush often to and from water. If a hippo or a herd of elephant use this track on a regular basis and you set up camp in their path, it could lead to an unpleasant confrontation. It is imperative that you never sleep with food stored inside your tent. You are very safe inside a tent, even against lion, hyena, hippo and elephant, as long as you follow this advice.

If you camp close to water, remember that game will want to drink and therefore you should ensure that there is easy access for the animals, especially if you are camped in an arid area. Animals made skittish by your presence may be too scared to drink and could die. Do not approach wild animals on foot unless you are accompanied by an experienced guide.

Washing and swimming in pools frequented by crocodiles and hippo is dangerous and should only be done once the area has been thoroughly looked over and there is somebody keeping constant watch. If you are going to swim, I strongly advise making the swim as brief as possible.

In many areas where animals are accustomed to the presence of humans, hyena, baboons and monkeys will raid your camp when your back is turned. It is important not to allow these animals access to your food. They will eat anything they can reach, and if they succeed they will become versed in the art of stealing which will only encourage them to try again.

NEVER, FOR ANY REASON WHATSOEVER, FEED A WILD ANIMAL

Once, while camping at Serondela in the Chobe Game Reserve in Northern Botswana, I placed two full 20-litre jerry cans on the lid of my cooler-box to prevent the baboons from getting inside. I walked about 20 yards away to do some fishing. After about five minutes I heard the clang as one jerry can hit the ground. I turned and ran towards camp. By the time I got there the lid was open and three rolls of Kodak film had been stolen. The baboon, more used to stealing citrus fruit, obviously thought that if it was yellow, then it must be tasty. I seethed as I watched the baboon climb the trees above the water, tear open the boxes, undo the plastic containers and drop my films into the river. Since that trip to Serondela, dozens of resident baboons have had to be destroyed because they became talented at tearing open tents. All this could have been avoided had they never been fed, or been allowed access to campers' foodstuffs.

Scorpions

An easy way to identify a harmless scorpion from a dangerous one is by the size of its pincers – the smaller the pincers, the more dangerous the sting. Scorpions with large pincers have less need for a highly toxic venom and hence the sting will be no worse than a wasp. Scorpions armed with small pincers will be armed with a more potent toxin in their sting, and a thicker tail. The venom is neurotoxic and the sting can result in cardiac or respiratory failure, or both. Some scorpions can spray their venom and envenomation of the eyes can result. It is therefore very wise to treat a scorpion as if it were a snake. Do not get too close, do not antagonise a scorpion or pick up a dead one. Scorpions seem to be attracted to camp sites and you may find one under a tent ground sheet when the tent is packed up, or under a jerry can or cool-box left sitting on the sand. They also like living in cracks in dead wood, and the risk of being stung while collecting fire wood is very real. Shake out your clothes and shoes before putting them on in the morning. Because scorpions and many snakes are nocturnal, do not walk barefoot at night.

While small, holding shovels are nice to have around the camp, they cannot double as a recovery tool. They are too small.

Snakes

Knowing about snakes, where and how they live, will go a long way in helping to avoid an unpleasant confrontation.

Most snakes depend on camouflage to protect themselves and unless they are moving they can become very difficult to see, even at close range. Fortunately snakes for the most part prefer to flee and will only attack in self defence. This is why more than 90 percent of recorded bites have occurred in people handling snakes. (Source: A Field guide to Animal Tracks – L Liebenberg) The puffadder on the other hand remains motionless when approached. This is why this highly venomous snake features very prominently in the list of recorded bites, as most are unwittingly stepped on and the snakes have retaliated by striking.

Here are a few simple rules:

- *Wear calf length boots and long loose fitting trousers when walking in the bush. If a snake strikes, it may bite into the loose trousers and miss the victim's flesh altogether.*
- *Step onto rocks and logs and not over them. A snake resting on the other side or under a log will not be seen, and a step onto and a*

This product, a brilliantly designed toilet and bath bag, is a tribute to my good friend, the late Charlotte Du Toit. She was instrumental in bringing some of the most ingenious and well-thought out camping gear to the market. Wherever you may find yourself camping you can be sure that evidence of Charlotte will be there somewhere. She will be missed by many who never knew her. Charlotte Du Toit. 19.. - 2001.

Flourescent lights are quiet and do not consume much electrical current. However, if you are running a fridge and are concerned about flat batteries, it may be a better idea to use gas for lighting.

glance over the log may reveal a snake which may otherwise have been stepped on.

• Avoid walking in very long grass where the visibility of the path is restricted.

• If you are picking up rocks or logs, do so by lifting or rolling them towards you, thereby allowing a path for a snake to escape by moving away from you.

• Never put your hand into a place in which you cannot see, like a burrow or a hollow tree trunk. A snake may have made it a home and will have nowhere to run to if it feels threatened.

• Do not walk around at night without a good torch – many snakes are nocturnal.

• Should you encounter a snake at close range, remain motionless until the snake retreats. Alternatively, withdraw very slowly – snakes have very poor eyesight and will strike at what they perceive to be threatening them. A sudden movement may induce a strike.

• Do not pick up a 'dead' snake unless you are absolutely sure it is dead. The rinkhals shams death when threatened and if it is touched will immediately strike.

• Do not approach snakes to get a better look unless you know what you are doing. Some species like the Mozambique spitting cobra and the rinkhals are able to spit their venom up to three metres and should the venom enter the eyes, thorough and continuous cleansing with water will be needed if the victim is to avoid permanent eye damage. Wearing sunglasses gives good protection against spitting snakes.

Ticks

Because ticks carry disease, some of which can be fatal, it is important to know how to avoid being bitten. Wearing boots with long trousers and applying insect repellent or paraffin to your socks will prevent them climbing up your legs. Ticks often sit on the ends of long blades of grass and wait patiently for a host to pass by. If you walk through long grass, inspect yourself thoroughly afterwards. If you find a tick, do not pull it off as it may leave its head behind. Smearing Vaseline, grease, disinfectant or alcohol onto the tick will make them release their grip. Some tick species bury themselves under the surface of the sand and lie in the shade of a tree waiting for a host to use the shade as a resting place.

Ostrich

We have encountered ostrich on many occasions on our travels and at no time have I felt comfortable with them when they have been bold enough to approach us and stay close by. In the Qwaqwa National

Park there are semi-tame ostrich which are frankly a nuisance and can become aggressive without provocation. These birds will run for kilometres alongside a vehicle and get uncomfortably close. I have been told by reserve staff that they are not to be trusted. When protecting its nest an ostrich becomes very dangerous, so never approach an ostrich nest even if it appears to be unguarded. This rule applies to every wild animal – threatening young offspring will produce a fearless defence from almost all animals, big and small.

A multi-tool is a real friend around the camp. I have used and owned several. The best: Leatherman Wave. The worst: Engel Multitool. My advice: Don't waste your money on a cheap multi-tool. If you have a limited budget get a small Swiss Army Knife.

Hippo

The hippopotamus accounts for more injuries and death than any other wild animal in Africa. They do not mock charge. Because of their poor eyesight a charge is normally wild and without direction. Moving sideways or climbing trees is the only escape route as outrunning a hippo is impossible for even the fastest athlete.

To avoid confrontation with hippo:

- *Do not camp on or too close to game paths leading to water.*
- *Do not shine bright lights at hippos, even if they are in the water. They have been known to charge at the headlights of a vehicle – so do not drive around at night in hippo country. This is one of the reasons why driving at night is forbidden in most game reserves in Southern Africa.*
- *Do not get between a grazing hippo and the water from which it has come – you will be cutting it off from its place of sanctuary and it may charge.*
- *If a hippo should rise up under and tip your boat, the best course of action – probably the only course of action – is to jump into the reeds and hide. And pray!*
- *If you are in a boat, keep at an extra distance if the hippo are with young. In this situation they can become very aggressive and will attack the moment they feel threatened. Hippo move with astonishing speed under water and a charging hippo may only be seen when it is too late.*

Lion

Like most animals, lions will usually move off when they become aware of approaching humans. The danger occurs when walking down-wind and the lion fails to notice your approach. Lions, especially when feeding or when they are with cubs, can become very aggressive and charge. The best course of action if you find yourself close to a lion or lioness is to remain motionless staring directly into the lion's eyes. If you turn and run, the lion's instinct may take over and you will be chased and brought down, whether the lion is hungry or not. If the lion charges, stand your ground, stare hard and shout at the top of your voice. Avoid high pitched screaming as this may be construed as fear. Throwing sticks towards the lion will help. The lion, realising that you have no fear of him will back away. Happily, I give this advice without first hand experience, but it comes from those who have.

Leopard

Shy and reclusive, leopard will more often than not move away when approached by humans. They can however become a threat if they are suddenly disturbed. In this situation, eye contact with the leopard should be avoided as this will let the leopard know that it has been seen which will promote a response, in most cases a quick withdrawal is advised. The other alternative is that the leopard will charge. Leopard do not mock charge and unlike a charge by a lion, shouting at it will have little effect. In short, if you come across a leopard that is uncomfortably close, do not look directly at it and immediately move away to a safe distance.

Tracking leopard is dangerous, especially if the leopard is injured or sick. Leopards have been known to back around their trackers and attack. Leopards are not a danger to people camping out in the open and only in very rare cases have leopards been known to attack humans for food.

Elephant

When on foot always establish in which direction the wind is blowing and walk into the wind. This rule applies to all wild animals if you wish to approach them safely and to a distance close enough to get a good look without their taking fright and moving away. This is particularly important when approaching elephant because, unlike most animals, elephant will not always turn and move away – they may not wish to have you around and may move towards you and chase you. Elephants use their trunks to smell and will raise them above their heads and point toward you. If they do this you can be pretty sure that they have smelt you – if they do not move away it is unlikely that they will be happy with the existing arrangement. This is a good time for you to retreat. Make sure that you then remain downwind until you are at a safe distance. Do not wait until the last minute to retreat. Elephants often mock charge. They do this with their ears flapping and they often accompany this performance by trumpeting. They may only mock charge once. The next may be for real and elephants do this with their ears held back. You will not outrun an elephant and climbing trees is of little use. If you are forced to run, run downwind. If you manage to get out of sight, hide in the thickest undergrowth you can find. Elephants have poor eyesight and rely on their acute sense of smell to locate their enemies. Elephants in a herd with young are the most likely to become aggressive. Elephants found in hunting areas are often very wary of humans and they should be kept at a good distance whether you are on foot or in a vehicle. Unlike buffalo, lone bulls are normally placid.

Buffalo

A lone buffalo is perhaps the most unpredictable of all African wild animals and will often charge without warning. They rarely mock charge. If you are on foot and come across a single, or a small group of buffalo, immediately look for a suitable tree to climb. Do not wait for a charge before looking for a tree because if it should charge, time wasted in finding a suitable tree could mean the difference between life and death. Large herds of buffalo are not dangerous – but if you do not spot a lone straggler and you get too close you could find yourself in trouble.

Rhinoceros

Like the elephant and buffalo, rhinoceros should be approached into the wind and never too close. The black rhinoceros is far more dangerous than the white, and is a particularly nervous and unpredictable animal. They have poor vision but an acute sense of smell and good hearing. Rhinoceros will mock charge, but this is often followed very quickly by a genuine charge. It will do this with its head held up for improved vision and it will only lower its head at the last moment. Climbing a tree is the best course of action. If there are no trees, do not run away but move sideways always staying downwind. Hide in dense undergrowth and remain motionless until the rhino loses interest.

An interesting fact about the white and black rhinoceros is that although the black is the more feared, there are more cases of white rhino charges than black. There are two reasons for this: the white rhino is more common and people know the dangers of the black rhino and respect it as a dangerous animal. The white is regarded with a casual attitude and people tend to get too close.

Hyena

Two species of hyena occur in Southern Africa – the brown and the spotted. The brown hyena is a timid animal and not aggressive, normally keeping away from humans. The spotted hyena however is a bold and resourceful animal. Although hyenas move off when approached on foot, they become dangerous and destructive when everyone is asleep. They can do damage to any food container left in the open at night. The jaws of the hyena are incredibly powerful and

InfoMap publish a range of unique road maps which include GPS co-ordinates, accommodation, fuel stops and other information found on no other maps. The following maps are available : Botswana, Namibia, Mozambique, Tanzania, Kaokoland, Lesotho and Angola (end 2004). In South Africa: Drakensberg and the Freestate Highlands, Richtersveld, Kruger National Park and the Lowveld, Northern Natal, The Garden Route (end 2004). Available from www.4xforum.com or by calling 27 21 852 9984 and from all good bookstores and outdoor lifestyle shops.

they put them to good use in getting at campers' foodstuffs. They will tear open a fridge or cooler-box with ease. They also attack plastics and rubber and there have been cases of them chewing and puncturing vehicle tyres. Covering tyres with thorn bushes will serve to discourage this practice. In areas where hyenas have become accustomed to the presence of humans, they are an even greater source of annoyance – aeroplane wings and tyres have to be guarded by piling up heaps of thorn bushes overnight.

In 1991 when running a camp in the Okavango, I attempted to discourage a spotted hyena from raiding our kitchen – which it had been doing regularly over the previous two months – by placing chicken bones on a plate flavoured with strong spices. The recipe included an entire bottle of Tabasco sauce, a tablespoon of curry powder and a tablespoon of hot English mustard powder. In the morning the metal plate on which this 'nouvelle cuisine' was served was licked clean! The spotty was back the very next night to take his revenge by tearing open a fridge, which strangely contained nothing other than green lettuce, cucumber and tomatoes. The hyena ripped out the plastic door lining, a quarter of which he ate!

The presence of spotted hyena is the most convincing reason why sleeping on the ground in the open is ill advised. There are some dreadful stories of hyenas attacking sleeping humans and with their powerful jaws they can easily take a life.

All wild animals should be treated with the greatest respect. Remember that you are the visitor in their world and they should never be interfered with. Animals like cheetah and wild dog, although carnivorous and potentially dangerous, will retreat and can easily be driven off a kill. In

situations where the food source is scarce, an approach too close to a kill could result in cubs going unfed, and prides breaking up. The nocturnal honey badger, although relatively small, can become very aggressive if approached too closely. It will attack with little provocation. There is one account of a honey badger bringing down a wildebeest! (Animals tracks of Southern Africa – Louis Liebenberg) Antelope such as roan, sable, gemsbok and bushbuck will defend themselves if cornered and their horns can inflict fatal wounds.

Game viewing and photography

The best time for both of these pursuits is in the early morning and late afternoon, when the animals are active and when the light is at its best. Lenses for landscape photography must include a wide angle of about 28mm, or my preference, a 24mm. Professionals shooting landscapes often use longer focal length lenses to do this – a 135mm is ideal.   For photographers keen on game, 180mm and 300mm lenses are ideal.

For successful bird photography you will need a focal length of 400mm or more. Remember that when using this type of lens, a tripod or some means of supporting the lens will be necessary. A film rated at an ASA of at least 200 will be required when using long focal length lenses because high shutter speeds will be needed to prevent camera shake from spoiling pictures.

If you are shooting pictures from inside a vehicle and are unable to use a tripod, have a small canvas bag filled with sand handy. Wind down the side window and place the sand bag on the edge of the door. Now you have a steady support which can be moulded and shaped for the lens, and the window can be raised for best viewing comfort.

Keeping your film in the refrigerator or cool-box is a good idea if the ambient temperatures exceed 35°C. Film rated at 100 ASA or lower can be stored for short periods up to 40°C without harm but film rated at above 100 ASA will be damaged very quickly if it is allowed to do so. The result of over heating a film emulsion will be a colour shift, in the case of transparency film, often towards the cyan-blue.

Bushbag easily mounts on a vehicle door and acts as a stabilizer for a camera with a tele lens. New to the market it is available from camera stores.

Do not photograph government buildings or employees. Do not even point your camera at a military installation or vehicle. Keep your photographic equipment packed away, but within easy reach when passing through border posts or road blocks. At some border posts you may need to declare your camera equipment and it is a good idea to have a list of each piece of equipment and its serial number from which you can copy the information down onto the declaration document. Never photograph a soldier in uniform or you may find yourself being interrogated as a spy.

A basic photograph equipment list is included at the end of this chapter.

MAPS AND MORE INFORMATION

Maps
Choosing maps for navigation in remote areas requires some understanding and know-how. This is covered in chapter-10.

4X4 Trails and Expedition book

The companion to this book is the Complete Guide to 4x4 Trails and Expeditions in Southern Africa by the same author. (ISBN 0-620-29698-4). The current edition is the 6th edition of the popular series which began in 1994. In addition to all provinces of South Africa, Botswana, Lesotho and Namibia, Mozambique and Zambia have been added. Trails appear in every country and province, catering for weekend travellers as well as two and three-week expeditions. For those still new to the 4x4 world and not entirely confident to venture out alone, there is also a chapter on self-drive guided safaris that can take you up as far as Uganda. Each trail is rated according to the required driving and overlanding skills and includes information on the routes, sights and facilities available on each trail. Many trails also feature GPS co-ordinates. Available from www.4xforum.com or by calling 021 852 9984. Also available in most bookstores and wherever good 4x4 equipment is sold.

VIDEO/DVD PRESENTATION
To supplement this chapter I have put together a DVD and VHS program called 'Working in the Wilderness'.

This one-hour presentation covers much of what is included in this chapter, namely how to take a vehicle and equip it to wander into the wilderness. The story begins in the Western Kalahari where we travel in a small convoy. The route has its challenges and as they are met the camera stays rolling. Finding water, grass seed problems, navigation, tents, packing, freezers, safety, towing trailers and a whole lot more are part of the story. This is a highly informative and entertaining video that captures the magic of off-road exploring. Guaranteed enjoyment.

This is one of a series of six 4x4 videos. The DVD version also contains the bonus video, "4x4 Adventure Stories", a 60-minute humorous and nostalgic look at the author's off-roading adventures between 1974 and 1994. Available from www.4xforum.com or by calling 021 852 9984. Also available in most bookstores and wherever good 4x4 equipment is sold.

LISTS

Copy these check lists and use them on your travels.
Tick the first block if needed. Tick the second when packed.

TENTS

Tent 1	☐☐	Tent 2	☐☐
Guy ropes	☐☐	Mallet	☐☐
Ground sheet	☐☐	Fly sheet	☐☐
Poles	☐☐	Tent brush	☐☐
....	☐☐	....	☐☐

BEDDING

Foam mattresses	☐☐	Folding mattresses	☐☐
Stretchers	☐☐	Duvet	☐☐
Sleeping bags	☐☐	Pillows	☐☐
Mosquito net	☐☐	Hot water bottles	☐☐
....	☐☐	....	☐☐

LIGHTING

Paraffin lamp	☐☐	Gas lamp	☐☐
Fluorescent strip	☐☐	Methylated spirits	☐☐
Spare mantles	☐☐	Matches	☐☐
Candles	☐☐	Torch	☐☐
Recharger	☐☐	Torch batteries	☐☐
Torch bulbs	☐☐	Spot light	☐☐
....	☐☐	....	☐☐

COOKING

Braai grid	☐☐	Fire lighters	☐☐
Charcoal	☐☐	Small stove & benzine	☐☐
Poitjie	☐☐	Flat iron pot	☐☐
Cooking pots	☐☐	Frying pan	☐☐
Kettle	☐☐	Gas bottles	☐☐
Gas bottle keys	☐☐	Spare jets & washers	☐☐
Gas extension tube	☐☐	Gas rings	☐☐
Smoker cooker	☐☐	Cutting board	☐☐
Aluminium foil	☐☐	Cling wrap	☐☐
....	☐☐	....	☐☐

CLEANING

Dust pan & brush	☐☐	Bucket and lid	☐☐
Basin	☐☐	Dish washing liquid	☐☐
Dish cloths	☐☐	Dish towels	☐☐

Scouring sponges	❑ ❑	Bottle brush	❑ ❑
Sink plug	❑ ❑	Swipes	❑ ❑
Paper towels	❑ ❑	Serviettes	❑ ❑
Washing powder	❑ ❑	Miltons	❑ ❑
Disinfectant	❑ ❑	All-purpose cleaner	❑ ❑
....	❑ ❑	....	❑ ❑

CUTLERY

Knives	❑ ❑	Paring knife	❑ ❑
Forks	❑ ❑	Utility knife	❑ ❑
Spoons	❑ ❑	Vegetable peeler	❑ ❑
Tea spoons	❑ ❑	Grater	❑ ❑
Serving spoons	❑ ❑	Tin opener	❑ ❑
Bread knife	❑ ❑	Wooden spoon	❑ ❑
Carving knife	❑ ❑	Egg lifter	❑ ❑
Bottle opener	❑ ❑	Cork screw	❑ ❑
Soup ladle	❑ ❑	Salad servers	❑ ❑
Potato masher	❑ ❑	Braai tongs	❑ ❑
Colander	❑ ❑	....	❑ ❑
....	❑ ❑	....	❑ ❑

CROCKERY

Plates	❑ ❑	Paper plates	❑ ❑
Bowls	❑ ❑	Kid's bowls	❑ ❑
Mugs	❑ ❑	Wine glasses	❑ ❑
Tumblers	❑ ❑	Containers	❑ ❑
Toothpicks	❑ ❑	Tea pot	❑ ❑
Tupperware jug & lid	❑ ❑	Tupperware bowl	❑ ❑
Plastic containers & lids	❑ ❑	Thermos flask	❑ ❑
....	❑ ❑	....	❑ ❑
....	❑ ❑	....	❑ ❑

MEDICAL

Antibiotics (infection)	❑ ❑	Antibiotic cream	❑ ❑
Antipyretics (fever)	❑ ❑	Antiseptics	❑ ❑
Anti-inflammatories	❑ ❑	Analgesics (pain)	❑ ❑
Anti-emetics (vomiting)	❑ ❑	Bandages	❑ ❑
Cortisone cream	❑ ❑	Eye drops	❑ ❑
Interflora	❑ ❑	Plasters	❑ ❑
Medical bag/box	❑ ❑	Malaria prophylaxis	❑ ❑
Mosquito repellent	❑ ❑	Insect spray	❑ ❑
Water purification system	❑ ❑	Survival blanket	❑ ❑
....	❑ ❑	....	❑ ❑
....	❑ ❑	....	❑ ❑

A hammock doubles as a handy tie-down on a roof-rack.

Birds	❏ ❏	Mammals	❏ ❏
Reptiles	❏ ❏	Insects/Butterflies	❏ ❏
Trees	❏ ❏	Stars	❏ ❏
4x4 Trails book	❏ ❏	4x4 Guide book	❏ ❏
Magazines/novels	❏ ❏	Children's book	❏ ❏
....	❏ ❏	....	❏ ❏

CAMP

Shovel	❏ ❏	Axe	❏ ❏
Water containers	❏ ❏	Clothes pegs	❏ ❏
Fire extinguisher	❏ ❏	Chairs – adult	❏ ❏
Table – catering	❏ ❏	Chairs – children	❏ ❏
Table – other	❏ ❏	Table cloths	❏ ❏
Shade cloth	❏ ❏	Taupaulin	❏ ❏
Catapult	❏ ❏	Pen knife	❏ ❏
Leatherman	❏ ❏	Bin bags (black)	❏ ❏
Newspaper	❏ ❏	Solar shower	❏ ❏
Coolbag	❏ ❏	Coolbox	❏ ❏
Ice bricks	❏ ❏	Freezer/Fridge	❏ ❏
....	❏ ❏	....	❏ ❏

Cooking grids must be folding to pack easily. I carry two grids: a broad flat one like this Makro item (middle) as well as a folding kettle grill (bottom).

CHILDREN

Games and toys	❏ ❏	Stationery & crayons	❏ ❏
Underwear	❏ ❏	Vests	❏ ❏
T-shirts	❏ ❏	Tracksuits	❏ ❏
Jeans	❏ ❏	Jerseys	❏ ❏
Jackets	❏ ❏	Balaclava	❏ ❏
Gloves	❏ ❏	Hats	❏ ❏
Pyjamas	❏ ❏	Boots	❏ ❏
Shoes	❏ ❏	Sandals	❏ ❏
Water wings	❏ ❏	Swimming costumes	❏ ❏
Rain wear	❏ ❏	....	❏ ❏

TOILETRIES

Bath plug	❏ ❏	Toilet rolls	❏ ❏
Soap	❏ ❏	Shampoo	❏ ❏
Aqueous cream	❏ ❏	Toothpaste	❏ ❏
Tooth brushes	❏ ❏	Cotton wool	❏ ❏
Deodorant	❏ ❏	Nail set	❏ ❏
Razor and blades	❏ ❏	Hair brush & comb	❏ ❏
Sanitary towels	❏ ❏	Lip balm	❏ ❏
Tissues	❏ ❏	Makeup	❏ ❏
Sunblock	❏ ❏	Lens cleaner, saline etc.	❏ ❏

A full-size axe is of little use in the bush. A panga and a hand axe are far more useful.

Contraceptive pill	❐ ❐	Condoms	❐ ❐
Towels	❐ ❐	Moisturiser	❐ ❐
....	❐ ❐	....	❐ ❐

DOCUMENTS & MAPS

Passports	❐ ❐	ID book/drivers license	❐ ❐
Visas and permits	❐ ❐	Travellers cheques	❐ ❐
Cash	❐ ❐	Credit cards	❐ ❐
Car registration	❐ ❐	Triptique	❐ ❐
Cheque book	❐ ❐	Booking receipts	❐ ❐
Vehicle registration	❐ ❐	Trailer registration	❐ ❐
InfoMaps	❐ ❐	AA maps	❐ ❐
Shell maps	❐ ❐	....	❐ ❐

FOOD – CONDIMENTS

Salt and pepper	❐ ❐	Sugar	❐ ❐
Sweetener	❐ ❐	Mayonnaise	❐ ❐
Tomato sauce	❐ ❐	Vinegar	❐ ❐
Olive oil	❐ ❐	Soy sauce	❐ ❐
Sun flower oil	❐ ❐	Spray and cook	❐ ❐
Herbs and spices	❐ ❐	Salad dressing	❐ ❐
Chutney	❐ ❐	Mustard	❐ ❐
Marmite	❐ ❐	Peanut butter	❐ ❐
Jam	❐ ❐	Honey	❐ ❐
Stock cubes	❐ ❐	Tomato paste	❐ ❐
....	❐ ❐	....	❐ ❐

FOOD – GENERAL

Tea	❐ ❐	Coffee	❐ ❐
Milk	❐ ❐	Powdered milk	❐ ❐
Bread	❐ ❐	Bread rolls	❐ ❐
Flour	❐ ❐	Bread mix	❐ ❐
Mealie meal	❐ ❐	Rusks	❐ ❐
Eggs	❐ ❐	Fruit	❐ ❐
Potatoes	❐ ❐	Onions	❐ ❐
Rice	❐ ❐	Pasta shells	❐ ❐
Spaghetti	❐ ❐	Sun flower seeds	❐ ❐
Tinned tomato & onion	❐ ❐	Cabbage	❐ ❐
Baked beans	❐ ❐	Sweet corn	❐ ❐
Tinned fruit	❐ ❐	Cake mix	❐ ❐
....	❐ ❐	....	❐ ❐
....	❐ ❐	....	❐ ❐
....	❐ ❐	....	❐ ❐
....	❐ ❐	....	❐ ❐

FOOD – BREAKFAST, SNACKS AND DRINKS

All bran	☐☐	Corn flakes	☐☐
Muesli	☐☐	Jungle Oats	☐☐
Chips	☐☐	Nuts	☐☐
Sweets	☐☐	Popcorn	☐☐
Chocolate	☐☐	Biltong/dry wors	☐☐
Marshmallows	☐☐	Fruit juices	☐☐
Tab/diet drinks	☐☐	Cokes/sodas	☐☐
Beer	☐☐	Wine	☐☐
Liquor	☐☐	Sherry/port	☐☐
Concentrate	☐☐	....	☐☐

FOOD – LUNCH

Tinned ham	☐☐	Tinned Tuna	☐☐
Tinned mussels	☐☐	Tinned corned beef	☐☐
Cheese spread	☐☐	Provitas	☐☐
Sandwich spread	☐☐	Cheese wedges	☐☐
....	☐☐	....	☐☐

FOOD COOLBOX/FRIDGE

Margarine	☐☐	Cheese	☐☐
Cold meats	☐☐	Yoghurt	☐☐
Cottage cheese	☐☐	Feta cheese	☐☐
Lettuce	☐☐	Tomato	☐☐
Cucumber	☐☐	Spring onions	☐☐
Avocado	☐☐	Carrots	☐☐
....	☐☐	....	☐☐

FOOD FREEZER

Chicken pieces	☐☐	Kebabs	☐☐
Lamb chops	☐☐	Steak	☐☐
Pre-prepared meals	☐☐	Mince	☐☐
Sausages	☐☐	Ribs	☐☐
Ice cubes	☐☐	Freezer blocks	☐☐
....	☐☐	....	☐☐
....	☐☐	....	☐☐
....	☐☐	....	☐☐
....	☐☐	....	☐☐

TRAILER, ROOF-RACK AND RECOVERY GEAR

License	☐☐	Padlock & keys	☐☐
Full gas bottles	☐☐	High-lift jack	☐☐
Full water tanks	☐☐	Battery secure	☐☐
Kinetic strap	☐☐	D-shackles	☐☐

Bow-shackles	❏❏	Chain	❏❏
Anchor/tree strap	❏❏	Snatch block	❏❏
Gloves	❏❏	Winch controller	❏❏
Anchor	❏❏	Stakes	❏❏
Tie-downs/rope	❏❏	....	❏❏

CLOTHES

Sun hats	❏❏	Balaclavas	❏❏
Sunglasses	❏❏	T-shirts	❏❏
Jerseys	❏❏	Jackets	❏❏
Underwear	❏❏	Shorts	❏❏
Jeans	❏❏	Tracksuit	❏❏
Socks	❏❏	Spare laces	❏❏
Tackies	❏❏	Boots	❏❏
Mud boots	❏❏	Slops	❏❏
Gloves	❏❏	Pyjamas	❏❏
Swimming costumes	❏❏	Rain gear	❏❏
....	❏❏	....	❏❏
....	❏❏	....	❏❏

MISCELLANEOUS

Cell phone & charger	❏❏	Inverter	❏❏
Chargers	❏❏	Compass	❏❏
GPS	❏❏	Fishing tackle	❏❏
Sewing kit	❏❏	Two-way radios	❏❏
Protractor and ruler	❏❏	....	❏❏
....	❏❏	....	❏❏

VEHICLE MAINTENANCE

Tool box	❏❏	Funnel	❏❏
Tyre pump/s	❏❏	Tyre repair kit	❏❏
Spare inner tube	❏❏	Spark plugs	❏❏
Workshop repair manual	❏❏	Globes	❏❏
Second spare wheel	❏❏	Fan belt/s	❏❏
Distributor cap	❏❏	Fuses	❏❏
Q-20 or equivalent	❏❏	Rotor arm & points	❏❏
Condenser	❏❏	Jerrycans	❏❏
Plug suppressor/HT lead	❏❏	Coil	❏❏
Hand cleaner	❏❏	Electrical wire	❏❏
Various nuts and bolts	❏❏	Spare keys	❏❏
Galvanised wire	❏❏	Radiator cap	❏❏
Gasket cement	❏❏	Epoxy putty	❏❏
Quick set epoxy glue	❏❏	Gearbox oil	❏❏
Exhaust sealing tape	❏❏	Hydraulic fluid	❏❏

Insulation tape	☐ ☐	Engine mount	☐ ☐
Locktite thread fastener	☐ ☐	Fuel hose	☐ ☐
Jump cables	☐ ☐	Fuel filter	☐ ☐
Engine oil	☐ ☐	Warning triangles	☐ ☐
Auto transmission fluid	☐ ☐	....	☐ ☐
Water paper	☐ ☐	....	☐ ☐
Various electric connectors	☐ ☐	....	☐ ☐
....	☐ ☐	....	☐ ☐
....	☐ ☐	....	☐ ☐

Photographic safari list:

Camera body/s	☐ ☐	Wide-angle lens	☐ ☐
Film/Flash cards	☐ ☐	Std./zoom lenses	☐ ☐
Telephoto lens	☐ ☐	Lens brush	☐ ☐
Plastic bags	☐ ☐	Close-up attachments	☐ ☐
Tripod/monopod	☐ ☐	Flash gun	☐ ☐
Compressed air	☐ ☐	Flash batteries	☐ ☐
Camera batteries	☐ ☐	Lens tissue	☐ ☐
Digital camera	☐ ☐	Laptop	☐ ☐
Blank CDs	☐ ☐	USB camera connection	☐ ☐
Camera battery charger	☐ ☐	Lens brush	☐ ☐
Bush bag/sand bag	☐ ☐	....	☐ ☐
....	☐ ☐	....	☐ ☐

BEFORE GOING AWAY

Cancel deliveries	☐	Disengage immobiliser	☐
Turn off geyser/s	☐	Inform next of kin	☐
Fish, plants and animals	☐	Domestic workers	☐
Engage light time-switches	☐	Inform security	☐
VEHICLE REG. no.	....		
Chassis no.	....		
Engine no	....		
TRAILER	....		
REG. no.	....		

Camera and valuables – serial nos.

....☐ ☐
....☐ ☐
....☐ ☐
....☐ ☐
....☐ ☐
....☐ ☐
....☐ ☐
....☐ ☐

If you drive through Third World African countries, carrying two warning triangles is required by law. Roadblocks will check this and fines are levied.

CONVERSION TABLES

VOLUME:

1 pint	600 ml	1 imperial gallon	4.54 litres
1 US gallon	3.78 litres	44 Imp. gallons	200 litres (one fuel drum)
1 litre	1 kilogram	20 litres	4.4 gallons (one jerrycan)
1 litre	1.76 pints	500 ml	.9 pint

DISTANCE:

1 inch	25.4 mm	1 foot	0.305 metres
1 mile	1.6 kilometres	1000 feet	305 metres
100 metres	328 feet		1 kilometre 0.63 miles

km	miles	km	miles
5	3.1	70	37.5
10	6.3	80	50
20	12.5	90	56.3
50	31.3	100	62.5

MASS:

1 kg	2.2 lbs	1 ton	1000 kilograms = 2200 lbs

TEMPERATURE:

To convert celsius to fahrenheit – double it, subtract 10% and add 32.

PRESSURES:

Kg/cm2 and PSI from 0.5 to 3.4 kg/ cm2
LPM (litres per min) – CFM (cubic ft per min)

FUEL CONSUMPTION:

Miles/gal	km/lit	lit/100 km	Miles/gal	km/lit	Lit/100 km
10	3.5	28.5	21	7.4	13.5
11	3.8	26.3	22	7.7	12.9
12	4.2	23.8	23	8.1	12.3
13	4.6	21.7	24	8.4	11.9
14	4.9	20.4	25	8.8	11.3
15	5.3	18.8	26	9.1	10.9
16	5.7	17.5	27	9.5	10.5
17	6.0	16.6	28	9.8	10.2
18	6.4	15.6	29	10.1	9.90
19	6.7	14.9	30	10.6	9.43
20	7.1	14.0	31	10.9	9.17

AA Travel

The AA now offers travel packages and holiday specials to local, African and popular international destinations.

Let the AA book your accommodation, arrange your car rental, help plan your route and provide you with maps to navigate your way.

Local Travel Solutions

- Car rental
- Accommodation bookings
- Road conditions
- Routes

Cross-border Travel Solutions

- Car rental
- Travel insurance at preferential rates
- Travel documentation
- Accommodation guides

International Travel Solutions

- Car rental
- Travel insurance at preferential rates
- International Driving Permits
- Flight bookings
- Accommodation bookings

Travel and Outdoor accessories

The AA has an exciting range of premium quality travel and leisure accessories that you can get from your nearest AA Auto Shop and leading retailer.

Show Your Card & Save

Your AA membership card gives you exclusive access to the SYC&S programme. This entitles you to CashBack rewards on every purchase you make at participating partner stores. AA members also get significant discounts at more than 135 000 participating international entertainment, travel, accommodation and leisure outlets.

Show Your Card & Save

Call 082 16 111   Click on www.aa.co.za   Visit your nearest AA Auto Shop

9. MAINTENANCE AND BUSH REPAIRS

MAINTENANCE

BREAKDOWNS

WELDING ON A VEHICLE

FILTERS

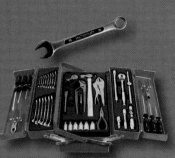

HANDLING FUEL

FOLLOWING YOUR VEHICLE manufacturer's service handbook recommendations when doing maintenance will get you going in the right direction. Get yourself a good workshop repair manual and carry it in the vehicle particularly when on an outback trail. This chapter gives advice on proper maintenance guidelines and how to avoid common mistakes as well as remedies for common vehicle breakdowns far from home.

MAINTENANCE

VEHICLE LUBRICANTS

Engine oils
Engine oils contain additives that make them specific for use in internal combustion engines. These are: alkalis to neutralise acids created by the combustion process, anti-foam agents to prevent air becoming trapped in the moving oil, anti-oxidants to prevent varnish deposits in the engine, and emulsifiers to keep any water contaminants suspended in the oil.

Automatic transmission fluid can be used as engine sump oil in an emergency. It should not be mixed with other oils and should be replaced with engine oil as soon as possible.

Transmission oils
Gear oils are labelled hypoy, hypoid or EP. Medium to heavy duty gear oils are specified GL 4 or GL 5. GL 4 oils are normally SAE 80 or 85/90. They have limited extreme pressure (EP) additive and are suited to gearboxes, transfer gearboxes and some hypoid differentials. GL 5 oils

are suited to heavy duty uses such as hypoid differentials and swivel pin/CV joint houses. The EP additive in GL 5 oils reacts with bronze synchronisers in main gearboxes and should not be used as the additive is so effective that it negates the friction required for synchronisers to synchronise gear changes. EP additives in GL 4 oils are often insufficient to handle the gear tooth loads in hypoid differentials.

Borate oils are superior gear oils containing boron additives. They offer superior performance to EP oils. They are however costly and are very sensitive to water contamination which severely degrades their performance. These oils are used in transfer gearboxes and differentials, areas that are vulnerable to water ingestion when wading, so they are not well suited to a working 4x4.

Oil changes

Cheap oils are the cause of a great many serious engine breakdowns. Although the manufacturers of cheap oils can give accurate information about the lubrication properties of their oils, seldom do they detail the cleaning and anti-sludge additives in their products. To make matters worse, rarely do the engine problems occur while the cheap oil is in the sump, and this is why: A cheap oil is run for one or more service intervals of let's say 10 000 kilometres . Then the vehicle is treated to a high quality oil either by the service centre or the owner who now has a little more to spend. Now, the excellent cleaning properties of the expensive oil have to do the work of the many kilometres run with the cheap, non-cleaning oil.

The sludge is cleaned from the engine and is filtered by the oil filter, which soon clogs up. If there is enough sludge to block the filter the engine's lubrication system fails and the engine seizes. This is then blamed on the new oil or the service mechanic. Oil is the life blood of your engine. Buy the best.

Service intervals

Many 4x4s are part-time and therefore low mileage vehicles. Engine lubricants degenerate even if the vehicle is not being used, whereas gear oils less so. Acid, oxidation and sludge formation are the chief villains. Six month intervals for engine oil changes and 18-month intervals for transmission oil changes should be adhered to.

When a vehicle is being operated in severe conditions, service intervals indicated in the handbook may have to be revised. For instance, if the vehicle is doing a lot of wading, water contamination of the axle and gearbox oils could mean that oil changes are required weekly. Heavy dust will mean that air and fuel filters will need to be changed frequently. Cleanliness of oils, filters and vehicle components has a direct effect on a vehicle's working life.

Service intervals and diesel engines

Diesel engines require servicing more often than petrol engines. I am told this is more the case in South Africa than elsewhere because of the very poor quality of most diesel fuel sold here. Atmospheric dust is also a contributor. If you operate a diesel engine and want it to last more than 300 000 kms, as they frequently do in Europe, it is recommended that the sump oil and filter are changed every 5000 kms, even if the manufacturers recommend less frequent changes.

BREAKDOWNS

Most breakdowns in the bush can be handled with a good tool set and spares such as fanbelts, rotor arm, points, spark plugs, gasket paper, silicone sealant, a packet of odd nuts, bolts and screws and a length of wire.

Don't start taking complicated components apart until you are absolutely sure that this is the cause of the problem. On my travels I have assisted with a number of breakdowns and it is startling how many times the carburettor is the first component to be accused as the villain and stripped only to find that it is not at fault. Once the carburettor is reassembled its settings have been altered and the vehicle now has an additional malfunctioning component. Remember, if you need to strip something, you will be working in far from favourable conditions and repairs will have to be improvised with what you have with you. With a workshop repair manual a repair job is made very much easier and one should always be carried, even if you think you know your vehicle well.

If you have a breakdown and intend to do what you consider to be difficult repairs, do not do these repairs too far away from the side of the road or track; do not hide your reasons for stopping. Nobody will stop and offer assistance if they think you have merely pulled over for a picnic.

Inspections

Regular inspection of a vehicle on safari is advisable. Check the undercarriage for bent suspension components, oil leaks, leaking shock-absorbers, loose wiring, loose transmission drain plugs, and any other parts about to drop off. In the engine bay, radiator caps, fan belts, battery clamps, high tension leads, engine oil, coolant, hydraulic fluid and battery electrolyte levels should be checked daily.

The following is a check list of vehicle support items that should be taken when travelling into unpopulated areas:

- Jerry-cans
- Tyre pump/s
- Workshop repair manual
- Spark plugs
- Fuses
- Fuel filter
- Distributor cap
- Points
- Plug suppressor
- Various nuts and bolts
- Galvanised wire
- Radiator cap
- Quick set epoxy glue
- Five litres gearbox oil.
- Insulation tape
- Locktite thread fastener

- Funnel
- Tyre repair kit
- Engine mount
- Globes
- Fan belt/s
- Rotor arm
- Condenser
- Coil
- Hand cleaner
- Electrical wire
- Spare keys
- Gasket cement
- Epoxy putty
- Hydraulic fluid
- Prestik

- Fuel hose – more than two metres – long enough to double up as a siphon hose.
- Second spare wheel (not essential if two similar vehicles are travelling together).
- Automatic transmission fluid (automatic gearboxes, power steering)
- Medium and fine water paper.
- Water repellent – Q-20 or equivalent.
- Carry enough engine oil for at least one complete engine oil change.
- Set of main leaves for springs – (well-used vehicles) an entire spring is not necessary. These can conveniently be carried by securing them to the front bumper and attaching a set of shackles and shackle pins onto which the leaves are fastened.
- Set of half shafts (Land Rover Series II), essential if vehicle is fitted with wide tyres.
- Exhaust sealing compound and tape.
- Various electrical connectors matching those used in your vehicle.
- Set of battery jump cables.

I recommend a toolkit that is versatile, containing a combination of sockets, spanners and vice-grips, hacksaws and pliers. This is the unit I carry, a Mastercraft toolkit with all items protected in a slim robust plastic case.

- Spark plug wrench
- Ratchet for sockets
- Two tyre levers
- Screw drivers
- Heavy chisel ±25 cms
- Circlip pliers
- Flat nose pliers
- Mole wrench

- Set of sockets
- Power bar for sockets
- Tyre pressure gauge
- Hacksaw
- Sharp nose pliers
- Wire cutters
- Feeler gauge
- Impact wrench

- *Watchmaker screwdrivers.*
- *Jump-cables.*
- *High lift jack – for breaking tyre beads.*
- *Set of spanners to fit your vehicle (metric and/or imperial sizes).*
- *Adjustable wrench – medium and large sizes.*
- *Ignition timing light or bulb and wire with crocodile clips.*

- *Valve spanner.*
- *Two hammers – 1/2 &2kgs.*

Carrying tools in a strong canvas bag is preferable to steel boxes. In canvas the tools will not rattle and will not be covered in a layer of fine iron filings as will be the case if carried in metal boxes.

Radiator damage

Big holes can be sealed with epoxy putty. Small holes can be fixed by breaking an egg into a bowl, removing the yolk, and pouring the white into the radiator. The water must not be hot when you do this. Do not replace the radiator cap until the temperature is up, otherwise the pressure will force the soft egg out of the holes. Remember to flush out your cooling system as soon as you can make permanent repairs. Porridge is an alternative to egg white.

Overheating

This is a common problem when driving in thick sand for long periods, especially when towing.

If a vehicle breakdown occurs far from home and help, take a break, make some shade and consider all options. Create a clear plan as to how to effect repairs and avoid deviating from the preset plan. All too often, breakdowns in the bush result in unnecessary panic. The result is unwise decisions made in haste which can even cost lives.

The following causes should be investigated, and in this order:

- *A broken or loose fan belt. A fan belt is an essential item in your spares kit.*
- *Low coolant level. Do not remove the radiator cap when the engine is hot. The sudden drop in pressure will cause the engine temperature to rise sharply and this could damage the engine. Scalding steam could also injure you.*

- Low engine oil levels. Oil cools as well as lubricates the engine. Make sure that the oil level is always at the high mark on the dip stick.
- Grass and grass seeds clogging the air gaps in the radiator.
- Vehicles with an air conditioner radiator sandwiched to the engine radiator – grass seeds and insects often clog the air gap between them. This cannot be seen unless one radiator is removed. Gradual engine water temperature increase over a long distance is often a result of this. Check your vehicle before your safari. Fit a grille net to prevent this build up.
- Badly adjusted ignition timing. You will need a timing light to set the ignition timing accurately. The timing specifications are given in the vehicle's handbook or workshop repair manual.
- Malfunctioning thermostat. Overheating will result if the thermostat is not opening to its full extent. Remove the thermostat and see if the overheating continues. If this does not help, replace the thermostat – it is not good practice to run an engine without a thermostat and one should be fitted as soon as a replacement is available.
- Auxiliary equipment badly positioned in front of the radiator. Overheating caused by a restricted air flow may only become apparent when the vehicle is worked hard.
- Research has shown that antifreeze increases the cylinder wall temperatures. If your vehicle does not live in a climate where freezing is a threat, remove all antifreeze and replace with a solution of pure corrosion inhibitor. An example is Motorcraft SXC103. The concentrations of water/antifreeze indicated on antifreeze product labels is often far too high for the Southern African climate. Reducing the concentration will aid cooling and reduce creep-seep. (The creeping properties of anti-freeze make it ooze from pipe connectors leaving green stains over parts of the cooling system).

Drowning an Engine

I have only once drowned an engine and in the event getting going again was painless and took about forty minutes. If water is sucked into the cylinder heads the process to safely evacuate the engine is as follows:

Recovery of a drowned engine:

- Remove the air filter.
- Remove water from the intake pipe and turbo. Check for deposits of sand.
- Chock the wheels and jack up one rear wheel. Engage two-wheel drive (or unlock the centre diff) and engage high-range fourth gear. Release the handbrake.

- *Remove the glow plugs (diesel) or spark plugs (petrol). An alternative for the diesel is to remove the injectors, but they are often more difficult to remove than glow plugs.*
- *Turn the engine by rotating the rear wheel. Rotating the engine in this way prevents the starter being stressed and prevents the possibility of a bent conrod at any stage of the flush because with hand-power, resistance can be felt and nothing is forced.*
- *Once all the water is out of the cylinders, clean, dry and replace the glow/spark plugs. Replace all seals. Only replace the air filter if it is dry, because a wet paper element could be sucked into the engine giving you a bigger problem than you started with.*
- *Have your mother-in-law stand behind the vehicle and start the engine. Why your mother in-law? Think about all the water in the exhaust pipe which has got to have some place to go when that high-compression engine starts up!*

Clutch failure

If your clutch fails, ascertain the cause of the problem. If you have a hydraulic clutch as do most 4x4s, check the level of the fluid. In the event of a fluid leakage from the master or slave cylinders this means that the piston rubbers are leaking. Bleeding the system may provide a temporary solution. If you dismantle and reassemble these components cleanliness is paramount. If you do not have hydraulic fluid almost any liquid will do. (In an emergency, add dishwashing liquid to water but avoid bubbles). Do not use mineral oils as they will soon rot the rubber plungers in the slave and master cylinders. If your vehicle has a cable operated clutch, check the tension of the cable. Adjust so that there is a very small amount of free play (±2mm).

If you are unable to get the clutch working, try changing gear without one. It just takes a little practice. When starting off, warm up the engine so that it will start easily and then switch it off. Engage first gear, and restart the engine. The vehicle will move forward and when the engine fires you will be on your way.

Gear changes are made in the following way: accelerate the vehicle until the engine is revving a little higher than for a normal gear change. By doing this you are allowing for the additional time it will take for each gear selection. Now, decelerate slightly until the engine is neither pushing the vehicle nor holding it back. The gear stick should move to the neutral position very easily. Now decelerate slightly until the engine revs match the wheel rotation as they would when engaged in the gear you are about to select. (If you are changing up a gear you will need to accelerate the engine). Change to the new gear slowly and gently – do not use force. When your engine revs are correct, the gear will engage quite easily and after a little practice you will make

quite smooth gear changes. For obvious reasons, I do not recommend doing this in stop-start traffic.

STARTING WITH FLAT BATTERY

A flat battery need not cause panic. Assuming that the battery has enough power left to be able to fire the engine but not turn the starter motor, and you are unable to push start the vehicle due to heavy sand, by jacking up a wheel and rotating it with a length of rope the engine can be restarted. Do the following:

- *Switch off all electrical equipment – conserve all of the power the battery has left in it.*
- *As the vehicle cannot be held by the handbrake the vehicle must be chocked. In sandy conditions one way to do this is to dig shallow holes behind the back wheels and push the vehicle into them. On hard ground, a heavy log, buried in a shallow trough and laid in front of the wheels, works well.*
- *Jack up one rear wheel but do not remove it.*
- *Wind a long length of rope tightly around the tyre so that when it is pulled the hub will rotate in the same direction as it would if the vehicle was moving forward. To do this make a knot in the end of the rope and wind the rope around the tyre crossing over at the knot. The rope must be wound as tightly as possible. Then wind the rope another two or three times, maintaining tension all the time.*

Being able to venture into the remote and unspoilt wilderness is the part of off-roading that gives me the most pleasure. I began with a vehicle (above) which was over twenty years old at the time. I carried a wide range of spares, a good selection of tools and a repair manual. It gave me peace of mind during my travels and on a few occasions was needed. Today, with a newer and considerably more reliable vehicle; while I do not carry the range of spares I once carried, I always carry a good set of tools and a box of odds and ends to enable me to effect a repair far from home.

- Gear selection depends on the size of engine and you may find that if the gear selected is too low, the vehicle may fall off the jack. Some trial and error may be required. A good ratio to begin with is high-range third.
- Switch on the ignition. Add choke if required.
- Depress the clutch and get someone to pull the rope. Release the clutch when the wheel reaches maximum speed and the engine should turn over.
- If your battery is totally dead and an alternator, as opposed to a generator, is fitted, this will not work. (most modern vehicles are fitted with alternators) It will also not work with automatic transmission.

Noisy suspension

During a safari a vehicle's suspension takes a great deal of pounding and if the vehicle is overloaded it is often the suspension which is the first thing to break. Wearing of components such as rubber bushes is accelerated by the combination of heavy loads and mud and dust.

The most common causes of suspension noises are:

- Shock absorber rubber bushes worn or missing.
- Shock absorber mounts badly worn so that the shock moves in the mount.
- Spring shackles worn (leaf springs) – replace
- Misaligned coil springs – park the vehicle so that the suspect spring is extended. Try and rotate the spring. A clunk can be heard as it returns to its correct mounting position. If the noise persists, slip a short length of plastic garden hose onto both top and bottom of the spring.
- Coil spring suspensions have many rubber bushes linking each component. Any of these bushes in a worn state could cause suspension clunks.

Steering vibration

Violent steering vibration, sometimes triggered by the front wheels hitting a bump, is caused by a fault with the steering damper. The steering damper is a shock absorber that lies horizontally in front of or behind the front axle. It links the steering system to the axle, absorbing vibration so that steering kickback over rough terrain does not rattle the driver to pieces. The fault can be a loose connection, a broken fitting, worn rubbers or a worn damper. The symptoms seem to be aggravated by well-worn front tyres.

Ordering spare parts

Ordering parts when in an outback village or town may be possible.

Parts dealers will require the following information:

- *Vehicle engine and chassis/VIN number.*
- *Part number if possible.*
- *Quantity of parts.*
- *Specify left or right side of vehicle. (This is indicated as if you are standing behind the vehicle and looking forward).*
- *If you do not know what the part is called but have to describe the part, avoid colourful language – keep the description as simple as possible.*

When the parts are received, check the packaging. Most genuine manufacturer parts are well packed and protected. Pirate parts are often mishandled, badly packed or damaged and may not be complete. Always order original parts if you can.

The accident scene after the collision with a Land Cruiser.

ACCIDENTS IN THE BUSH

Northern Botswana 1988:

I opened my eyes. The view of the road ahead was obliterated by the bonnet which had been torn from its hinges. I looked around. Everyone was motionless – staring forward in stunned silence. The driver's door was jammed shut, so a little shaken I climbed out through the window.

The repair scene before three days of work got us back on the road. Christened the 'Strange Rover', my highly modified vehicle took us home almost without a hitch.

We had been game viewing on the narrow dirt track that links Serondela camp site and Ngoma, the bridge over the Okavango river and the border post between Botswana and Namibia. I looked around – resting in the bush was the Toyota Land Cruiser that had rounded the blind bend at high speed, and smashed into my Range Rover. The Toyota did not appear to be badly damaged – the rear canopy was torn and the driver's door was badly dented.

The road was totally blocked and in the middle my 1971 Range Rover lay with bits of it strewn around. Soon a large truck appeared. It was full of locals and to my surprise ...tourists! Local transport consists largely of open flatbed trucks used by the villagers and smaller four-wheel-drive vehicles used by government personnel and wealthier tourists. These tourists were American students bumming their way around Africa on dollar-a-day, and for them our accident scene was a welcome break in the monotony of their overland travels.

Closer inspection of the damage was made after the Land Cruiser towed the Range Rover to Ngoma Gate, a place to work in the open, safe from lions and elephants. On first inspection it appeared that we would not be driving anywhere for some time! The entire right fender

and valance had been twisted beyond recognition and the battery had split in two. The wheel rim was wrecked and the drag link, tie rod and radiator fan were badly bent. The radiator appeared undamaged, but the header tank had been holed, a problem easily solved with some epoxy putty, one of the many 'quick fix' items taken on our overland trips.

Many times during my travels in the bush had I been called upon to make repairs, but these had always been simple problems. I remembered repairing sheared bolts on a front shock turret and an oil pump failure. What confronted me now was my pride and joy with half of its front end torn up. We were a long way from home – three days of travel and the prospect of having to tow the Range Rover all the way, in searing heat and in heavy sand and corrugations. The motivation was so great to get our vehicle going again that we set about out task with intense enthusiasm.

We began by removing the front fender. The wheel arch was unbolted and the metal had to be cut to free the brake lines which would now have to be supported with some wire. The strut supporting the bonnet slam tray was removed and mounted at an angle from a bolt on the steering box to a long bolt fixed to the top of the radiator. This would prevent the radiator from moving backwards and hitting the fan. Wire from a coat hanger, another 'quick fix' item, supported the bottom. The expansion tank, once sealed and the epoxy left to set, was mounted on the now bent front bumper and secured with some shock cord, normally used as a tie-down on the roof rack. It soon seemed possible that we may just be able to get driving again. We worked tirelessly through the heat of the day and by now we had consumed most of the rest of our beer – new motivation for getting the Range Rover back on the road.

The auxiliary battery used to drive the winch was rewired in place of the main battery and the cables tied down with plastic ties. It would have been unwise to have used wire for this because the constant vibration due to the bad roads and the choking dust would have caused the wire to wear through the cables likely to result in a short circuit. A hot fire, a four pound hammer and a large flat rock were needed to straighten the steering drag link, tie rod and the fan blade. Finally the winch cable was attached to the top of the radiator as added security. It took almost two days to complete the repairs, after which we really felt as if we had accomplished something. We filmed the entire repair process with my home video camera and when I got home I edited the sequence to music – Monty Python's 'Always Look On The Bright Side of Life'.

4x4 Adventure Stories is a one-hour DVD and VHS video witnessing the author's early days of adventuring in a 4x4. Between 1974 and 1984 the program follows two decades of travel and adventure, sometimes into the remotest parts of Southern Africa, learning what he now teaches so many. Humorous and entertaining anyone vaguely interested in 4x4s will thoroughly enjoy this one. The accident spoken of in this chapter is part of the story. Available from all good 4x4 and outdoor stores.

The following day we packed up our 'Strange Rover' for a test run to Kavimba, a small town about 20 miles away on a reasonable dirt road. Because we no longer had a bonnet fitted, I could see the engine running in front of me. After about ten miles I noticed the radiator moving about a bit too much so we stopped to sort out the problem. The right side of the radiator was not properly supported but tying the invaluable four-pound hammer to the chassis member under the radiator quickly solved the problem.

The effort that we had put into the repair had paid off and the drive home was easier than anticipated. The border post officials, pedestrians and motorists were very amused by our Rover as it created a lot of attention whenever it was seen. At the border the customs official showed utter amazement. He walked around and around shaking his head, pausing to look more closely at the four pound hammer supporting the radiator.

"How!" He yelled.

"It's the bad roads here. Everything just fell off," I explained with a smile. After a thoughtful pause he asked,

"Was it the Nata – Maun Road?"

Readers who know the Nata – Maun Road as it used to be will understand the irony of this comment. This story is told on my DVD/ Video, 4x4 Adventure Stories.

Welding on a vehicle

You will need two batteries connected in series to give 24-volts. (12-volts is not enough). Use a pair of jump leads to connect the two batteries and a third lead as the welding cable. Commercial welding rods are best, but if these are not available the carbon stick from a torch battery works well. Wrap aluminium foil around the back end of the carbon to prevent the lead from melting. Round the end and taper the rod slightly. You will need goggles. If you do not have any you will require a minimum of three pairs of sunglasses. Be warned, eye damage caused by arc welding without sufficient protection can be permanent! Coat hanger or fence wire or even winch cable will work as a metal filler.

Disconnect the battery and ground the positive terminal as close as possible to the welding site. Use a jumper lead to connect the negative terminal to the positive of the other battery. Connect the negative terminal of the second battery to the carbon stick. If welding is being done off the vehicle, run the engine to keep up a good charge. If welding is being carried out on the vehicle, disconnect the alternator to prevent possible damage.

This welding technique is a cross between gas and ordinary arc welding. Heat is controlled by the arc length – the arc is started by scratching the part with the carbon rod and then pulling it away. When the weld area is molten, feed in the filler metal and proceed along the joint. Have someone keep an eye on the temperature of the ends of the jumper cables as these could melt. A field welding kit should include two heavy jumper cables with soldered connections, a third cable of the same length with eyes to fit onto the battery, eye protection, a coat hanger and welding rods.

Filters
In very dusty conditions, the bigger the air cleaner the better. Air pre-cleaners, designed to filter out heavier dust particles before they enter the standard air filter, are a good idea if extended desert travel is intended.

Cleaning a paper element air filter is possible, although it is always preferable to fit a new one. Soak the element for up to 60 minutes in a solution of a biodegradable, non-sudsing type washing powder as used in automatic washing machines. Rinse well and allow to dry in a dust free area out of direct sunlight. Drying the element too quickly could damage it. Do not refit a damp element as the engine suction could collapse the paper. Cleaning a paper element fuel filter is done by thoroughly rinsing it in clean fuel. Wipe the filter bowl with a clean, dry cloth before refitting. See also Safari Snorkel air cleaner extensions in chapter-3.

If in-line fuel filters are fitted, a spare should be carried as these are not reusable. In Third World countries, it is wise to fit at least two fuel filters as the fuel is often full of sediment. Resultant clogged fuel lines and misbehaving carburettors are a common cause of vehicle breakdowns in these countries. Bowl-type fuel filters can be reused in an emergency after thorough rinsing in clean fuel. Be careful not to over clean the element as the paper becomes fragile as it gets old.

HANDLING FUEL

Decanting fuel
Whenever aircraft are refuelled in the field, one end of a steel cable is clamped into a metal part of the airframe and the other end to the fuel drum. This allows any static electricity which may have built up to be discharged before any filler caps are removed. An electrical discharge occurring during refuelling could cause a catastrophic explosion. This is done because aircraft fuel is of a high octane and the fuel is extremely flammable. Motor car fuel, although not as flammable, could still ignite.

- Discharge any static build-up *BEFORE OPENING ANY FILLER CAPS OR JERRYCAN LIDS* by touching the jerrycan against any bare metal part of the vehicle.
- Open jerrycans slowly, especially if they are hot. Pressure builds up inside the can as it is shaken about and heats up on the roof rack. The pressure release can spray precious fuel everywhere.
- Empty jerrycans are more dangerous than full ones as they contain an explosive air-fuel mixture.

Funnels & Spouts

A small green spout designed to clamp onto the spout of a jerrycan is the only method I have found of pouring into a fuel tank without spillage. They are cheap and are a real boon to the 4x4 adventurer. They are, however, only suitable for use with steel jerrycans. Unlike the jerrycan spout, a funnel is versatile. When selecting a funnel get one that will allow you to pour fuel single-handed and which can be placed in the filler pipe and stay there unaided. Wide brimmed plastic types with a removable pipe and a gauze strainer are easy to use and easy to stow. Rigid steel types that have a bend in the filler pipe are bulky to pack and are prone to rust. A gauze filter through which the fuel is poured either in the funnel or the vehicle's filler pipe is highly recommended. To repeat warnings I have issued a number of times: fuel purchased in Third World countries, especially in remote areas, is often dirty. Some older vehicles have fuel pipe gauze fitted as standard.

Buying fuel

If you are filling up with fuel from an electrical or mechanical fuel pump, make sure that the pump gauge registers zero before pumping

Refuelling in the bush or purchasing fuel in remote villages introduces the possibility of vehicle trouble caused by contaminated fuel. Avoid buying fuel taken from drums that are labelled with any non petroleum chemical. Keep funnels and hoses clean.

begins and keep a good look that it does not stop turning while fuel is still flowing. There are cases of thievery by petrol pump attendants who 'suddenly notice' after some time that the pump has broken and then claim that they have pumped far more than they actually have, and demand vast sums before allowing their customers to proceed. They then threaten to call the police. The entire affair can turn into a very unpleasant incident.

Dirty or contaminated fuel is a common cause of vehicle breakdowns in all remote areas of the world. When buying fuel from old drums, check the labels on the drums. If it appears that the drum once contained another liquid, beware of contaminants or residues that may have dissolved in the fuel. For example, resin dissolved into fuel will cause severe damage to a vehicle's fuel system.

Fuel sampling

Testing can be done with the use of a length of PVC tubing, your nose, your eyes, a litre-measure and a small scale. It is an advantage if you are familiar with the appearance and smell of 'healthy' fuel. The PVC tube should be at least one metre in length and should be bound to a piece of stiff wire to keep it rigid.

Taking a sample

The density of the contaminant will have a different density to the fuel itself, causing the heavier liquid to sink and the lighter liquid to float. This is why tipping the barrel to take a sample will not be an accurate way of establishing what is inside.

Lower the PVC tube into the fuel until it touches the bottom. Place your thumb over the hole and withdraw it. A level-by-level sample will be contained in the tube. Release the contents of the tube into a clear glass container. Plastic containers may soon be clouded up as the petrol chemically attacks many plastics. An empty whisky or gin bottle is ideal.

Next, smell your sample. Shake the contents and then smell it again and note any difference. If possible, weigh one litre of the sample.

Diesel fuel

Diesel engines can be difficult to start in very cold weather. The answer to this is a high capacity battery in good condition. To prevent diesel from freezing it can be mixed with petrol in a ratio of one part petrol to fifteen parts diesel.

PHYSICAL PROPERTIES OF FUEL

Petrol	Volatile, highly flammable vapour. Light straw or pinkish colour. Distinctive smell.
Paraffin	Some models are very noisy
Diesel	Non-volatile. Light straw colour with a pungent smell.
Fuel oils	Non-volatile. Black with a smell similar to diesel.
Foreign Bodies	Can be seen settling to the bottom. Very fine particles may remain in suspension but will be filtered out by vehicle's own filtering devices.

DENSITIES OF LIQUIDS

Water	1.00	Antifreeze	1.114
Petrol	0.78	Battery acid	1.28
Diesel	0.86	Lubricating oil	0.91
Alcohol	0.79	Kerosene	0.76 to 0.86
Silicone Oil (WD40)	0.76-0.98		

DIESEL FUEL CONTAMINATION CHART

Contaminant	Consequences	Test method
Water	Damage to pump and injectors. Rapid rusting.	Visual inspection of sample of settled fuel. Water will be seen as a separate layer.
Foreign Bodies	Damage to pump and injectors. Possible pump seizure.	Visual inspection of sample (dirt). Large particles will settle at bottom. Small particles can be filtered out. No loss of smell.
Petrol (Gasoline)	Fire risk - 2%. Contamination makes diesel as hazardous as petrol. Damage to pistons.	Petrol is less dense so will settle at top. Strong gasoline smell. Poor hot start.
Kerosene (Paraffin)	Can be seen settling to the bottom. Very fine particles may remain in suspension but will be filtered out by vehicle's own filtering devices.	Only detectable by the weight/density test. No detectable change in smell
Fuel oil (Boiler)	Carbon build up in injectors and cylinder head.	Colour jet black. No detectable change in smell
Oxidisation	Only heavily oxidised fuel is a risk.	Colour darkens. Acrid smell. (Source - Land Rover's Manual For Africa - Land Rover LTD.)

NAVIGATION

COMMUNICATION

THIS CHAPTER IS in two parts, GPS navigation followed by traditional map, protractor and compass navigation. Despite the accuracy of a GPS, much of what is required in traditional map work still applies when using a GPS.

THE GPS

Global Positioning System (GPS) receivers receive signals from a constellation of 24 GPS satellites and tapping into this $14 billion resource is free of charge. This system is owned by the United States. Russia owns a similar system, but it is used for military purposes and civilians do not have access to it.

Not all GPS receivers are the same because not all users require the same thing out of them. Decide in what sphere you need the GPS to work. Is it needed in the city, in the country or in the remote wilderness? Answer this before you shop, not the other way round.

The receivers or plotters can be described as hand-held satellite tracking computer receivers which are extremely accurate for determining three dimensional position fixes (latitude, longitude and altitude). It is essentially a time measurement system in which signals sent from a series of satellites are received and time differences measured. Ranges are measured simultaneously from a minimum of four satellites (for a 3-dimensional fix) and providing that the satellites' positions are known the receiver's position can be established. The GPS updates its position fix continually.

Below top: Magellan Sportrak, an excellent value basic GPS with a super-sensitive antenna.

When the GPS is moved it provides a host of other information useful to the navigator. Speed, track, distance covered, distance to go, estimated time to go to destination, track to starting point etc. The GPS gives a sense of security to the traveller, and as a pilot it has taken much of the stress out of long distance flying.

Bottom: In a vehicle a large screen is a real advantage. This is the one of the best value big screen units available today, a Garmin 176C.

Once coded to reduce accuracy with a system called Selective Availability, a GPS with ten satellites can today read with an accuracy of between eight and five metres, anywhere inside our atmosphere. Only three years ago this book's previous edition spoke about regular accuracy measurements of 100 metres. Now we tend to take it for granted, but isn't that incredible?!

Choosing a GPS

Like everything relating to computers, the moment you take your GPS receiver home it will be superseded by a better, smaller and faster model. All modern GPSs are much alike but a four-wheel driver will demand different things from a GPS than a pilot, GPSs can no longer be regarded to be the same. Firstly an aircraft travels faster and in a straighter line than a vehicle and secondly, for a vehicle, a backtracking feature is very useful if not essential. Units with fewer buttons often used to be more complicated to operate because of the dual functionality of the controls, but many current models are

Where the only landmarks are few and man-made, a GPS can be a real advantage. But, while a GPS can almost magically give your position, this is not much use without something to reference it to, like a map for example. Because of this, basic map reading and compass skills are still essential.

designed for single-handed use, where the GPS is held in the palm of the hand and the buttons are pressed with the thumb. This system is ergonomically pleasing and easy to use.

When perusing the range of GPSs, glance through the instruction book of the one that catches your eye, look specifically at one particular function and go through the routine. By doing this you will see if the instruction book is well laid out and well written, as you will need to study your GPS and its instruction book to enable you to use it to its fullest advantage. Size and battery life are important features if you also want to use a GPS for hiking. Backtracking features are very useful.

An external antenna is required for use while travelling, especially in vehicles with flat windscreens. Vehicles with well slanted windscreens may not need an external antennae to operate but look out that the incoming signal is not weak.

Breaking the technology barrier between paper maps and GPS is difficult for many. I produced this DVD and VHS program to address this issue. If you are new to GPS I guarantee after watching this program just once, you will take a giant leap forward and will almost immediately be confident and compitent with your GPS. It is available where GPSs are sold as well as from www.imap.co.za. Or, call 021 852 9984.

Important features to look for:

- *Ease of use*
- *External antenna (some flat windscreens)*
- *External power supply*
- *Backtracking*
- *Protective bag*
- *Size (hiking)*
- *Battery life (hiking)*
- *Connectability (mapping on a PC)*
- *Software availability and internet support*
- *Maps of where you intend to travel.*

HAND-HELD GPS RECEIVERS

The world's leaders in hand-held GPS technology are Magellan and Garmin. No single product stands out as the very best and it is unlikely, whatever your choice, that it will be a disappointment. Like all technology, changes are swift and new models become old models very quickly.

Although there are other GPS manufacturers I have intentionally restricted this buyers' guide to the two main contenders. Both are high-quality units with excellent maps.

Garmin

The agents for Garmin products are Avnic Trading, 011 701 3244. The range is considerably wider than Magellan. Both Garmin and Magellan share a similar map base (It comes from the same organisation) Garmin's PC software is called MapSource

Magellan

Magellan products are available from Pertec, 011 805 1996 (Johannesburg), 021 419 4450 (Cape Town). Magellan have a broad range starting with the Sportrak and onto the Meridian. All Magellan units feature an especially sensitive antenna and dare I say it, which is considerably more sensitive than Garmin's. The Magellan software, MapSend is also superior in many ways to Garmin's Map Source.

Like all products in the IT world, things change rapidly and so I suggest a good look at both of these manufacturer's products.

USING A GPS RECEIVER

A GPS receiver (depending on features) can accomplish the following:

- *Pinpoint your position.*
- *Give you direction from your position to a given waypoint.*
- *Tell you which way to travel to get to a waypoint. It will give a compass bearing which must be followed. If no compass is available then the trip must be begun by guessing the direction until the GPS reads a position change and corrects the course.*
- *Calculate a speed over the ground.*
- *Calculate an average speed between two waypoints.*
- *Estimate the time it will take to reach a given waypoint/s.*
- *Calculate the distance to a given waypoint/s.*
- *Calculate the distance covered.*

- Record a path taken to allow the navigator to find the way back to the starting point covering the same path.
- Store waypoints for instant retrieval, such as favourite fishing spots and secret campsites.
- Record a journey in the finest detail to be played back in real time on a computer screen.
- Converting latitude and longitude measurements from the GPS to a map and vice versa.
- Plot and record positions on a map.
- A compass converts bearings supplied by the GPS into a direction in which to travel.

The most common use of a GPS is simply to follow given directions and as more 4x4 trail books and maps are being published with position fixes, the GPS is becoming more popular. Even in this, the most basic use for the GPS, a compass is required as all the GPS will tell you is where you are and supply a compass bearing in which to travel. A bearing is a number in degrees – you need a compass to point the way or to plot it on a map.

Converting co-ordinates onto a map

Let's say for example, the co-ordinate (in this case Sylvia Shoal, Mozambique) is your position fix. Your GPS reads: 23° 13′ 15S, 35° 29′ 15E. Translated into English this means: 23 degrees, 13 minutes and 15 seconds south of the equator, line of latitude by 35 degrees, 29 minutes, 15 seconds east of the zero meridian, line of longitude. To pin-point this onto a map do the following:

Make sure the GPS datum is the same as the map and the notation is the same (e.g. degrees, minutes, seconds or degrees, minutes, decimals, etc.) If they are not, inaccuracies will result.

The ideal maps for pin-point navigation are topographical as they are small scale with an accurate grid. Doing this with large scale (e.g. 1: 1000 000) road maps is likely to result in major inaccuracies.

At the extreme top and bottom of the grid there is a ruler displaying longitude co-ordinates. Always read off and measure the latitude (flat lines) first. Run along this line and locate your co-ordinate and make a mark. In this example 23° 13′ 15S. For the latitude co-ordinate do the same thing by following the rulers down either the left or right side of the grid – in this example 35° 29′ 15E. The final step is to run lines parallel to the grid from the marks you have made and where the lines intersect indicates your position.

MAP READING

From this point you will use a map to navigate and convert the position marked on the map to a bearing on which to travel. With knowledge of how to use a GPS and compass, how to convert bearings taken from the compass and plot them on a map you have all the power at your fingertips to navigate with full confidence in any terrain.

The Compass

Not all compasses are the same and their features will determine their versatility. For use in conjunction with a GPS as well as for regular map navigation the prismatic type compass is ideal. The prismatic compass has the card (the part that rotates, indicating bearing) enclosed in a small case with a lid. The lid consists of a frame and a window with a hair line running vertically down it, and an extension on the opposite end to the hinge. The extension is known as the tongue and has an indentation in it that runs parallel to the hair line. Below the lid is another window which is marked in degrees. It can be rotated and has a pointer. On some models it can also be locked by a thumb screw clamp on the side of the compass body.

Prismatic Compass

Below this is yet another window under which is the compass card, marked off in degrees 0° – 360°, together with the four cardinal points; east, south, west and a pointer indicating magnetic north. On the outer rim of the compass card, the degrees are printed in reverse so they can be viewed through the prism the correct way up. On the inner ring of the compass card, the degrees are marked off in 20° intervals.

The Divider

A divider is used by using measurements from the linear scale printed on the map to gauge distances on the ground. Although this can be done with a simple ruler, a divider is more accurate, faster and more versatile. They can be purchased from any stationery shop. Place the left point onto a whole number on the linear scale and the right leg on a whole number to the right of zero. Then by placing the left point on a place on the map, quick distance calculations can be made. To the left of zero on the linear scale, the distance is divided into fractions. These fractions are used in the same way.

Maps

Topographical maps are referred to in this chapter as they are the most useful type of map for ground navigation. Topographical maps are drawn from stereo aerial photographs. They represent an area's topography, or the physical features of an area.

Scale

The scale of a map is the ratio between the distance represented on a map and the horizontal distance between the same two points on the ground.

One rises 250 metres in 1 kilometre
or   250 metres in 1 000 metres
or $\frac{1}{250}$ metre in 1 000 metres
or   1 metre in 4 metres

The most common scale of topographical maps of Southern African is 1:50 000. The entire map normally represents a square measuring 25 X 25 kilometres. This totals 625 square kilometres. Maps are also available at a scale of 1:250 000, but these will lack some detail that may be of use to the ground navigator.

What the scale represents

For example, 1:50 000 means that for every 1mm represented on the map, 50 000 mm is represented on the ground. No matter which measurement system you are using, the same applies; for every 1 inch represented on the map, 50 000 inches is represented on the ground. This scale is also called the representative fraction, and in this case it is 1/50 000. With a 1:50 000 scale map, 2 centimetres represents 1 kilometre. This is obvious if one considers the calculation; 2cms = 20mm. 20 X 50 000 = 100 000 or 1000 metres = 1 kilometre. Don't let this confuse you – just remember that 2 centimetres represents one kilometre on a 1:50 000 map.

The scale of a map is of great importance to the navigator. If you are working in a small area of ten kilometres, then a small scale map will be of greater use, because the smaller the scale, the more detailed the map will be. If you are working in a large area, for example 300 kilometres, then a larger scale map will be of more use as more area will be represented on the same map. Heights on a map are represented by contour lines. On a 1:50 000 map, they are normally drawn at intervals representing 20 metres. Intervals in feet are drawn on older maps. This interval will be stated in the map key or scale. Orthophoto maps are available for some areas, and are particularly useful. These are prints of aerial photographs with the contour lines over-printed. They combine the advantages of photographs and topographical maps.

Using the compass

Taking a bearing:

*   *Bearing: the angle measured clockwise from True North, Magnetic North or Grid North.*

The GREAT OUTDOORS just got smaller...

Tame the wild with Magellan GPS... Many models to choose from with features such as colour screen, electronic compass, barometer, expandable memory to 80Mb and detailed street maps.

Backed by a 2 year warranty and an excellent trade-in program, you can't go wrong with Magellan.

- Open the lid to a vertical position, the hair line running down vertically.
- Fold the prism over so that it lies flat on the compass window. Place your thumb in the ring and hold the viewing prism up to your eye, supporting the compass with your forefinger. The compass must be held as horizontally as possible.
- Swing around and view the object on which you wish to take a bearing.
- Line up the hair line to the exact point on the landscape, and let the line cut through it.
- Cast your eye downward. You will see that the hair line also cuts through numbers written on the compass card. When the compass card has come to rest, read off the number. This number is the magnetic bearing of that object.

A magnetic compass can give a false reading if it is placed in the following places:

- Inside a vehicle.
- Close to a vehicle. Walk 20 metres away if it is a light car or truck, and 60 metres away if it is a large truck.
- Electrical power cables. Move at least 40 metres away.
- Spectacles and jewellery made from steel or other magnetic material.

If you are in any doubt that a reading may be inaccurate due to external influences, take more than one bearing. Walk some distance away from or towards the object on which you are taking a bearing, and the reading should be the same. If it is not, then you know that one of the readings is false. To confirm which one is false, you must then take a third bearing. If all three are different, then some common magnetic source is affecting all your readings and you should move a considerable distance away and start the process again. This may occur if you are in an area of rocks containing large deposits of magnetic material.

THE THREE NORTHS

When working with bearings and maps it is essential to know about the three norths: magnetic north, true north and grid north.

Magnetic north

This is the direction to which the compass card pointer will always point. It is the direction on a map that is clearly marked 'Magnetic North'. It is also the bearing which a GPS receiver will display, although true north can be selected in the GPS set-up menu.

Converting a grid bearing to a magnetic bearing

The best way to find out if you should add or subtract the 12° is to draw a diagram. Draw a line to true north. The variation is 12° west, so draw another line 12° west of the line to true north.

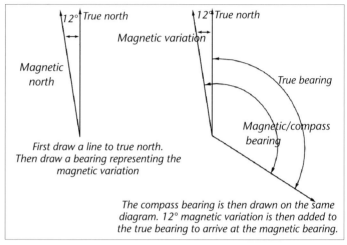

12° True north

Magnetic variation

Magnetic north

First draw a line to true north.
Then draw a bearing representing the magnetic variation

12° True north

True bearing

Magnetic/compass bearing

The compass bearing is then drawn on the same diagram. 12° magnetic variation is then added to the true bearing to arrive at the magnetic bearing.

Converting a magnetic bearing to a grid bearing

Converting from a compass bearing to a map/grid bearing is a similar procedure but the process is reversed. First draw a diagram of the magnetic bearing that you have taken from your compass. You will now want to convert this bearing to a grid bearing so you can plot it on your map.

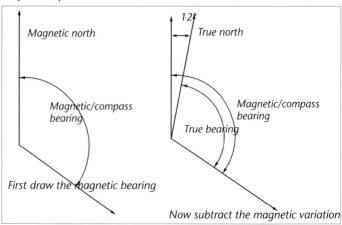

Magnetic north

Magnetic/compass bearing

First draw the magnetic bearing

12°

True north

Magnetic/compass bearing

True bearing

Now subtract the magnetic variation

True north
True north never changes. The North Pole is the most northerly point and is situated at 0° true north.

Grid north
Maps are covered with lines, running both vertically and horizontally, dividing the map into squares. In fact an entire country is divided up into squares on a grid system. It follows that if these squares are in fact square, and the earth is round, not all of the vertical lines will point to true north. (Remember a map is a three dimensional area represented in two dimensions). The difference between grid north and true north is very slight, so for practical purposes they will be regarded as the same.

THE THREE BEARINGS
Because of the three norths, there are three types of bearing:

Magnetic bearing
This is the direction in which the compass card pointer will read and relates to magnetic north.

Grid bearing
This is measured on a map with a protractor.

True bearing
Because of the curvature of the earth, the grid lines on a map do not always point to true North. For practical purposes we shall regard the grid bearing and the true bearing to be the same.

Magnetic variation
The magnetic variation is the difference between the north measured by a magnetic compass and true or grid north plotted on maps. This difference is written as the magnetic variation on all maps with a workable grid. For the exercises on the left it is 12° west. This means that whatever grid/true bearing you have measured on your map, will be 12° more or less than the magnetic bearing.

Plotting bearings on a map
The conversion of bearings is necessary if you wish to use your map, compass and GPS together. Another important tool to the navigator, the protractor, a link between the compass and the map, will be used. It enables a bearing taken in the field to be plotted on a map, or a bearing taken on a map to be measured and then used in the field to find your way with the aid of a compass or GPS.

- Draw a pencil line between two positions on a map from which you wish to take a bearing.
- Place the protractor on the map so that the base line is absolutely parallel to the grid lines on the map. If the bearing to be measured is between 0° and 180°, place the protractor to the right of the point on the map and if the bearing to be measured is between 181 and 360°, place the protractor to the left of the point on the map as follows:
- Place the zero edge, or base line (from where the degrees marked is zero) over the pencil line so that it precisely cuts through it. It can be placed anywhere along the plotted line.
- Read off the degrees from the degrees scale on the protractor. This is the grid bearing from one point to the other.

If this bearing is now going to be used to travel to an object, it must first be converted from the grid bearing taken to a magnetic bearing so that a compass can be used to follow it. In the case of navigating with a GPS, the two positions can be stored as waypoints and the GPS will do the rest.

CONVERTING DEGREE TO GRADIENTS

1° = 1 in 57.29	14° = 1 in 4.01
2° = 1 in 28.63	15° = 1 in 3.73
3° =1 in 19.08	16° = 1 in 3.48
4° = 1 in 14.3	17° = 1 in 3.27
5° = 1 in 11.4	18° = 1 in 3.07
6° = 1 in 9.5	19° = 1 in 2.9
7° = 1 in 8.14	20° = 1 in 2.75
8° = 1 in 7.11	25° = 1 in 2.14
9° = 1 in 6.31	30° = 1 in 1.73
10° = 1 in 5.67	35° = 1 in 1.43
11° = 1 in 5.14	40° = 1 in 1.19
12° = 1 in 4.7	45° = 1 in 1
13° = 1 in 4.33	

FEATURES OF MAPS

Contour lines

Heights on a map are represented by contour lines, continuous lines drawn on a map that join all the areas of equal height above sea level thereby indicating the shape of the landscape and gradient of slopes.

Other ways of indicating height are trig beacons, spot heights and colours. Using these for navigation will result in improved accuracy.

Trig beacons

These appear as a small triangle with a dot in the middle. They have a figure printed underneath or alongside which indicates the exact height above sea level.

Spot heights

Black dots usually on a hill, or on the highest point on a road, also indicate the exact height above sea level.

Contour lines and gradients

For the off road driver, an understanding of gradients and how they appear on a map is of great importance.

Where a series of contour lines run equidistant to each other the slope has an even unchanging gradient. Where contour lines are close together, the slope is steep and where contour lines spread far apart the slope is gentle. How gentle or how steep the slope is, determined by the vertical scale. If the contour lines are drawn at 100 metre intervals (this interval can be seen by reading the numbers written on each contour line) then with the aid of a ruler or a pair of dividers to measure the distance between each contour line, and by referring to the scale of the map, the angle of the slope can be calculated.

The distance between two points on a map is called the Horizontal Equivalent (HE). The difference in altitude between these two points is known as the Vertical Interval (VI).

To calculate the gradient of a slope, the formula is as follows:

- *For example, the distance between two points (HE) is one kilometre or 1000 metres, and the height difference (VI) is 200 metres:*
- *Contour lines drawn at height intervals of 20 metres which are 2mm apart mean that the slope rises 20 metres every 100 metres. (2mm converted to scale of 1:50 000 is 100 metres).*
- *Likewise, contour lines drawn at height intervals of 20 metres which are 50mm apart means that the slope rises 20 metres every 2500 metres. (50mm converted to scale of 1:50 000 is 2500 metres = 2 kilometres).*

Another example is a one in one slope. This is a slope that for every one metre covered horizontally, there is also a one metre gain in height. The contour lines will be 0.4mm apart. For some off road vehicles, a one-in-one slope is technically possible, but the calculation of a vehicle's ability to climb a gradient is measured when driving on a smooth concrete surface offering ideal traction to all four wheels. Driving over ground is very different, as there will be other obstacles to halt your progress.

Colours

Areas of height can also be coloured to assist in quick recognition of landmarks. Greater heights are normally shaded darker. You will notice that the edge of each shaded area runs along a contour line.

FINDING YOUR WAY WITHOUT A COMPASS

The Southern Cross

This constellation is best viewed between January and September because it is during these months that the Southern Cross is highest in the sky. So many people travelling from the northern hemisphere to the south often ask about this famous constellation that is represented in the national flags of Australia and New Zealand.

The stars of the Southern Cross constitute the constellation Crux, a Latin word meaning cross. It is the smallest of the 88 constellations in the sky. To face south, estimate the position on the horizon where the sun sets and then turn anti-clockwise for approximately 90°. The stars of the Southern Cross are bright and well defined, so if you know what you are looking for it will be easy to locate. As shown in the diagram, the Cross is often seen lying on its side. There are also two bright stars, although not strictly part of the same constellation, that point to the 'top' of the crucifix, and aid in its location. They are called the Pointers. These two stars form the two front feet of the half-man, half-horse constellation of Centaurus. One of them, Alfa Centauri, is the closest star to our solar system and is a mere 4.3 light years from earth. (The measurement of distance when talking about the stars is the light year. It is the distance at which light travels in one year which is 9.4607 million, million kilometres).

The other star, Beta Centauri, is 330 light years from earth. The Cross itself is made up of five stars and an area that appears devoid of stars which is called the Coal Sack, which is what astronomers call a dark nebula. It is an area sufficiently opaque as to hide the stars behind it.

Another interesting feature of the constellation is that the colour and brightness of each star varies, and this can be seen easily with the aid of binoculars. The stars are named after letters of the Greek alphabet, Alfa being the first letter. The others in order of brightness are; Beta, Gamma, Delta and Epsilon Crucis. The colour variation tells us how hot each of the stars are. Gamma Crucis is red, indicating a relatively cool star whose surface temperature is close to 2000°C. Epsilon Crucis is orange and a little hotter while Alpha, Beta and Delta are blue white stars with surface temperatures exceeding 25 000°C. As the diagram illustrates, by creating an imaginary line along the long axis of the Cross and a line perpendicular to a line drawn between the two pointers, the intersection lies directly due south (not magnetic south).

Finding your way

In the event that you are lost and you have neither map, compass or GPS, the most obvious thing to do is to follow your tracks and retrace your steps. But if you have been driving around lost for some time, following your tracks will probably be of little use.

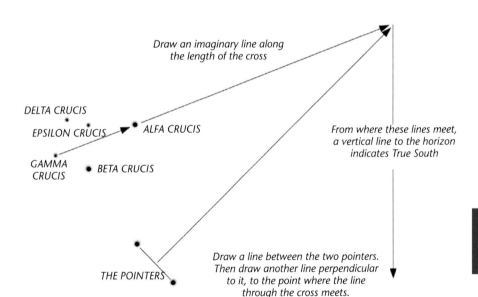

Draw an imaginary line along
the length of the cross

DELTA CRUCIS

EPSILON CRUCIS   ALFA CRUCIS

GAMMA
CRUCIS   BETA CRUCIS

From where these lines meet,
a vertical line to the horizon
indicates True South

THE POINTERS

Draw a line between the two pointers.
Then draw another line perpendicular
to it, to the point where the line
through the cross meets.

InfoMap, the publishers of a wide range of maps developed for the adventurous traveller, is engaged in mapping South Africa. GeoOrigin are supplying high-tech digital maps with the accuracy down to just two metres. The result is stunning visual maps accurate enough for survey use, usually reserved to topographic maps. In addition InfoMap's 'Information map' content is added. This information can be adapted for any user. In the case of the Leisure-Traveller Series, the information relates to holiday travellers: Accommodation, holiday activities, places of interest etc. Unlike any other maps produced, this information is icon-based in information blocks. These blocks contain not just names but contact numbers, GPS coordinates, types of accommodation, lists of activities available and a whole lot more. The beauty of icons is that lots of information can be packed into a small space and they are not language sensitive. An section of Drakensberg and the Eastern Free State, 1:250 000 is shown on the left.

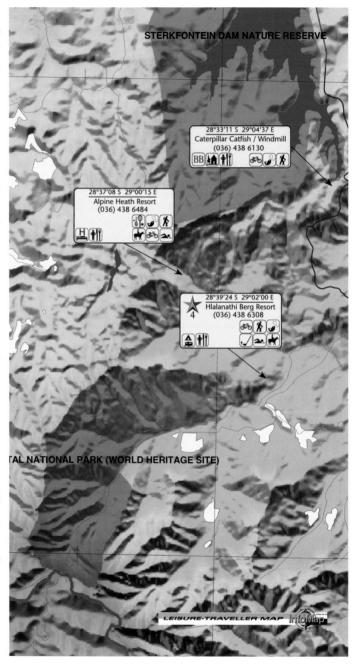

STERKFONTEIN DAM NATURE RESERVE

28°33'11 S 29°04'37 E
Caterpillar Catfish / Windmill
(036) 438 6130

28°37'08 S 29°00'15 E
Alpine Heath Resort
(036) 438 6484

28°39'24 S 29°02'00 E
Hlalanathi Berg Resort
(036) 438 6308

TAL NATIONAL PARK (WORLD HERITAGE SITE)

LEISURE-TRAVELLER MAP InfoMap

- Think back on landmarks that you drove close to before you became lost or disoriented. Rivers or dry river beds, small hills, villages or settlements, cattle or game watering holes and very tall trees are all things that you could make your way back to.
- Now calculate where north is. If you have no compass use the methods described previously. Finally, work out the approximate direction from which you have come and write it down; north-east, south-west etc.

LANDMARKS

Rivers and dry river beds.
The one thing that rivers, dry or flowing have in common is trees. Walk to the highest point that you can find and stand on your vehicle's roof or climb a tree. Scan the horizon. A river valley will appear to be a long stretch of trees that are greener and taller than those surrounding them. Knowing where north is, write down the bearing of the trees to which you are heading. If the ground is flat you may have to re-establish north and/or look for the landmark periodically.

Villages and settlements
Paths with human footprints or litter will either lead to a settlement or a source of food or water. It may be necessary to walk in front guiding a vehicle along at walking pace.

Cattle or game paths
A little tracking knowledge or a book about animal tracks will help you determine whether a path is cattle or game. If the path is well trodden, it will probably lead to a watering hole or river. If it goes in the approximate direction from where you remember seeing a familiar landmark, such as a water hole, follow the path.

MAPS
Using a map designed for an application unsuited can lead to frustration.

Topographic maps
Normally 1:50 000 or 1:250 000, they are highly detailed with topographic features such as contours, rivers, roads and railways. They are used by anyone needing high detail and accuracy and are suitable for reading off the grid lines and imputting into a GPS. InfoMap Leisure-Traveller maps feature the accuracy of a topo map with road and tourist information with stunning digital 3D computer imagery.

Road maps

Scales range from 1:50 000 to over 1:1 500 000. Their primary task is to illustate roads and tracks for the motorist. They are not suitable for accurate navigation using latitude and longitude grids.

GPS maps

Those published by InfoMap are often referred to as GPS maps. They can be regarded as a combination topo and road map. While the scales of over 1:500 000 does not permit the reading of grid lines and inputting into a GPS, they contain actual GPS co-ordinates. The coordinates are simply inputted into the GPS as waypoints. These maps are available in paper and electronic formats.

COMMUNICATION

No matter what you do with your four-wheel drive vehicle, communication makes it safer and often a lot more fun. Whether you are off-roading in a club environment, touring or overlanding in remote terrain you can have confidence that someone else knows where you are which lets you push the limits a little further.

The technology explosion over the last 20 years has resulted in efficient radio communication products becoming smaller and smaller; in some cases the size has been reduced to 1/20 of the size of radios of the 1970s. Batteries last longer, weigh less and reliability has been dramatically improved with some manufacturers obtaining Mil.Spec (military specification) approval for their equipment. Competition between the manufacturers has also created an environment for better, cheaper, more reliable and smaller products and in such a market the consumer always wins. A number of duties and surcharges have been dropped and or reduced, compensating for the jump in the dollar – rand exchange rate, with some products being cheaper now than they were five years ago.

EQUIPMENT

Before investing in radio equipment ask yourself the following questions:

- *How far do I need to communicate?*
- *Will I be on foot or in a vehicle most of the time?*
- *Are the radios going to be for emergencies, fun communications, business control or for safety of clients.*

A typical HF rig.

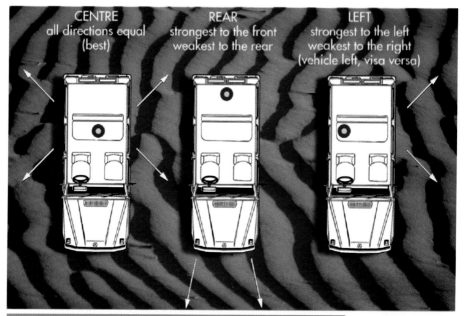

CENTRE	REAR	LEFT
all directions equal (best)	strongest to the front weakest to the rear	strongest to the left weakest to the right (vehicle left, visa versa)

Radio equipment is available in the following modes:

- FM (frequency modulation) – crystal clear communications.
- AM (amplitude modulation) – noisy communications, clear for short range.
- SSB (single side band) – gives the best range and even if no signal is present on the built-in meter the voice quality can be excellent.

Radio equipment will give you the following ranges:

- FM Equipment – up to one kilometre.
- HF Equipment (also called SSB or long distance radio) – up to 5000km
- VHF Equipment (Midband range) Mobile radio up to 70 km, hand-held up to 3 km.
- VHF Equipment (Highband range) Mobile radio up to 25 km, hand-held 0 to 3 km
- AM Equipment (similar to above but better penetration through concrete) 29 MHz (Ski boat type) mobile radio up to 15km, 27 MHz CB radio up to 30km

The information above is approximate and ranges are dependant on output power of equipment, antenna type, terrain, altitude, and in the case of HF, time of day and solar activity and frequency. Hand-held radios are ideal for very short range communications (line of sight).

UHF (FM) radios have enough range for short convoy communications (line of sight). They arer not designed for multiple vehicle convoy communication.

With a full charge and intermittent conversation the battery on a typical hand-held, the Motorola P110 gives about 7 hours of use. Extra batteries can be purchased and they are small enough not to get in the way in your pocket or backpack. Batteries can be charged from 220v AC supply or from a cigarette lighter socket, with an optional adapter. Accessories are available to make the use of the hand-helds easier, such as speaker, microphones, headsets with boom microphones, carry cases, etc. Advice on purchasing hand-helds is to look for well-known brands that will be well supported with a spares network in most countries. Motorola products have proved themselves and are probably the most used hand-held radios in the world.

MOBILE RADIOS VHF MIDBAND AND HIGHBAND

Mobile radios will give you a range of up to 70 km depending on the frequency and antenna installation. Mobiles are 5 times more powerful than hand-helds. These are ideal for vehicle convoy applications as well as for hunting, game counting, rescue, hot air balloon recovery, boating and fishing.

The advantages are:

- *High power*
- *Range of up to 70km*
- *Cannot be dropped or lost.*
- *Vehicle antenna is efficient*
- *These radios are very versatile in that they can be programmed for repeater use, the prime source of communications in urban areas.*

MOBILE HF LONG RANGE SYSTEMS

HF or high frequency systems offer communication from your vehicle for a range of 5000km plus. There are numerous factors affecting the range of HF systems such as:

- *Installation quality*
- *Frequency selection*
- *Time of day*
- *Transmitter power*
- *Antenna position*
- *Solar activity*

If you need to communicate with your office, make telephone calls and require communications for safety purposes in remote areas, HF is the way to go. With a professionally installed system (including an automatic antenna tuner) you can expect to have good communications for 90% of the day (daytime hours). Communications are usually good in sub-equatorial Africa and always better than the rural telephone systems. For trans-Africa trips specific frequency predictions can be carried out to ensure that communications are successful from Cape Town to London. The HF system can be directly linked to numerous telephone systems, and with the use of an operator you can make telephone calls to any location in the world. These telephone systems, which are similar to the system used in the Australian outback, are used extensively in Africa. With a similar system at your office you can go touring for weeks and still keep control. By linking a laptop computer to your radio you can send and receive data files from your office.

Advantages of HF:

- *World wide communications*
- *Telephone facilities*
- *Vehicle antenna is efficient*

HF radio systems are not easy to install and will not work unless the correct frequency selection is made and applied for by the dealer. When selecting a dealer to install a system ensure that he has successfully installed HF systems in the past (ask for references) and that he can undertake computer simulated frequency predictions for your application. Insist that the equipment is synthesised, not crystal controlled, and that the equipment will automatically reduce power if antenna problems occur.

29 MHZ AND CB RADIOS

These systems are the cheapest available and are ideal when travelling in convoy with communications up to 15 km. The system is AM and is therefore associated with the usual snap, crackle and pop of this mode. These radios only put out 4 watts of power and have limitations in terms of versatility. When a single side band CB is used, power output increases to 12 watts and you will be able to communicate up to 30 km, albeit with worsening voice clarity.

Advantages:

- *Range*
- *Price*
- *Sound quality*
- *Low power consumption*

Top: Glass mount VHF.
Middle: Body mounted HF with built-in single-frequency coil.
Bottom: Body mount VHF.

With all radio communications the single most important factor is well-engineered and accurately tuned antennae. There is no point in spending thousands of rands on a top quality transceiver if you cannot

Convoy communications are not only fun, but in driving in unknown territory it contributes to safety, as the lead vehicle can warn the convoy of dangers lying ahead.

hear anyone because the antenna has not been properly installed. There are basically three types of antennas on the market- magnetic, glass mount and body mount antennas.

Magnetic antennas have the advantage of being easy to remove and install but have a number of distinct disadvantages. With vehicles having aluminium bodies the antennas do not stick, even a small amount of dust will cause damage to the vehicle paintwork and overhead bushes can knock it off. Also the antenna cable will have to be fed into the vehicle through the door or window and will result in dust entering the vehicle and the chance of damaging the antenna cable is increased. The only real application would be in a hire vehicle in which you cannot drill holes.

Glass mount antennae are neat and easy to mount and also do not require holes. These antennae are the least effective of all and the only application that they have is on radio repeater systems and then only if you are close to the repeater.

Body mount antennae are therefore the best way to go. If installed properly the vehicle will not rust around the antenna and the antenna's earthing system will be sound. The antenna cable is mounted permanently and is therefore less susceptible to damage by friction or passengers. In general the higher the gain an antenna has, the better the range over flat ground will be. However, this will be a slight disadvantage in hilly terrain.

INSTALLATION

The radio, no matter which type, should always be connected directly to the battery via a fuse, and not to any convenient wire under the dashboard. By doing this, you will isolate any interference from the vehicle's electrical system which could be misinterpreted as poor reception. A filter can be wired between the power supply and the transceiver to reduce interference. The fuse is purely a protective measure against short-circuit and fire.

Positioning of the radio

The actual transceiver should be positioned so that you can see it without taking your eyes off the road but out of direct sunlight which will damage it. Consideration should be given to keeping the unit out of reach of rising water should you venture into deep water. The perception that radio communication systems can be installed by anyone is generally incorrect all antennae have to be adjusted to resonate at the correct frequency and if this is done incorrectly a transceiver can malfunction and can require repair. Sometimes, only when a home installation is compared with a professional's can the difference be appreciated. The reasons for this are simple; If an error is made in the wiring of the system a fire can occur with disastrous results. Don't select an antenna for its looks – go for one that works.

License and regulations

The Department of Post and Telecommunications is the management body of radio spectrum in South Africa and controls the use of transceivers, radio equipment specification and the assigning of frequencies. All equipment must be type approved and licensed before it can be used and when travelling in the third world, special licences are often required.

Maintenance

Prevent water from entering your antenna cables by sealing them with silicone prior to any trips. Once water has got into the cable, corrosion will occur and the cables must be replaced. Check the power and antenna cables are not getting pinched under plastic linings and in doors. Check your antenna to make sure that it is still secure on the vehicle as you will be amazed what vibration can do to locking nuts. Check to see that the whip has not been bent or broken, and if it has, replace it immediately and get your local dealer to set up the new antenna before you use it. Using an antenna without tuning it can result in overloading and burning out your radio. Before a trip check that the equipment works, clean all fuse holders and fill them with non-conductive silicone grease. When transmitting the transceiver draws a lot of current from your battery, especially if it is a high-power HF rig. Connect it to your deep-cycle auxiliary battery if you have one.

11. CONSERVATION

ON THE BEACH

CAMPING

RESPONSIBLE
BEHAVIOUR

LET'S STOP PAYING lip service in the cause of conservation. Talk is cheap. Every one of us has a contribution to make. The most valuable contribution is to stay on existing tracks and encourage other motorists to do the same. Do not assume that a vehicle track, if it is visible but not well used, is an official track. It may be that the driver ahead of you has been thoughtless and has made his own track over virgin ground. Should you now follow the new track it won't be long before it becomes a well-used track – adding yet another to the vast maze criss-crossing our continent.

It has become apparent that in Southern Africa some of the most outspoken members of the 4x4 community, who advocate responsible driving practices, who are recognised by the country's environmental protection institutions and claim to be the leaders of the cause when it comes to protecting the environment against the damage done by 4x4s are themselves the worst offenders. For obvious reasons I am not at liberty to give names, but in one case, an individual 4x4 tour guide and outspoken champion of eco-friendly practices took a 70-vehicle convoy on a Cape West coast beach drive. This same individual frequently takes ten or more vehicles onto the Botswanan salt pans and encourages the vehicles to drive alongside one another. Not a single track is created across the pan, but 10! In the video footage I saw, he encouraged his party to collect as much firewood as their roof-racks could carry and burn several massive bonfires.

It is no surprise that South Africa's beaches have been closed to 4x4s and the Botswana wildlife department are suggesting the closure of the Magkadigkadi Salt Pans to general traffic.

ON THE BEACH

In mountainous terrain what begins as a vehicle track soon becomes runaway erosion.

Although beaches have been closed across South Africa it is still worthwhile discussing beaches and the effects vehicles have on them. The University of Cape Town has done research on this subject. They divide the beach into four regions, the glassy layer, the intertidal, the drift line and back beach and the dune field.

The glassy layer is the shallow surf where most animals are tolerant to disturbance and can handle the effects of humans and vehicles. However, effects are seen as large molluscs respond to the liquefaction of the sand by 4x4s because they 'think' that the tide is rising and come to the surface. This then makes them very susceptible to damage by vehicle convoys as they are crushed while on the surface. Plough shells also occur here and are often seen feeding on jelly fish and other drift material. Research has shown that 10% of these animals are destroyed for every 50 vehicle that passes. Large convoys increase the percentage.

The intertidal region is quite tolerant of beach traffic. The finer the sand the less the damage. Course grain beaches have vehicle tracks that are deeper. During low tide, most animals found on fine and medium sandy beaches are plough shells, juvenile sand mussels, sand lice and worms. Less than 15% of the juvenile mussels are damaged per 50 vehicle passes.

Drift line and back beach. This is a narrow stretch of beach frequently used by vehicles as they move at high tide. This is unfortunately the home of the giant isopod (Tylos granulatus). Approaching the endangered species list, this animal, which grows to 55mm in length, is now absent from most South African beaches. They remain buried during the day and at night feed on the driftline material. As the tide begins to rise again they bury themselves to hide from predators, sun and water. However they have the tendency to bury themselves in disturbed sand which, if it is a vehicle track, may be fatal if the track is used by other vehicles. The most serious hazard to this isopod is driving at night when the percentage killed by passing vehicles is alarmingly high.

The success of indigenous dune-stabilisers such as Scaevola are critical to beach survival.

Dune fields are without question the most vulnerable region of the beach. The general consensus is that there should be a total ban on driving on dunes, tidal marshes and the back-shore because of the extreme damage caused by vehicles in these areas. Not only do vehicles disturb the nesting sites of birds such as Oyster catcher and terns, sanderlings and plovers but also the salt crusts and dune-stabilising bacteria and vegetation. The results are blow-outs which destabilise the dunes and vegetation. Recovery takes a long time.

In addition to the conservation aspects of driving on beaches, most beach users hate vehicles. People who love to walk for long distances to escape other people are often disturbed by vehicles, which are

The beach at Sodwana during the heyday of 4x4s on the beach. This picture was taken before the real crowds arrived!

usually racing across the beach. The beach is not a vehicle playground, it is a people playground. Due to irresponsible driving and today's self-centred attitude among so many people, I advocate the principle that on a beach people and vehicles don't mix. Vehicles should therefore be banned on beaches where people regularly find relaxation as well as the total ban on driving on all beaches at night.

Conservation when driving on the beach:

- *Never drive on the dunes. It leads to dune erosion and 'sand blows' which ultimately results in the destruction of coastal forests. Many animals, including turtles and some sea birds, nest in the dunes.*
- *Vehicles pose a hazard to people walking on, and sunbathing amongst the dunes.*
- *Driving on a beach at night severely endangers beach dwellers. Even shining bright lights on nesting creatures disturbs them and can cause them to abandon their nests.*
- *Keep the area which is used for launching boats clear when parking.*
- *Do not bury your litter on the beach.*
- *Don't drive on the beach as though it's your right of way. It is surely unreasonable to ask people strolling or children playing on the beach to look left and right as if they were on a street in a town. Give them right of way and drive slowly.*
- *Because conservation opinions differ, it is important to read conservation literature relevant to the area. This is often readily available and free to the public.*

CAMPING

Surely one of the main reasons why we enjoy four-wheel driving as a hobby is to enable us to explore the untouched wilderness? Then why do we not take better notice of good camping practices in order to preserve it?

Sound camping practices:

- *Dig a deep latrine. Faeces simply covered with a layer of soil is not sufficient. Jackals dig up shallow latrines. The deeper the hole the faster the decomposition. Bury the minimum amount of toilet paper. Burn the rest. Use unbleached toilet paper.*
- *Never bury rubbish. Wild animals dig it up and spread it around.*
- *Most cleaning chemicals contain phosphates, which contain nitrates. These run into water courses after rain and pollute the water. Water containing excess nitrates promotes the growth of algae to unnatural proportions, and eventually waterways can become*

A destructive fire swept accross 30% of the south eastern portion of the Okavango Delta. Tourists were accused of starting the blaze.

choked with algae, starving the water of oxygen. Therefore wash well away from water courses.

- *Avoid setting up camp on animal tracks. These look like human paths – they often lead to water.*
- *Never feed wild animals – you may be signing their death warrant. Animals which become accustomed to being fed usually end up making a nuisance of themselves. Often they have to be destroyed by wildlife department officials. Those that feed them are the real killers.*
- *When camping in arid areas, do not camp close to a water hole. If it is the only water hole in a large area, desert dwelling animals will travel great distances to get to the water. If you are camped too close they may be scared away and this could cost them their lives.*

Lighting Fires

- *Dig away an area and make sure that the surrounding grass cannot catch alight.*
- *Do not burn newspaper without breaking it into small pieces and rolling it up. Large pieces can catch the wind and be blown into the air.*
- *Never leave a fire unattended. Don't go to sleep inside a tent and leave a fire blazing away.*
- *Bury a fire after it has turned to ash.*

- Use existing camp fire sites if you can. It's very unsightly when the ashes from old camp fires are scattered all over the place.
- Be aware that buying wood from roadside vendors could mean damage to indigenous forests.
- Do not take wood from a live tree, make a fire under a tree or on its roots. If possible, take your own firewood – you may think you're not doing much damage yourself by burning a single dead branch, but when all campers do it a single dead branch soon becomes an entire tree.

RESPONSIBLE BEHAVIOUR

Poor driving techniques and irresponsible driving are the biggest cause of damage to tracks and the resulting erosion. Drivers who repeatedly spin their wheels or apply accelerator in frustration when a tyre battles for traction unsettle the surface layer. The rain falls and the unstable topsoil washes away.

This concept is not new, but what is, is the attitude if some off-roaders to try and make it over an obstacle no matter the cost. If all of the off-road obstacles we encounter were easy, there would be no thrill of overcoming the tougher ones. But, challenging obstacles to the point where vehicles are damaged and the track is destroyed is not worth it.

Two examples illustrate the point:
In the Western Cape there is a 4x4 trail beginning from the Cederberg town of Wupperthal. The trail is scenically splendid from beginning to end, but nowhere more so than about two-thirds along the route where the track runs on the edge of a deep valley before descending sharply to the valley floor. The descent is potentially dangerous in the most ideal conditions, even for experienced drivers. It is about 300 metres in length, as steep as 40 degrees in places and is surfaced with loose rocks, sand and deep holes. Towards the end of 1998 a team tackled the trail and over 20 vehicles, driven by both experienced and novice drivers successfully completed the trail. The trail guides, all of whom were experienced, coached each driver through. Everything was professionally and safely orchestrated until someone asked if they could try and go up. The response should have been 'no'. But, the go-ahead was given and the specially prepared Hilux with front and back diff locks engaged made it over the top. The climb was dangerous and a few times the driver almost lost control. The damage to an already hazardous descent was severe and made even more dangerous for those coming down. Many men pay for one selfish man's prize.

The second example took place while I was driving on a large dune field, ideal for experimenting with vehicles, tyre pressures and driving techniques. It is operated by experienced off-roaders who should know better. I was at the head of a group of novice drivers. After an hour or so most of the drivers had gained confidence and were looking for something a little more challenging. The guide suggested that they attempt a short but very steep dune climb in two-wheel drive. At this moment I made the mistake of letting it happen. A vehicle will climb anything, it will even fly, if it goes fast enough. And that is exactly what happened – a vehicle took off. At that moment everyone looked a little embarrassed that things had got out of hand. The Hilux involved sustained no damage. It is this same attitude that promotes reckless use of our environment. Alcohol may have played a part in both of these scenarios. Alcohol and driving, including off-road driving don't mix. Unfortunately, I feel as I write this, that my words will be like an ant trying to persuade a buffalo to give way.

Source: Mail & Guardian, 'The Thoughtful Tourist', and a selection of works compiled by Ronel Nel of the Zoology department, UCT, Rondebosch, 7701. Email PNEL@BOTZOO.UCT. AC.ZA

Other good off-roading practices:

- *After digging a vehicle out, fill in the holes.*
- *Bull bars are not for clearing bush in front of your vehicle. They are to protect against impact.*
- *When winching off a tree never tie cable around the it as it ring-barks the tree and kills it.*

These unique, easy to read road maps for every kind of traveller include GPS co-ordinates, accommodation, fuel availability and 4x2/4x4 suitability.
No map is updated as regularly or has as much really useful information as an InfoMap!

INFOMAP:
PREMIER, ADVANCED TOURING GPS MAPS OF SOUTHERN AFRICA

LEISURE-TRAVELLER MAP

InfoMap Leisure Traveller Maps are unique, easy to read road maps for the holiday traveller. Small-scale maps packed with details of type of accommodation and activities on offer, GPS co-ordinates, and more! The base map is 3-dimensional relief showing an astounding amount of detail. These maps are the first of their kind found anywhere with more information found on any other map!

By the end of 2004 the following LEISURE-TRAVELLER MAPS will be available:
DRAKENSBERG AND EASTERN FREESTATE
KRUGER NATIONAL PARK AND THE LOWVELD.
NATAL NORTH COAST
THE GARDEN ROUTE
NAMAQUALAND FLOWER GUIDE

I TRAVEL THEREFORE IMAP

A

Ablutions 224
Accidents 253
Air jacks (see jacks)
Allucab 209
Altitude 5,7
Ammeter 94
Anchor straps 22,168
Anchors 168,178,179
Angles 18-20
Approach angle 19,20
ARB 83
Army surplus vehicles 32
Asia Rocsta 41
Awnings 222
Axe 245
Axle articulation 21,23,149
Axle straps: see suspension
Axles: see suspension

B

Bejing Jeep 77
Baillies Off Road 88,105
BATTERIES
batteries cyclic 95
charging 97-100
deep cycle 95
Delco 100
discharge 97,98
split-charge systems 95-99,215
Bearing damage 17
Bilstein 84
Blowouts 158
BMW X3/X5 38
Border posts 209

Brakes 27
Breakdowns 258-253
Break-over angle 19,20
Bribes 209
Broad tyres 113
Buffalo 239
Bull Bars 82,83
Bumpers 29
Bush-bag 241
Bushes (suspension) 87

C

Cable guide 164
CAMPING
fires 298,300
on the beach 296
cooking 221
lighting 222,243
Capstan winches: see winches)
Caravan 194
Centre diff locks: see diff locks)
Centre-of-gravity 21
Chains 168
Charging batteries: see batteries
Chassis numbers 31
Chlor-floc 232
Chlorine 233
Cibie 92
Citizen band radio 288
Clearance 21
Clothing 225,227,248
Clutch failure 260
Clutch misuse 132,139
Commode 223
Compass 277
Compression ratio 6

Communications 288-293
Conqueror Trailers 196
Conservation 394-303
Consoles 109
containers 208,209,210
Conversion tables 250
Corrugations 86,155,156

D

Deep cycle batteries: see batteries
Departure angle 19,20
Desert Wolf trailers 198,199
Diahatsu Rocky 41
Diahatsu Terios 41
Diesel engines 24-26,256
Diesel versus petrol 24-26
DIFFERENTIALS
after-market diff lock 16
auto-locking diff lock 17
axle diff lock 10,15,18
centre diff lock 9, 15,18
diff lock vs lim.slip diff 16
front axle diff lock 15
limited-slip 16
using diff locks 133
Driving DVD video 159
Driving schools 159
DRIVING
ascending slopes 137,139
basics 131
beach 147
descending slopes 137,138,142
driving at night 157
mud driving 140, 141
dunes 144,145
engaging 4x4 131
engine stall on slopes 139

grasslands 155
push-pull technique 151
ridges 149
river beds 153
rocking 142
rough tracks 153
ruts 153
salt pans 153-155
sand tracks 145
sand 143-147
side slopes on sand 145
side slopes 140
snow and ice 157
troughs 149
uneven terrain 149
V-shaped gullies 151
wading 28,147-149
Drowning an engine 259
Drum brakes: see brakes
Dual battery systems 95
DVDs 159,189,242,252,273

E

Echo Trailers 199
Eezi Awn 222
Engine choice 4,5
engine modifications 7
Engines 4
Exhaust gas temperatures 24-26,93
Exhaust systems 8

F

Fender guards 84
Filters 266
Filtration (water) 232,233
Fire extinguishers 224
Fires 295
First aids kits 227
Flat battery 261
Food (containers) 208,209
Food (lists) 246,247

Footware 227
Ford Courier/Ranger 28,46,83
Four-wheel Drive: see Transmissions
Free wheel hubs 17,18,134
Front Runner 96, 209,229
Funnels 267
Fuses 97
FUEL
carrying fuel 88
contamination 268,269
decanting 266
cooking 221
economy 8
pouring spouts 88
pumps 88
tanks 88,89
Third World fuel 6,257,258
FRIDGE/FREEZERS
compressor 212
current draw 213,215
Engel 213
heat exchange 213
National Luna 213
selecting 213
setting up 214
thermo-electric 213

G

Game Viewing 241
Garmin 272-274
Gas tank mounts 233
Gauges 93,94
Gearbox 10
Gemeni 95
Generators 101
Global Positioning System (GPS)
Gloves 168,178
GPS receivers 272-287
Grids (cooking) 221,245
Grille nets 107

Ground clearance: see Clearance
GUAGES
exhaust gas temp 93
oil pressure 93
oil temperature 93
volts 94

H

Hammock 244
High lift winch 187
High-lift jack: see jacks
Hill descent control 11
Hippo 237
Hub capstans 164
Hummer 77
Hydraulic winches (see winches)
Hyena 239
Hyundai Terracan 63

I

Inflation pressures 140
InfoMap 239,293
Insect repellents 224
Inspections 256
Insurance 109
Inverters 101
Isuzu KB/Frontier 46,23,63
Isuzu Trooper 23,63

J

JACKS
air 171,172,158
bottle 173
high-lift 171,172,185
Jack and pack 187
Jack and push 186
Jack nappy 173
Jack plates 173
Jacking points 185

jacking techniques 216
scissor jacks 173
Jeep Cherokee/Sport 4,64
Jeep CJ 41,42,13
Jeep Grand Cherokee 64,135
Jeep Wrangler 42

K

Keeping warm 222
Kettle 222
Kia Sportage 37
Kinetic straps care 184
Kinetic straps 170,171,183

L

LA Sport
Lada Niva 42
LAND ROVER
Defender 8,15,23,54,55
Discovery12,15,65,66,13, 141
Forward Control 50
Freelander 19,24,37,133
history 13,47-51
Series 1, 2 and 3 6,51,162
Range Rover 4,12,23,24,6 6,67,87,103,138,141
Leaf springs 22-24
Loading 26,104
Leopard 238
LIGHTS
colour of light 91
driving 91
fog 91
metal halide 92
quartz halogen 92
rear lighting 92.93
sealed beam 92
shields 92
Lists 243-249
Lubricants 254,255

M

Magellan 272-274
Mahindra 43
Makro 216
Maps (types) 239,242,246,286,287
Maps (working with) 275-287
Mastercraft 257
Mazda B/Drifter 56,148
Mercedes Gelandewagen 13,15,19-25, 69-72
Mercedes M-class 12,40
Mercedes Unimog 18,77
Milemarker winch 164
Mitsubishi Colt 20,56
Mitsubishi Outlander 37
Mitsubishi Pajero 43,23,70,71,133
Mitsubishi Shogun: see Pajero
Mud flaps 109
Multi-tools 237

N

Navigation without a compass or GPS
NISSAN
Hardbody 56,57
Patrol 23,73,74
Sani 75,134
Terrano 44,148
Tracker 23
Xtrail 38

O

Oil pressure gauge 93
Oil temperature gauge 93
Oils: see lubrication
Old Man Emu 84,85
Ostrich 236

M

Outback roller drawer 209
Outdoor Warehouse 226
Over loading 27
Overdrive 10
Overheating 258,259

P

Packing roof racks 210
Packing systems 209
Packing vehicles 208,221
Payload 20
Petrol engines 4
Photography 241,249
Phutsi Fly 228
Pinzgauer 24
Plastic sand ladders 174
Porsche Cayenne 40,142
Portable power 200
Portal axles 18
Power steering 28
Pre-combustion chamber26
Pressure Gauge 177
Protection plates 19, 107
Proto 230
PSP plate 175
PSP versus tank tracks 175
Pumps: see tyre pumps
Puncture repairs 122-124
Punctures on slopes 124

Q

Quadra-Drive 12

R

Radiator protection 107
Radio installation 291,292
Radios (types) 287-292
Range (vehicle) 28
Range Rover: see Land Rover, Range Rover
Recovery DVD video 189

Recovery gear list   165
Recovery kit   173
Recovery techniques
175-189
Refuse   224,225
Responsible behaviour
301-303
Rhinoceros   239
Road blocks   209
Roll-over angle   20,21
Rubber mats   174
ROOF RACKS   101-105
  foot design   102
  gutterless   103
  packing   211
  slat design   103
  steel   102
  versus tents   195
Roof top tents   210-212
RPM   4,5
Running boards   83

S

Safari Centre   108
Safari Snorkel: see snorkel
Safety straps 169,178, 178
Sand ladders   174,175,188
Sand: see driving
Sanyo solar panels   220
Scorpions   235
Seat belts   132
Seat covers   106,107
Secondhand vehicles 29-32
Security   109,249
Service intervals 30-31,255
Shackles   165
Shock absorbers   22,26.85
Showers (camp)   231,234
Side steps   83
Sleeping inside a vehicle 221
Snake bite kits   227
Snakes   235
Snatch block   167,181,182

Snatch straps (see Kinetic
straps)
Snorkels   104,105,149
Soft Roaders   36-38
Solar panels   218-221
Sound systems   232
Southern Cross   284,285
Spades/shovels using
175,177
Spades/shovels167,168,235
Spare parts   257,253
Spare wheel locations
27,118,119
Spline shaft damage   17
Split charging: see Dual
battery systems
Springs   22-24,86
Ssangyong Korando   44
Stakes   179
Stings and bites   228
Streamlight torches   222
Super Roaders   39-40
Super-Select 4wd13,14,133
SUSPENSION
  axle articulation   21,23
  axles independant   21
  axles solid/live   21
  choice   20,21
  coils versus leaf springs 22
  configurations   23-24
  noise   252
  torsion bars   86
Subaru Forster   38
Suzuki Samurai   45
Suzuki SJ40   45
Suzuki Vitara   45
SVM   45

T

Tables   223
Takla Seat Covers   106,107
Tanks: see water/fuel
Tent poles (carrying)   103

Ticks   236
Tides   147
Tie-downs   212
TJM   83,84
Tool kits   248,257
Torches   222,223
Tow bars   167
Track-mats   174
Traction control   12,135
Tuggum straps: see Kinetic
straps
TOWING
  off-road   203,204
  on-road   201-203
  stability   198,201-203
TOYOTA
  Condor   75
  Hilux
  57,58,116,139,144,149
  Landcruiser
  4,7,11,15,23,58,59,83,62,
  76-78,84,102,147
  Prado   75,76
  RAV4   38
TRAILERS
  axle breakage   197
  C of G   203
  design   196-200
  dust proofing   199
  electrics   204
  equipment   199,200
  over-run brakes   204
  fridge & freezers   215
  racks   199
  jockey wheel   199
  over-run brakes   198
  rust protection   198
  storage systems   200
  suspension   197
  trailer top tents   199
  tow hitch   195,197
  wheels and tyres   197
  Trailers vs roof racks 195
  weight restrictions   199

TRANSMISSIONS
4x4 systems   9,18
diffs: see differentials
full-time 4wd - system   13
full-time 4wd – using   133
full-time vs part time   13
main gearbox   9
manual vs automatic 10,11
part-time 4wd - system
13,14,133
Transfer gearbox   9,133
Turbochargers diesel   5,6
Turbochargers petrol   6
TYRES
all-purpose tyres   115
balancing and rotating 124
broad tyres in mud   113
broad tyres in sand   113
chains   169
cross-plies   116
deflators   121
fitting   118
footprint   118
load rating   115
load rating   115
maintenance   120
mud   112
pressures 118,136,137,145
radial versus crossply   116
radials   117
rough country   114
sand   112
selection   112
self-cleaning   112
sidewall   115
snow   114
speed rating   115
temperature rating   115
tube versus tubeless   117
Tyre indicator tables   123
Tyre pumps   120
Tyre repair kits   123

U

Uaz   77
Understeer   15
Used vehicles   29-32

V

Vacuum diff locks: see diff
locks)
Valve stems (tyres)   118
Vehicle buyer's guide 34-79
Videos/DVDs
159,189,242,252,273
Viscous coupling   9,13,14
Voltage meter   94
VW Syncro   24,78
VW Taureg   40

W

Warn Multi-Mount   165
Washing clothes   209,232
WATER
bladders   231
carrying   229
filters   232,233
heater   229
positions   89
purification   232
showers   231
survival   228,229
tanks   89,228,231
taps   89
Wading: see driving
Washing   232
Welding on a vehicle   265
Wheel carriers   27,119
Wheel rims split   121
Wheel rims   119,120
Wheel spin   141
Wheelbase   20
Wild animals   234-241
Wolff packs   208

WINCHES
capstan   163
drum winches   163
hand   165
hub capstans   164,180
hydraulic   164
mounting   165
portable   164
pulling power   164
using   178-182